Carole Greenhalgh
Rica Design
September 1994.

Victorian Style

Victorian Style

Judith & Martin Miller

Photography by James Merrell

MITCHELL BEAZLEY

VICTORIAN STYLE
Judith and Martin Miller

Photography by **James Merrell**
Chief Contributor **John Wainwright**

Edited and designed by Mitchell Beazley International Ltd,
part of Reed Consumer Books,
Michelin House, 81 Fulham Road, London SW3 6RB

Art Director **Jacqui Small**
Senior Executive Editor **Judith More**
Art Editor **Trinity Fry**
Assistant Art Editor **Helena Stendahl**
Senior Editor **Sophie Pearse**
Production **Sarah Schuman**

A CIP catalogue record for this book is available from the British Library

ISBN 1 85732 098 0

The publishers have made every effort to ensure that all instructions given in this
book are accurate and safe, but they cannot accept liability for any resulting injury,
damage or loss to either person or property whether direct or consequential
and howsoever arising. The authors and publishers will be grateful for any
information which will assist them in keeping future editions up to date.

Typeset in Bembo 10.5/15 and Bembo italic 10.5/14
by Dorchester Typesetting Group Ltd, Dorset, England
Colour reproduction by Mandarin Offset, Singapore
Produced by Mandarin Offset
Printed and bound in Singapore

The CONTENTS

INTRODUCTION

Although Queen Victoria ascended the throne in 1837 and reigned until 1901, she gave her name to a period of history – the Victorian era – that is better understood as beginning in 1815, following the demise of the Emperor Napoleon's expansionist policies in Europe, and extending to 1914 and the outbreak of World War I. The political, economic and military effort that was expended over some twenty years on defeating Napoleon had left Europe exhausted.

Yorkshire and Scotland. The harnessing of coal and steam power, combined with the exceptional skills of engineers such as Isambard Kingdom Brunel, produced an extensive network of railways which further fuelled the expansion of manufacturing industries by expediting the transportation of coal and other raw materials, notably those essential to the construction industry, to those regions where they were either scarce or non-existent.

Right: the furniture in this music room was purchased in 1823 and shipped from North Carolina. The boat sank en route and the furniture lay underwater for three months. When it was raised the only damage were water stains on the fabric.
Above far right: an illustration of an elegant Grecian revival drawing room, published in 1838.

Below right: the sumptuous ceiling of a tent room is made of white and green cotton billowing out from a central medallion or rose adorned with gold tassels.
Below far right: an early Victorian illustration by Mary Ellen Best depicts a family dining table in Yorkshire, England, laid with a printed Staffordshire-ware service.

However, the peace that followed the battle of Waterloo witnessed a gradual recovery and a process of re-energizing that allowed many nations – in particular Britain, her colonies in Australasia, India and South Africa and the independent states of North America – the opportunity to enjoy the fruits of the Industrial Revolution and an increase in international travel and trade.

The Industrial Revolution effected profound changes in society during the 19th century. First and foremost, in Britain it turned what had been a primarily rural population into a predominantly urban one. Giving additional impetus to a process of social mobility that had begun with the Agrarian Revolution of the mid-18th century, it sucked surplus labour from the farming communities in the countryside into the towns and cities that were growing up and expanding around new industries, such as the iron foundries of Shropshire, the textile mills of Lancashire, the potteries of Staffordshire and the coal mines of Wales,

To meet the needs of a rapidly expanding British population – London's quadrupled during the second half of the 19th century – a vigorous programme of building ensued. For many among the working classes this took the form of "back-to-backs" which were inexpensively constructed regimented row or terraced houses with poor or non-existent sanitation, very few of which have survived to this day. However, the row or terraced residences built in the cities for the growing ranks of the middle classes were of far better construction and a substantial proportion have survived; as have the suburban rows or terraces and "semi-attached" middle-class dwellings that replaced the market gardens around the perimeter of the cities.

The growth of middle-class suburbia was fuelled not only by the need for more accommodation, but also by a desire to escape the overcrowded and often dirty and insanitary city slums. The feasibility of commuting to work in the cities offered by the railways and the decline in the need to grow perishable commodities close to urban areas now that they could be rapidly transported in from the countryside also contributed substantially to expanding areas of suburbia.

The notable increase in prosperity that accompanied the Industrial Revolution was largely based on the accumulative benefits of inexpensive imports from the colonies, improved technologies that gave rise to increased mechanization and mass-production and the existence of captive markets abroad for home-produced products. While the chief beneficiaries of this in terms of a rise in their standard of living were the upwardly mobile middle classes, even the poorer sections of society began to reap some of the benefits during the second half of the 19th century.

Increasing concern for the welfare of its citizens saw succeeding governments of the day introduce State legislation to improve general working and living conditions. While various Factory Acts in Britain went some way to curbing the exploitation of inexpensive labour and the introduction of basic housing standards and building regulations resulted in better accommodation for manual workers, a series of major public and private works to improve standards of hygiene benefited all. Advances in medicine and the accompanying greater understanding of how diseases spread, the desire to do something about it, together with the necessary technological know-how and sufficient wealth to make it possible, resulted in the installation of an increasingly efficient sewerage system and the introduction of mains water, gas and also, by the end of the century, electricity into many houses. Related improvements in sanitary equipment and methods of heating water combined to improve the day-to-day quality of life for all but the poorest members of society.

Of all the political, economic and social developments that took place during the Victorian era, one of the most significant was the expansion of an increasingly better-off middle class. Greater political representation, and therefore power and influence, had come as early

as 1832 with the passage of the first Reform Bill through Parliament, while greater purchasing power came with the rising dividends, salaries and wages provided by a prosperous economy. This new-found affluence and status was naturally echoed in the types of houses and apartments or flats that the middle classes lived in and the styles in which they decorated and ornamented them. Aesthetically uncertain, at least at first, they turned for reassurance to the tried and tested – in other words, to styles of architecture and furnishing that had previously been the preserve of the aristocracy and the upper classes. Increasingly, better education, the growth in trade and the opportunity to travel abroad also led to a greater appreciation of the products imported or brought back by architects, designers and tourists from different countries and cultures overseas.

One of the consequences of this in terms of architecture was the profusion of various historical-revival styles that became fashionable either throughout or for specific periods during the Victorian era. In Britain, the Classical style, derived from the architecture of ancient Greece and Rome, and the various re-interpretations of it made during

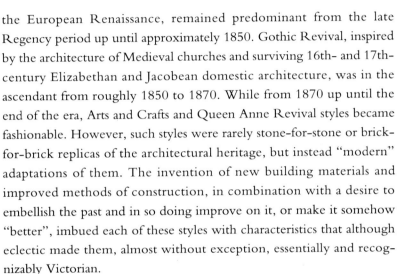

the European Renaissance, remained predominant from the late Regency period up until approximately 1850. Gothic Revival, inspired by the architecture of Medieval churches and surviving 16th- and 17th-century Elizabethan and Jacobean domestic architecture, was in the ascendant from roughly 1850 to 1870. While from 1870 up until the end of the era, Arts and Crafts and Queen Anne Revival styles became fashionable. However, such styles were rarely stone-for-stone or brick-for-brick replicas of the architectural heritage, but instead "modern" adaptations of them. The invention of new building materials and improved methods of construction, in combination with a desire to embellish the past and in so doing improve on it, or make it somehow "better", imbued each of these styles with characteristics that although eclectic made them, almost without exception, essentially and recognizably Victorian.

Architectural styles in the United States and in British colonies such as Australia, New Zealand, South Africa and India, largely echoed those in Britain, but were obviously adapted to accommodate locally available building materials and methods of craftsmanship as well as different climatic conditions. For example, in India Neo-classical and Gothic Revival buildings were embellished with various indigenous motifs and patterns. (The exportation of architectural styles was not of course all one way: Oriental bungalows and verandas were to become fashionable in Britain during the latter part of the Victorian era.) Similarly, in the warmer climates of Australasia, South Africa and the southern states of North America, architectural features such as the partly enclosed porch and balcony were usually larger than those in Britain as the intention was to provide a sitting area that offered protection against the sun while at the same time taking maximum advantage of any cool breezes that were available.

In the United States architectural styles became increasingly diverse. In terms of what was considered fashionable, the momentum was broadly from Gothic, Italianate and Second Empire Revival, to Queen Anne Revival and Stick-, Eastlake- and Shingle-style buildings. However, the fact that in many parts of the country wood was the least

expensive and sometimes the only building material available resulted in an architecture which was generally lighter and more colourful than was usually the case in Britain. Wood was often painted or stained in a variety of fashionable colours in order to protect it against the effects of the elements, while in Britain drabber brick, stone and slate were the primary building materials.

The influx of European immigrants into the United States during the Victorian era, each bringing with them the architectural traditions of their own countries of origin, also resulted in the predominance of certain styles in specific areas: for example, the Irish influence was notable in Boston, the Swedish in the Mid-West, the German in Baltimore and the Spanish on the western seaboard. While the European influence has survived in the Victorian buildings still standing today, a truly distinctive American style of architecture only began to gradually emerge after the Centennial Exhibition of 1876 and is best seen in the work of indigenous architects such as Louis Sullivan, father of the modern skyscraper, H.H. Richardson and Frank Lloyd Wright.

Just as the prosperity resulting from the Industrial Revolution fuelled an unprecedented boom in both the number and styles of houses built in the Victorian age, particularly during the 1850s, 1860s and 1870s, so it also gave rise to a profusion of decorative materials and styles for the furnishing and ornamentation of the home. Prior to the advent of mass-production, hand-made furniture, fabrics and wallpapers had been relatively expensive. As a consequence, while the exteriors of, for instance, many Regency houses had appeared opulent, their interiors were often quite sparsely decorated with an elegant simplicity that was determined as much by the cost of furnishings as by current ideas as to what was fashionable or in good taste. However, by the beginning of the Victorian era, the combination of a relative reduction in the cost of mass-produced furnishings and a notable increase in the disposable income of a substantially expanding middle class, had begun to reduce the financial constraints on interior decoration. Ordinary middle-class home-owners could now increasingly afford to furnish their homes in a manner that was both as comfortable and fashionable, at least to them, as the homes of the wealthier upper classes. However, to many Victorian commentators of the day decorating the home was more than just a matter of comfort and fashion or style. An influential American book, *House and Home Papers*, written in 1864, exhorted: "the man and woman who approach the august duty of creating a home are reminded of the sanctity and beauty of what they undertake". And in 1891, an edition of the American magazine called *The Delineator* took this ethos a stage further by actually suggesting in its pages that poor standards of decoration and bad housekeeping were tantamount to being immoral. By the second half of the 19th century interior design had become a serious business.

In terms of style, during the early years of the Victorian age the Neo-classicism of the Regency period remained the height of fashion among the wealthier sections of society. However, furnishing manufacturers, interior designers and their clients gradually began to turn to a host of other historical styles for inspiration. Complete historicizing schemes based on, for example, English Baronial, European Renaissance, Louis XIV and Rococo designs became popular in grander houses and were soon echoed in the furnishings of detached middle-class suburban homes.

One of the primary means through which designers, craftsmen and clients could learn about what was in vogue during the first half of the 19th century was the pattern book. An early and influential example of one such publication was John Loudon's *An Encyclopaedia of Cottage, Farm and Villa Architecture and Furniture*, which appeared in 1833. The book contained comprehensive illustrations and advice on virtually every element of interior and exterior design, from furniture, fabrics and wallpapers to architectural fixtures and fittings and even drainage systems. The popularity and widespread availability of such books and periodicals in Britian and her colonies, Europe and North America, and the fact that local tradesmen were able to make accurate copies of the various designs and schemes illustrated in them, contributed in no small part to an increasing uniformity of decorative styles, especially in middle-income Victorian households.

Throughout the 1840s and 1850s the choice and availability of products, materials and styles with which to decorate the home gradually increased. The Great Exhibition of 1851, held in the Crystal Palace, London, England, and similar international events held in Paris in 1855, Brussels in 1860 and Philadelphia in 1876, were intended as a celebration of the major advances that the Victorians had made in the fields

Above far left: a fashionable mid-1870s town-house drawing room. The serpentine-back couch with an antimacassar is typical. The decorative plasterwork on the ceiling and the ornamental mirror frames are in Neo-rococo style.
Above left: a blue, white and gold bedroom in Louis style, c.1885, illustrated by Samuel Rayner.
Right: the dining room in the Old Merchant's House, New York, with chairs made in the Duncan Phyfe workshops. The pier mirror in-between the windows was a common feature in Victorian rooms: giving the illusion of an additional window, as it afforded extra light.

Above: in this corner of a New York Village home the furniture is the epitome of American Gothic. Most of the pieces date from 1830 to 1850 and are by the master craftsmen of the period, A. J. Davis, Crawford Riddell and Joseph Meeks.

of technology, manufacturing and the arts and crafts. While providing a showcase for the numerous manufacturers of, for instance, furniture, fabrics, wallpapers, ceramics, sculpture, silverware and glass, they also gave the Victorian public (who attended these exhibitions in vast numbers) an additional opportunity for "window shopping" for their homes over and above what was on offer via pattern books and periodicals on interior design.

While these international exhibitions fuelled the appetite for decoration and ornamentation of the home, they also provided a focal point for leading architects and designers who had become increasingly critical of both the style and quality of many mass-produced products. For example, the ever-increasing choice of colours made available by the invention of chemical aniline dyes during the middle of the century, coupled with the development of power-loom weaving and machine-printing from metal rollers, had resulted in the production of a wide selection of furnishing fabrics, wallpapers and carpets with highly colourful and complex pictorial patterns.

While they proved popular with the public, particularly the middle classes during the high-Victorian period, to architects and designers such as A.W.N. Pugin, Owen Jones and Richard Redgrave, such patterns depicting naturalistic, "three-dimensional" flowers, plants, animals, landscapes and panoramic views were often seen as garish and essentially dishonest. Jones, who wrote his highly influential *Grammar of Ornament* in 1856, believed that supposedly accurate, "three-dimensional" replicas of images that naturally occurred in Nature did not actually constitute a pattern and were in poor taste. Instead, he felt that

on the grounds of honesty and aesthetics, man-made patterns should be flat, highly formalized and stylized interpretations of Nature.

The aesthetic debate triggered by a reaction to the excesses of high-Victorian style also extended to furniture. For instance, the fashion for over-stuffed and padded upholstered sofas and chairs was made possible by technological advances in manufacturing, such as the invention of coil-springing, the cast-iron metal framework and the perfection of techniques for deep-button backing, the latter was a popular style of upholstery. However, in his *Hints on Household Taste*, which was published in 1865 and proved very influential in both Britain and the United States, the English architect Charles Eastlake criticized what he saw as the unnecessary deception and vulgarity of such furnishings and argued instead for a return to a more robust, open and honest style based on Gothic principles of craftsmanship and design.

Similarly, William Morris – a founder of the Arts and Crafts movement and, according to the German commentator Hermann Muthesius writing at the end of the 19th century, the most authoritative and influential designer of flat-patterned fabrics and wallpapers during the Victorian era – reacted to high-Victorian fashions and the relatively poor quality of mechanized production of furnishings by returning to pre-industrial patterns and motifs for inspiration. He also favoured hand-crafted methods of construction based on the traditions of the Medieval craft guilds.

The critics of high-Victorian style, who collectively made up what came to be known as the Aesthetic movement, objected not only to the style and quality of machine-made furnishings and ornaments but also to the manner in which they were used in the home. For example, the typical middle-class drawing room or parlour during the third quarter of the 19th century was crammed full of furniture, fabrics were used in abundance (it was the era of the "cover-up") and every available surface and display cabinet was overflowing with all manner of ceramics, glass, silverware and other assorted knick-knacks and bric-a-brac. To the middle-class home-owner such displays were a means of showing off their new-found cultural interests, prosperity and status. They were also in accord with the fashionable notion that bareness and insufficient ornamentation in a room was in poor taste. However, to the aesthete the sum total of all the trappings of a middle-class lifestyle amounted to little more than clutter.

well-to-do, and some time later, during the 1870s and 1880s, they became fashionable among the more educated and cultured sections of the middle classes. However, throughout this period most middle-class homes continued to be decorated in high-Victorian style – a fact that can to some extent be explained by the substantial cost of Aesthetic and Arts and Crafts furnishings and ornaments which were hand-made using traditional methods of craftsmanship, compared with relatively inexpensive mass-produced items. For example, William Morris's Arts and Crafts hand-blocked patterned wallpapers and fabrics and also his pieces of furniture were well beyond the pocket of most ordinary home-owners who instead had to content themselves with machine-made copies (some of which were actually of very high quality).

Above left: "My Neighbour's House" by Frederick Elwell shows a recreation of a mid-Victorian hallway. The wooden panelling, fireplace and gas-light chandelier are typical and the Jacobean Revival chair and sideboard are reminiscent of the latter part of the 19th century.

Left: many Victorian houses had tiled entrance halls, as shown in the Steamboat House, Galena, Illinois. The wallpaper is an accurate copy of a 19th-century French design. The American clock is c.1870 and the locally made furniture dates from the late-Victorian period.

The decorative style advocated by men such as Eastlake, Morris and other followers of the Aesthetic and Arts and Crafts movements primarily consisted of Queen Anne Revival style for the outside of the home. Inside, furniture was inspired by Medieval, Elizabethan, Jacobean, classical Greek and traditional Georgian forms. Fabrics and wallpapers were generally lighter and more subtly coloured, using traditional pigments instead of the richer, more vivid colours obtained by the use of the new chemical aniline dyes. Ornaments also tended to be simpler in terms of colour, pattern and form; Japanese prints and Chinese export blue-and-white china were much admired both in themselves and as a source of inspiration for both the form and decoration of new designs and production.

In the mid 1860s Aesthetic-style interiors were almost exclusively confined to the houses of leading artists and designers and of the

However, during the last decade of the 19th century and right up until World War I, Arts and Crafts furnishings did begin to replace high-Victorian style as the fashionable ideal for middle-class aspirations, particularly in suburbia. The William Morris-inspired cottage with its low-ceilinged living-hall, large-hearthed inglenook and plain and simple oak furniture, fulfilled an increasing nostalgia for the rural idyll of the pre-industrial age, as did some of the English Art Nouveau interiors designed by C. F. A. Voysey. Ironically, the railways, which had contributed in no small part to the growth of industry and manufacturing, the general movement of populations toward the towns and cities and the attendant urbanization of the landscape now helped to fuel that wave of nostalgia by providing city dwellers and suburbanites with the opportunity to visit and enjoy the tranquillity of the surviving rural communities.

In terms of decoration and ornamentation of the home perhaps the greatest irony of the Victorian era is that in an age of rapid and significant advances in the technology of manufacturing – particularly in the production of such things as architectural fixtures and fittings, furniture, fabrics, wallpapers, ceramics, glass, silverware and a variety of household appliances – architects, designers, craftsmen and their clients consistently looked to the past for inspiration.

The wave of nostalgia for a pre-industrial past seen at the end of the era in the gradual acceptance by the middle classes of Arts and Crafts as well as Aesthetic-inspired designs, was in fact little different from the high-Victorian yearning for the splendours of sumptuous interior decoration commonly found in France during the Second Empire, or the early to mid-Victorian admiration for Classical, Gothic, Renaissance, Louis XIV and Rococo styles. Looking to the past and also to other cultures for inspiration and embellishing or refining their designs and products to suit either modern methods of manufacturing, new social needs or fashionable notions as to what was aesthetically pleasing or seen to be in "good taste", was therefore a consistent theme throughout the 19th century. Indeed, in many respects it can be usefully considered as the essence or hallmark of Victorian style.

It is important to remember this fact when recreating a Victorian interior today. Successful Victorian-revival decorative schemes do not have to be exact replicas of 19th-century interiors such as those illustrated in period pattern books, photographs or, indeed, in illustrations in this or any other books on the subject. Unlike recreations of Neoclassical, Regency or Federal interiors – where for authentic results you are obliged to pursue, often at great expense and with considerable difficulty, what Osbert Lancaster called "the fatal will-o'-the-wisp of period accuracy" in its entirety – in fact, the characteristically eclectic nature of Victorian style, particularly during the second half of the 19th century, conveniently lends itself to judicious combinations of the old and the new. For example, just as the Victorians happily married original or copies of 18th-century furniture with contemporary furniture, fabrics and wallpapers, so it is equally possible and even desirable to create an effective Victorian domestic ambiance today by combining a display of Victorian antiques, collectables and original or reproduction fabrics within a modern setting.

During the 1850s and 1860s numerous Victorian houses on both sides of the Atlantic were modernized – a regrettable process that involved the destruction of many of the orginal architectural fixtures and fittings. However, the recent and widespread interest in all things Victorian has led an ever-increasing number of manufacturers and specialist suppliers today to offer a broad and comprehensive selection of original or reproduction features, including fire surrounds, doors, floors, stained glass, staircases and wooden and plaster mouldings (*see* The Directory, pages 220-33).

Original and high-quality reproduction tiles, fabrics and wallpapers have also become readily available from a variety of sources, including antique dealers, auction houses and, again, specialist suppliers (*see* The Directory, pages 220-33). Junk or thrift shops, garage or jumble sales and swap meets or boot sales can also be useful sources of Victoriana. In addition to a number of specialist manufacturers, most of the leading paint companies now supply a wide choice of reproduction period paints. Antique Victorian furniture can be bought via auction houses and antique dealers or, if you are lucky, discovered in the loft and

good-quality, reproduction 19th-century furniture can even be found in many leading department stores.

The eclectic and adaptable nature of Victorian style and the availability and affordability of the numerous elements of that style, in both original and reproduction form, collectively offer the would-be Victorian revivalist of the 1990s and the future beyond the opportunity not only to recreate and so celebrate the past but also, just as the Victorians themselves did in one of the most dynamic periods in our history, adapt, refine or even embellish it to suit ever-changing present-day needs and circumstances.

Left: designed by Jonathan Hudson, the impact of this Victorian set piece relies on a rich variety of colours, fabrics, plants, pictures and furniture. Above: Louis C. Tiffany's "Morning Room" of 1881 shows his fondness for gilt papers, coloured glass and exotic textiles, all set off against dark wood. Right: a fireplace and overmantel in typical high-Victorian Gothic style.

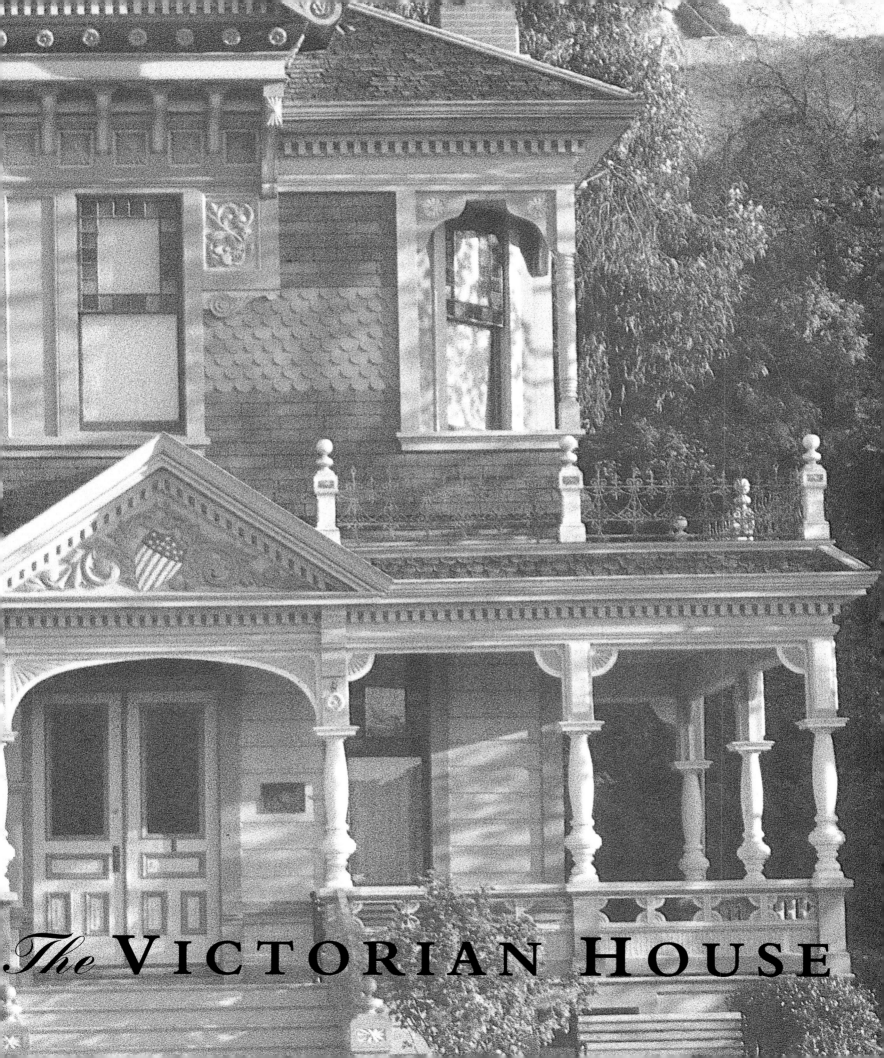

The Victorian House

ARCHITECTURE

At the beginning of the Victorian period, after some fifty years of independence, the East Coast and a few of the major river junctions were the only truly urbanized parts of the United States. Even by the end of the era large cities of today such as Los Angeles and Dallas were still only in the early stages of development. Nevertheless, as the country was opened up and agriculture and industry expanded during the 19th century, a vigorous and substantial programme of building ensued to meet the needs of a growing and increasingly prosperous population.

For much of the Victorian era architectural styles in North America were influenced by prevailing fashions on the other side of the Atlantic. So, during the first half of the century many East Coast town houses bore a close resemblance to their European and, in particular, their British counterparts. For example, the row or terraced houses in Boston, Massachusetts and the brownstone residences of New York hardly differed in appearance from their equivalents in Kensington, London, England.

The architectural legacy of the early settlers of North America was primarily Neo-classical in origin and many of the buildings that had been constructed during the Federal period at the end of the Georgian era were in the Greek Revival style, with its attenuated columns and the use of Greek (instead of Roman) orders and details. The Federal

Left: a detail from the Queen Anne-style Hale House in Heritage Square, Los Angeles, California, which has been restored in its original colours.
Right: the Eastlake veranda with turned porch posts, spindles and fan-like brackets and the different roof slopes of Kearfoot-Bane House in Martinsburg, West Virginia, built in 1901, are characteristic of the Queen Anne style.

Constructed c.1897, this late-Victorian house with a steeply pitched roof and turret is on East Main Street, Middletown, Maryland.

Durfee House in St James Park in Los Angeles, California. Known as a "pink lady", it was built c.1880 in Eastlake style.

A 19th-century weather-boarded Victorian cottage in Vicksburg, Mississippi, painted in typical cream with brown shutters and detailing.

Classical style, seen for instance in the work of architects such as William Strickland, was to remain fashionable to varying degrees, particularly in the state capitals, for the rest of the century. Similarly, Italianate-style mansions and town houses based on Italian *palazzi* were erected in large numbers, especially during the early years of the Victorian era. Generally square in proportion and with few columns, most featured mansard or low-pitched roofs, deep architraves around the windows and heavy moulding or cornicing. Architects working in this style included C.F. McKim, W.R. Mead and Stanford and White.

Around the middle of the century mansions and houses built in the Gothic style also began to appear. The ensuing "battle of the styles" between Classical and Gothic echoed that in Britain. However, the Gothic influence in North America was initially inspired by the French interpretation of the style. Many leading architects travelled to Paris to learn their trade at the *Ecole des Beaux Arts*: R.M. Hunt, for example, went there in 1846 and returned to New York to build a substantial number of large houses with features such as steeply pitched roofs, dormer windows, finials and parapets – all characteristic of the perpendicular face of Gothic architecture. Although lived in by only the most affluent members of the community, these ornate residences provided the inspiration for the façades of numerous smaller, albeit less elaborately ornamented,

Another detached suburban house on East Main Street, Middletown, Maryland, constructed c.1905. The porch shows decorative wood carving.

A grander residence also on East Main Street, Middletown, Maryland, constructed c.1902, with a prominent dormer window and deep porch.

The Inn at Antietam in Sharpsburg, Maryland. The wood-clad house dates from pre-Civil War years and overlooks the Antietam battlefield.

Gothic Revival houses built during the second half of the century.

The Gothic influence was also prevalent in the work of the renowned Victorian architect H.H. Richardson, who had followed Hunt to Paris in 1860. While many of his buildings, which were essentially a synthesis of Gothic and Romanesque styles and typified by heavy stonework and deep rounded arches, were best-suited to a non-urban environment, adaptations of them are still evident in the down-town areas of numerous North American cities to this day.

Both Richardson and Hunt were also to prove influential in the emergence of the American Stick style of architecture during the second half of the century. Richardson's

Watts Sherman House and Hunt's summer houses, built at Newport, Rhode Island, were based on the English half-timbered Tudor style and provided the inspiration for less sophisticated architects and builders who erected a large number of somewhat naive timber-structured houses which boasted picturesque features such as decorative millwork, deeply overhanging gabled eaves and patterned exterior walls.

The Gothic Revival inevitably co-existed with other architectural idioms during the second half of the Victorian era, many of which were either adaptations or a synthesis of different revival styles that also had their origins in Europe. For instance, houses built in the American Queen Anne style were

inspired by the work of the English architect Norman Shaw and early examples combined Classical detailing with various vernacular forms such as complicated projections, steep gables, patterned masonry and decorative wooden shingles. Later examples designed, for instance, by the architectural firm of McKim, Mead and White in the 1890s, were a hybrid of Queen Anne style and the traditional clapboarded architecture of the East Coast. This highly practical synthesis, better known as Colonial Revival, was to become the typical face of the American home well into the 20th century. Many examples have a regional or vernacular quality and are single-storied edifices with clapboard walls, large roofs and pedimented dormers and sash windows; some

Above: a mid 19th-century wood-clad Italianate-style house in Los Angeles, California, with a low-pitched roof, broad eaves and narrow windows.
Right: an elaborate veranda with balusters and Classical-style columns and capitals.
Below: part of an Italianate-style row or terrace of Australian homes, built c.1860s.

Griswold House in Newport, Rhode Island. A literal interpretation of the English half-timbered tradition which influenced the Stick style.

A Shingle-style house in Newport, Rhode Island, built 1881-2. It is notable for its plain shingled surfaces and asymmetrical planning.

The broad gables and elements of half-timbering on this house, built in 1875 in Newport, Rhode Island, are characteristic of the late-Victorian era.

of the more ostentatious examples feature a portico similar to those found on the plantation houses in the South of the country.

Other notable developments of Queen Anne style included the relatively plain yet highly attractive and imaginative Shingle-style houses constructed from the 1880s to approximately 1900. Often planned asymmetrically, the roofs, exterior walls and columns of these residences were usually covered with wooden shingles – hence the name. Similarly, the robust furniture designs of the English architect Charles Eastlake were transposed from the 1870s into a popular domestic building style not unlike Queen Anne, but distinguished by more ornate carved and turned ornament and scrollwork.

As the Victorian era drew to a close the British and European influences were in some

respects nearly as strong as they had been at the start of the period. This influence could be seen in architectural idioms as diverse as the fine Arts and Crafts-inspired houses built on the West Coast by C.S. and H.M. Greene (which also drew on simple Japanese designs) and the blocks of apartments or flats which were first built in Europe and later erected in American cities at roughly the same time as the phenomenon of grouping residences together under one roof began in London, England, toward the end of the 19th century.

While most of the various revival styles fashionable at one time or another throughout the Victorian era had their origins on the other side of the Atlantic, a number of factors combined to distinguish American architecture (as well as that in Australia and New Zealand) from its counterparts in Britain and Europe. First and foremost among them was the presence, unlike in Europe, of huge forested areas which yielded vast supplies of lumber and ensured that wood was a predominant feature of buildings as diverse as the large Classical plantation houses of the South to the log cabins of the Rockies.

One of the most innovative and distinctive ways in which wood was used was in the development of the prefabricated house – a system of building which facilitated the rapid expansion of many American cities after the Civil War. Initially advocated by the landscape gardener Andrew Jackson Downing in the 1840s and made possible by technological advances that enabled commercial mills to mass-produce uniformly shaped timbers, such houses became available via mail-order suppliers during the last quarter of the century. Transported by rail, the components arrived on site numbered for immediate assembly. The frames were usually hung with wooden shingles, either elaborately finished to resemble brick or stone, or given a "rustic" effect. Ready-made doors and windows were then attached to the frame and a wide selection of

Left: Hale House in Los Angeles, California. Right: the Barn in Devon, England built c.1900 has huge chimneys and "butterfly" wings. Far right: the Grange in Philadelphia, Pennsylvania; a late 19th-century Gothic Revival house with "gingerbread" eaves and gables.

decorative details could be added as required. By the end of the century the development of balloon framing had even made it possible to incorporate more complex architectural features such as overhangs, bay windows and towers.

The extensive use of wood in combination with the publication and widespread availability of numerous pattern books also had a profound influence on the exterior detailing of American houses. For example, *Palliser's*

Modern Homes, published in 1878, offered local carpenters an enormous choice of elaborate designs by architects such as Charles Eastlake, which they could copy or adapt to meet the various needs of their clients. One

The Steamboat House in Galena, Illinois.
A two-story Gothic Revival house built in 1855
for Captain Daniel Smith Harris.

Husted House in Galena, Illinois. The house was
built by Lyman Husted in 1856-8 from red
Galena brick and is painted in the Italianate style.

Designed in brick by William Dennison in 1860,
the Ulysses S. Grant home is typical of the
Italianate bracketed style.

of the consequences of this was a tremendous diversity of vernacular and "one-off" styles across the country. The results of such embellishments can, for instance, be seen in Martha's Vineyard in Rhode Island, where a substantial number of small houses, each designed according to the original owner's whim, display vast carved bargeboards or vergeboards shadowing small Gothic windows and doors.

While immigrant craftsmen and carpenters also brought their own native styles of construction and embellishments with them – resulting in, for example, a visible German influence in Baltimore, Swedish in the

Mid-West and Spanish on the West Coast – local climatic conditions also played a part in distinguishing much North American architecture from that in Europe.

For instance, in the warmer South and South-West, large porches, balconies and verandas designed to circulate air around the exterior walls and provide a seating area protected from the sun were a common feature. Naturally they offered tremendous scope for elaborate embellishments and given the availability of inexpensive mass-produced frets and turnings (either locally or via mail-order), decorative exterior woodwork was both

uninhibited and abundant. Hence the popularity of the distinctive and highly decorative "gingerbread" houses that were such a feature of the late-Victorian period.

However, it was the need to protect wooden structures and exterior features from the elements that indirectly gave North America a lighter and more colourful architecture than was generally found in Europe. From the so-called "painted ladies" in San Francisco to the Stick-style vertical-board-sided houses in New Jersey, exterior paint schemes in a multitude of complementary and contrasting hues abounded.

Left: Belvedere Mansion in Galena, Illinois,
1857. The windows and woodwork are original.
Below: Dezoya House, Galena, Illinois, c.1830.

Garth Woodside Mansion in Hannibal, Missouri.
Built as a summer home in 1871,
it is an example of Second Empire architecture.

Constructed c.1890 by the Rhoderick family who
still retain ownership, this late-Victorian home is
on East Main Street, Middletown, Maryland.

The all-pervading impact of the Industrial Revolution, in particular the harnessing of steam power which triggered the expansion of the railways and so brought about widespread mechanization, changed the face of 19th-century society beyond recognition and, in so doing, played a highly influential part in the development of the British Victorian house. Poorer people living in rural and farming areas migrated to the expanding conurbations throughout the century in the hope of

Above left: South Lodge at Mentmore Towers in Buckinghamshire, designed by George Devey. Above right: a stone-banded cottage in Edensor, Derbyshire which was remodelled in the 1840s.

making their fortunes; for example, the number of inhabitants in the City of London more than quadrupled from 1840 to 1900. The second half of the Victorian era saw an unprecedented population explosion which went hand-in-hand with vigorous building.

Today much town and city housing – and approximately one-quarter of London's stock – survives intact from the Victorian period.

As the railways transported materials from all over the country – cast iron from Scotland, glass from Lancashire and bricks from the claybelts of southern England – many new products became available to builders, enabling them to adopt a new diversity of architectural styles. Large builders' merchants and well-stocked warehouses were established close to

Queen-Anne style town houses in Cadogan Square in Belgravia, London, England.

Built in 1877, an early 18th-century style house with a hipped roof and a crowning balcony.

Pilasters, balconies and classical swags embellish the façade of a late-Victorian house.

Above left: Gothic details integrated into pre-Victorian Southwick Hall in Northamptonshire. Above right: Wightwick Manor's half-timbering and red brick shows William Morris influence.

railway depots and goods were delivered "carriage free" by rail or canal. As trains increased the speed and mobility with which perishable commodities could be relayed from country to town, so market gardens moved away from the urban fringes they had traditionally occupied and made way for houses to be built in their place. Speculators were quick to build accommodation for manual workers as rapidly and inexpensively as possible, which resulted in the regimented rows or terraces of so-called "back-to-backs" where three sides of every house formed party walls with neighbouring dwellings. This type of low-class housing was particularly prevalent in the industrial Midlands of England. The walls were made of thin, often porous brickwork, roofs tended to leak and sanitation was non-existent. Many of these hastily built houses have not survived and the numerous Victorian homes still intact today are examples of more superior workmanship. The grim reality of life in the overcrowded city slums so shocked Prince Albert that he introduced housing standards for the poor and in an attempt to institute reforms he assisted in designing "model dwellings", some of which survive in Camberwell, south London. In a similar vein, Henry Roberts designed blocks of "model" apartments or flats for labourers in London in the 1840s. However, it was only toward the

end of the 19th century that mansion apartments or flats became popular town residences for the well-to-do.

Victorian rows or terraces and smaller semi-detached houses (known as "semi-attached" during the 19th century), were often the homes of shopkeepers, artisans and clerks. There was little regional variation in their design: early versions were typically two stories high and two windows wide, with a plain brick front and a tiled or slated roof behind a parapet. Later, as parapet gutters frequently leaked into front rooms, they were supplanted by eaves gutters. These rows or terraces were usually set back from the road and had a basement set behind iron railings or a modest front garden behind a low wall surmounted by a cast-iron balustrade. Away from the lower-class housing areas, larger detached houses were built for the more affluent members of society. The upper classes in particular favoured more ostentatious and idiosyncratic domestic architecture.

Houses were constructed in a host of eclectic styles during the Victorian era. In the early years there was a broad division of two

architectural camps – the Gothic Revival which harked back to Medieval designs and the more sombre Classical style. The so-called "Grand Tour" of Europe, in particular Italy, prompted architects and the wealthy, travelling members of Victorian society to admire and emulate the classical Italian Renaissance style. Queen Victoria and Prince Albert had a palace built at Osborne on the Isle of Wight in the mid 1840s, a gesture which patronized the Classical cause. In contrast, other patrons, inspired by the romantic writings of such as Sir Walter Scott and Alfred Lord Tennyson, preferred the broken skylines so characteristic of Gothic style. The artist John Ruskin encouraged "polychromy" or the use of colourful banded brickwork which went firmly against the Classical grain. And it was common for the entrepreneurial industrialists of the day to live in huge Gothic houses or "baronial" halls, such as those designed by A.W.N. Pugin, where an abundance of towers and spires aimed to give a convincing, though false, impression of family lineage.

As more and more trade publications gained larger circulations, speculative builders used these journals as guides and often mixed Gothic and Classical detailing so that some houses juxtaposed polychromy with plain stone dressings. Later in the century there was a general tendency toward lighter façades

influenced by the architect Richard Norman Shaw's so-called Queen Anne style, which was characterized by moulded brickwork, ornate gables and terra-cotta.

The Victorians were conscious that the first and most important impression that a visitor gained of a house was its porch and front door. Because of this the very grandest residences

sometimes incorporated a *porte cochère* into which carriages could drive, so allowing their passengers to dismount under cover. The homes of the well-to-do almost invariably had a porch which was richly embellished, and even modest row or terraced houses usually featured porches decorated with ornamental glazed tiles and a polished red-tiled floor. Many front doors had stained glass panels and transoms or fanlights above them in order to allow daylight into the entrance hall. Gothic-style doors were particularly popular and they were generally made of plain oak boards and strap hinges; they also featured black iron bell pulls and brass knobs and knockers. Houses built in the Classical idiom tended to have brass furniture on darkly painted doors – particularly dark green – in the Georgian panelled tradition.

Throughout the Victorian era the standard sliding sash window, despite being difficult to keep clean, was universally popular. Once large sheets of plate glass became readily available, windows were far less costly to produce than earlier blown panes had been.

Above and right: Holly Village in Highgate, London, England, was built in 1865 by Henry Darbishire. It was conceived as a pastiche of a village green surrounded by Medieval cottages. Left: Hall Place in north London, England, was built in the late 1860s. The Gothic architecture has a hint of the German schloss.

Above left, middle and right: Queen-Anne style façades in Cadogan Square, Belgravia, London, England. The ornamented brickwork echoes Flemish Gothic and Renaissance styles of architecture which were typical during the 1880s. The houses on the west side of the square display exuberant windows and exterior details, including eclectic combinations of terra-cotta, red brick and Portland stone. This residence was built in 1886 by the flamboyant architect Ernest George.
Right: the symmetry and detailing of the windows and transom or fanlight of this house in London, England, are typical of the early 19th century.

Below left: Lonsdale Square in Barnsbury, London, England is an early example of a complete square in Tudor style. The houses were designed by R.C. Carpenter and built in 1843 (far left). A typical Gothic front door of a high-Victorian middle-class house. The steps add a note of grandeur and the pine painted doors are woodgrained to simulate hardwood. The number of the house is incorporated into the transom or fanlight – a popular Victorian feature.
Below right: the bay window, which allowed more light into the front room, was almost a universal feature of middle-class Victorian homes.

A consequence of this was that mid-Victorian houses were designed with numerous windows, and conservatories also became fashionable – a development given additional impetus by the disappearance of the window tax in 1851. During the second half of the 19th century, with the advent of the Arts and Crafts movement, hinged casement windows – thought to be picturesque and often with small panes of leaded glass – came back into vogue. In the late-Victorian years windows became noticeably larger, reflecting a general desire to have more light and air penetrating interiors. As the fashion for better-ventilated interiors grew, so roofs were broken by all sorts of ornate turrets, chimneys, cowls and belfries which often disguised ventilation outlets. And small towers atop the house sometimes indicated the presence of an out-of-the-way "smoking room".

One of the most dominant ornamental features of Victorian houses was cast iron, although evidence of this has been largely erased because so much was scrapped during World War II. Virtually every town or suburban house was fronted by a low brick wall and elaborate cast-iron railings; most entrance gates were also made of iron. Fashioned metalware changed throughout the Victorian period, reflecting current design trends, so that by the end of the 19th century it was often free-flowing, in keeping with the fluid lines of Art Nouveau.

Whatever form they took, late-Victorian British houses incorporated a wealth of varied styles and architectural influences. Documented by such devotees as Hermann Muthesius, the homes of the more prosperous members of society gained the reputation of being models of domestic comfort.

Below and right: an elaborate glass-covered porch in Kensington, London, England. Gilded leaves atop a railing show the influence of the late 19th-century Art Nouveau movement (top right).

Right: wrought-iron railings and balconies still survive on many of London's town houses. Linley Sambourne House on Stafford Terrace, built 1869-74 in the Italianate manner.

INTERIOR DETAILS

$\mathcal{T}$he rich variety of 19th-century architectural fixtures and fittings lent much to the distinctive character of the Victorian house. For example, the fireplace was the cornerstone of domestic life in many homes, and also the visual focus of most rooms. Surrounds made of marble, slate, wood and metal appeared in a host of historical-revival styles. Embellished with overmantels, chimney cloths, fenders and impedimenta of the hearth, they also provided a surface for the display of numerous decorative wares that were a hallmark of the Victorian era.

Just as the fireplace was more than a source of heat, so internal doors were as decorative as they were functional. While some were made from richly coloured and intricately figured hardwoods, others were extravagantly woodgrained, stencilled or concealed with heavily draped *portières*. Similarly, staircases featured newel posts and balusters turned in a multitude of shapes, hardwood board or parquet floors were augmented with oilcloths, rugs, carpets or linoleum, and encaustic or inlaid tiled floors boasted patterns inspired by Medieval designs. Decorative plasterwork was also much in evidence; typical examples included ornate arches, ceilings and a variety of mouldings or cornices.

For the would-be Victorian revivalist not fortunate enough to own a period house that has survived intact, high-quality reproductions of these essential elements are widely available.

Left: a fireplace with a marble slip, carved acanthus leaf and dentil mouldings. Right: an elaborate Gothic Revival fire surround. Gold metallic paint with a bronze antiquing glaze has been applied to wood and plaster mouldings and the carved woodwork is mahogany-stained and waxed. The red and gold wallpaper is a mid 19th-century documented pattern by Watts & Co.

In North America, from the parlours of large town houses to wooden homes in more isolated regions prone to extreme winters, efficient stoves were designed to give off warmth and the fireplace was often preserved for its ornamental qualities, acting in the main as a status symbol.

During the first half of the Victorian era the display of wealth was not considered ostentatious, and consequently a variety of elaborate surrounds, mantel shelves and overmantels embellished the original cast-iron grate. In the dining rooms of large Gothic residences fireplaces tended to feature dog grates and andirons which were especially designed to carry massive logs and recreated the style of hearth found in a Medieval banqueting hall.

In Britain in particular the design of fireplaces echoed all levels of what was a strictly hierarchical society so that the grandest examples, found in principal rooms where they could be admired by visitors, bore little resemblance to their humble counterparts sited in the attic bedrooms reserved for the servants.

The fireplace consisted of two main parts – the cast-iron grate and the chimneypiece or surround. In larger houses the surround was generally made of marble or slate and, later in the period, of cast iron. In smaller houses and servants' quarters more modest wooden surrounds were installed. If the wood was of high quality or had an interesting grain then it would have been varnished. Less expensive woods would have been painted or grained in order to simulate the look of hardwood, and

Fireplaces

The fireplace was an intrinsic feature of most Victorian rooms. Serving much more than a functional, heat-providing purpose, it had an important role as a focal point and, as such, was a prominent part of the overall decorative scheme. The fireplace was also regarded as a measure of wealth, implying that servants were on hand to feed it. The expansion of the railways during the 19th century meant that coal could be transported with ease from the mining areas to the towns and cities – where

it was the predominant fuel. While in rural parts, where supplies of lumber abounded, log fires were generally more common.

Above and right: a dominating Greek Revival Belgian black marble fireplace made in the 1860s (top). Victorian embellishments on a Classical fireplace (middle). A plain fire surround in the Morris Jumel Mansion in New York (right).

Above: a wide variety of designs for fire surrounds were illustrated in 19th-century trade catalogues.

it would certainly have been quite inconceivable to leave the wood completely bare.

Victorian scientists spent much time, effort and expense improving the efficiency of heat transmission from the grate to the rest of the room. By the 1840s, after years of research, the enterprising American inventor Benjamin Count Rumford designed and then tirelessly promoted the Rumford grate. A simple but effective innovation, the grate had splayed sides or cheeks which reflected heat into the room and much less heat escaped up the chimney. Rumford's comparatively efficient and economical prototype was then universally adopted in the form of the standard register grate. The latter was cast as one piece combining the grate, fireback and inner frame

Right: a plain marble slab was a popular form of mantel shelf in the early Victorian period. Below: an intricately undercut Gothic Revival frieze in a home in London, England, c.1860.

and featured a moveable iron plate in the flue to regulate the updraft. From the 1850s onward register grates were popular. Produced in a variety of sizes and often characterized by semi-circular arched heads, they were usually decorated; the more intricate embellishments being an indication of the affluence of the household. As recommended by Rumford, the fireback was splayed and the coal was contained in an open basket fronted with iron bars. The ash simply dropped into a bin underneath, or else fell directly onto the

hearthslab, from which it could be shovelled away. Dampers were also fitted into the chimney throat to regulate the supply of air. Later in the century a rectangular-topped register grate became popular, and from the 1870s onward hoods and surrounds were often decorated with coloured tiles. Initially, these tiles were confined to the drawing rooms or parlours of large town houses, but once mass-produced, they became popular in smaller

Left: a 19th-century cast-iron fireplace with a patriotic eagle motif on the lintel and cheeks. Below: modest cast-iron fireplaces painted white to emulate marble were found in upstairs rooms.

homes, nursery rooms and servants' quarters. Those designed by prominent artists of the day such as Walter Crane, William Morris and William de Morgan are now much sought-after by collectors. Today's Victorian houses, from

Below left: a black marble fireplace with brass fender and andirons in a secondary reception room. Below right: from the late 1850s cast-iron fireplaces with built-in grates were mass-produced.

the most modest to the grandest, often retain their register grates and these can also be found in profusion in architectural salvage depots.

At the beginning of the Victorian period there was a predominance of plain, Classical fire surrounds which were made usually of stone or marble; the sides could be fluted to suggest Classical pilasters and the lintel might have had a decoratively carved central panel. As the period progressed surrounds became more and more elaborate. For instance, they were enriched with carving and gilding and heavily scrolled brackets were used to support the mantel shelf. Panels of different types of stone were sometimes set into moulded surrounds to embellish the lintel and sides.

From the 1860s onward fireplaces became valued increasingly for their aesthetic impact. Their design and construction moved away from utilitarian origins into the realm of furniture. Grates, which were sometimes also called "interiors", were enhanced with a huge variety of mantel shelves and overmantels. As the Victorian period progressed, fire regulations affecting chimney construction were introduced in Britain and non-combustible marble, slate and cast-iron surrounds were favoured for safety reasons.

In America revivals of Rococo, Renaissance and Neo-classical styles led to a vogue for heavily ornamented marble and

wooden surrounds and as mass-production of fireplaces increased so English firms such as the Carron Company and C. Hindley & Sons answered the demand for reproduction Elizabethan, Queen Anne and Neo-Georgian surrounds. In Europe, plain fireplaces were ingeniously disguised with new paint effects in order to resemble stone, marble, exotic wood or high-quality veneer. Even though fire surrounds were fixed to chimneypieces, in

Below: plain fireplaces of almost Grecian simplicity were produced throughout the Victorian era (left). A Rococo Revival surround in New York, many were imported from Europe (right). Far right: a late-Victorian solid wood fireplace.

Top: three styles of overmantel: Neo-classical (left); Georgian Revival (middle); Classical (right) Above: intricately cast gas fires arrived late in the Victorian period, here are a pair of typical designs with asbestos heat elements.

Brass fire accessories often adorned the hearth.

A slate surround with a simulated marble finish.

A modest tiled marble fireplace, 1892.

the most fashionable houses they were treated as furniture to such an extent that they were often changed when rooms were redecorated.

The designs of mantel shelves were generally in keeping with the predominant style of the rest of the home. A fairly simple marble slab, or one made of slate as a less expensive alternative, was frequently installed in the dining room. These surfaces were considered more hygienic than wood, which tended to gather dust and was considered undesirable in a room given over to eating. In the drawing

Above: a cast-iron register grate, c.1860, with an oval flap behind to prevent debris falling down the chimney (left). More ornate register grates were produced by the William Owen foundry in the late 19th century (middle and right).
Right: today reproduction Victorian fireplace surrounds are widely available in all sorts of designs. Far right: by the end of the Victorian era tiles and tile panels were mass-produced. These are from the Pryke and Palmer catalogue of 1896.

room or parlour a more elaborate wooden structure was usually installed and by the late 19th century the fashion for overmantels with a central mirror encased with columns, turned supports and compartments for displaying ornaments was well-established. In contrast, bedroom fireplaces were typically small and sometimes featured a so-called "combination" consisting of an all-in-one cast-iron mantel shelf and register grate. Servants' rooms usually had even smaller grates which held only a minimum amount of fuel; they would probably have carried away a few lumps of red-hot coals from the kitchen range on retiring to bed.

In smaller houses belonging to the less affluent the family tended to live around the kitchen range during the winter months and fires in other rooms were only lit for special occasions or when there were guests. Smoky chimneys and drafts were continuous

drawbacks so cowls were fitted to the tops of chimneys. However, their effectiveness was often defeated by householders blocking cracks which prevented air reaching the fire, so filling the room with smoke. Small sliding ventilators were later incorporated in the front of the hearth to help diminish the problem. By the end of the 19th century the re-appearance of the Medieval inglenook – a recessed space beside a fire often with a built-in seat – became popular. The Arts and Crafts and the Aesthetic movements revived an interest in plain surrounds – bringing the evolution of fireplace styles almost full circle.

This four-panelled wood-grained door would have been found in a modest Victorian home.

Painted double doors of the late 1880s, showing Aesthetic freehand and stencilled decoration.

Etched glass panels were a feature of houses throughout the Victorian period.

Doors

Most early Victorian doors were made of inferior fir or pine and a diagonal piece of wood or "brace" was placed across the horizontal ledges to reduce warping; the whole was often finished with lead-based paint or woodgraining. Battened doors were reintroduced in some middle-class homes much later in the period as part of the vernacular revival brought about by the Arts and Crafts movement. In contrast, these well-constructed late-

Mahogany sliding doors framed by columns in the Old Merchant's House, New York.

Victorian examples were generally made of oak and often featured the heads of carefully spaced iron nails. Usually lightly stained or polished and fitting snugly into their detailed frames, they had hammered black wrought-iron hinges and ingeniously hand-carved oak latches with wooden pegs or wedges which served as locks.

However, the most common interior door throughout the Victorian period was "framed and panelled" and its quality varied enormously according to the decor of the rest of the house. Modest residences, whether detached or row or terraced, as well as the servants' rooms in grander homes, often featured four-panelled doors set in frames less than 1in (2.5cm) thick which were commonly made from pine. They were usually fitted with surface-mounted "rim" latches or locks which were placed on the room side of the door so that they could not be tampered with from the corridor. Plainer doors were sometimes painted or woodgrained to imitate more expensive wood and even the simplest architraves – the moulded frames around the door – were embellished to some degree and often featured a "mousemould", so-called because in cross section it had the profile of a mouse.

The suburban homes of the more well-to-do featured heavier architraves and doors, the latter with six or even eight panels. It was generally considered unattractive for a door to be higher than double its width. In larger rooms "reception" doors were popular. These sometimes had pediments or other architectural features above the door head, which were Gothic or Classical depending on the overall decor of the house, or sometimes a confused mixture of various styles. Two-leaved doors were another feature of spacious

Heavily ornamented brass push plates or fingerplates are part of the door furniture.

rooms, allowing one room to open into another. In many town houses the two principal rooms on the entrance floor could be separated by either a pair of wide folding doors or else "pocket" doors which slid into hidden "pockets" in the walls; both types could be drawn back to accommodate large gatherings. Double doors dividing rooms were sometimes lined to prevent servants from listening in to conversation and to minimize kitchen noises and smells penetrating the drawing or dining room. Decorative dummy doors were also installed to create symmetry within a hall or a room, a treatment which appealed particularly to Classical architects. Later in the 19th century it was felt that too many large internal doors made rooms cold and drafty. Consequently doors became noticeably smaller so that less air circulated in-between rooms and as a result large pieces of furniture had to be taken in and out via the windows. Heavy drapes or *portières* were sometimes hung over doorways in order to eliminate drafts.

High-quality doors were usually made of white deal – a superior type of pine – and then oil-painted. Oak, mahogany and other exotic woods were also popular and tended to have a polished finish. In some houses the servants' quarters were concealed behind secret entrances built into panelled walls, or, more commonly, servants passed through a door in the entrance hall which was often covered in green baize designed to block off noise from "below stairs".

Whatever its appearance, on almost every Victorian door there was a pair of "push" or "finger" plates, above and below the typically circular- or oval-shaped door pull or knob. These protected the paintwork from greasy fingerprints and came in pressed *repoussé* metal, brass, silver gilt, ceramic or carved wood.

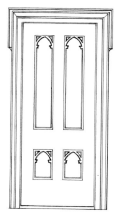

Above right: a door showing Aesthetic design (top). A dining-room door with Gothic-style tracery (middle). An escutcheon or metal plate around a keyhold and a selection of china door knobs: usually found in black or white and frequently decorated with a gold line.

Above: during the late 19th century, particularly in the reception rooms, the door was very much a part of the overall impression of the interior. Here the painted upper panels echo the motif on the walls of the room, the lower panels are ornamented with coats of arms and the brass door furniture is very elaborate. The door is swamped with heavily trimmed drapes and a matching pelmet fills the space in-between the moulding or cornice and the picture rail.
Left: because hardwoods were expensive, the Victorians often grained their softwood doors.

Scale of the Plan.

Plan.

Section from A to B.

Decorative Plasterwork

In affluent Victorian houses the baseboards or skirtings and dados were sometimes fashioned from plaster, although these were more commonly made of wood. But it was ceilings in particular which offered plasterers ample opportunity to demonstrate their skills. Many were embellished with intricately patterned friezes, panelling and ribs. Overdoors, mouldings or cornices, mirror and picture frames, columns, arches and ceiling medallions or roses were also dressed in decorative plasterwork and typical relief patterns included flower and leaf motifs, scrolls and loops, as well as beaded, fluted and Greek key designs. Although some ceilings were left white, others were painted, papered, gilded and stencilled for decoration and to disguise cracks and discolouring caused by the fumes emitted from oil and gas lamps.

At the beginning of the Victorian period ornamental enrichments were moulded as small, individual components and then placed

Above: an enriched plaster ceiling, 1868.
Below: a distressed-finish moulding or cornice.

Below left and right: Classical columns were popular as purely decorative features.

Above: a design for a moulded plaster ceiling in the Renaissance style, c.1885.

Right: decorative ceiling medallions or roses were made of papier mâché *or fibrous plaster.*

in position. The plaster mould was taken from an original clay model and then covered in grease to prevent the casts from sticking to it and forming imperfectly. The process of pouring liquid plaster into the mould to make the casting was very labour-intensive and so it was only the more affluent sections of early Victorian society who could afford the most ornate plasterwork.

The advent of precast fibrous plaster strengthened with canvas made decorative plasterwork more affordable. It was moulded into all sorts of patterns and mouldings or cornices and ceiling medallions or roses arrived on site in standard sizes to be simply screwed into place. Fibrous plaster was both easy to mould and suitable for working in deep relief; it was the main material used for all manner of high-Victorian plaster enrichments. The introduction of gelatine moulds increased the scope of decorative plasterwork further and these flexible moulds were ideal for casting busts, figures and deeply embossed plaques.

In the bedrooms, where plainer moulding or cornicing sufficed, the plasterer usually prepared wet plaster and ran a template over the mixture to form the chosen profile. This was a skilled process and an unsteady hand produced unsightly blemishes. Wet plaster took a long time to dry out and in the winter fires were lit to try and accelerate the process. In spite of this, several weeks needed to elapse before it could be painted. Mouldings or cornices were often painted in several colours to highlight their relief and match the colours of

the walls. Unfortunately decorative plasterwork in many of today's Victorian houses has often been so heavily overpainted that the original detail has been lost. However, careful cleaning and restoration will bring back the crispness of the relief.

Another less expensive and versatile alternative to plaster was *papier mâché*. Although this did not have the same intricacy as plaster casts it was often used to make ceiling medallions or roses which served as a suspension

point for gas lamps in modest houses and chandeliers in grander homes. As with other ceiling and wall plasterwork dressings it was often painted to match the decor of the rest of the room. In general the entrance hall and the reception rooms, important parameters of wealth and status, boasted the most ornate decorative plasterwork in the house.

Below left: reproduction plaster mouldings.
Below: Classical staircase mouldings, c.1847.

Left: mass-produced late-Victorian balusters.
Below left: a pair of heavy Italianate newel posts.
Below: a spiral staircase with a scroll pattern
on the treads and stair-ends.

Above: the self-supporting winding circular staircase with tapering balusters in the Bartow-Pell Mansion, New York, dates from c.1842 and rises from the entrance floor to the attic.

Above: the late 19th-century staircase in Leighton House, London, England was designed by George Aitchison. The carpet features a recreated pattern taken from a historic "Tree of Life" rug.
Right: a heavy, square newel post from the 1880s (left); an intricate 1870s cast-iron newel post (middle); and a highly decorative wooden newel in a New York home, dating from the 1830s – the design was probably meant to be executed in stone but here has been made in oak (right).

Stairs

The simplest staircases found in humble homes consisted of a steep flight of narrow wooden stairs. Usually made of inexpensive pine, they rose directly from the hall or a room on the entrance floor. In row or terraced houses it was customary to have a "dogleg" stairway, so-called because it was divided by a half-landing at the back of the house. This was situated at the rear of the hall – usually a narrow passageway connecting the front door with the entrance-floor rooms. In town houses which had rooms in a semi-basement there was a lower flight of "dogleg" stairs and the half-landing led directly into the back yard or garden. In some instances the entrance floor was raised above street level and the front door approached by several steps. The latter external feature, as well as variations in levels of floors and landings inside the house added an element of grandeur to the overall impression of the building.

A typical early Victorian staircase featured plain square balusters and a touch of refinement may have been added in the form of a

newel post and a polished oak or mahogany handrail. The edges of the stair treads were usually painted or stained and visible on either side of a strip of carpet or floorcloth that ran up the middle of the staircase.

With mechanized lumber industries developing apace, large commercial joineries began to mass-produce all sorts of building components made from wood. Some manufacturers exercised great skill in making continuous handrails which were able to turn corners and terminated in scrolls. By the 1880s small-scale construction firms could purchase ready-turned balusters and newel posts so that staircases became much more elaborate. Fretwork was also popular: fashioned from flat planks pierced and cut into fancy shapes it was then used to make balusters or decorative panes in spandrels and screens. Many builders selected such products by mail order from a wide variety of illustrated trade catalogues.

The houses of well-to-do Victorians often had a large stair hall or reception area for visitors which was furnished with seats and a fireplace. The open stairwell was designed to impress and was typically finished in polished oak or mahogany and had richly

Above: cast-iron balusters, c.1850, embellished with foliage in a house in Glasgow, Scotland.

turned balusters and bulky newel posts surmounted by a decorative finial such as a ball.

In the grandest houses and also in blocks of apartments or flats, where the stairs were subject to heavy wear and tear, the steps were often made of polished marble or stone and the balustrades were cast iron. Cast-iron fixtures and fittings were supplied to builders

Above: Richard Norman Shaw's oak staircase in Cragside, Northumbria, England, c.1876.

in much the same way as joinery. Later in the 19th century the influence of the Arts and Crafts movement led to an interest in wrought ironwork. Also by this time, tall blocks of apartments or flats were served by ascending carriages or elevators; they looked like ironwork cages and were built into the existing stairwell.

Above: a newel post with an unusual carved patera, the turned tapered balusters are typical of the late-Victorian period (left); in an 1830s New York home simple balusters are set into a round banister and the newel post has a facetted shaft (middle); painted pine balusters in a hallway in London, England, c.1880, and a polished hardwood handrail (right).
Right: late-Victorian taste demanded that a large residence featured an impressive staircase – this panelled staircase hall was built in the 1880s.

Above and below: parquet floors and borders were composed from different-coloured hardwoods.

Above: instead of leaving floorboards bare, the Victorians covered them with rugs.

However, by the end of the 19th century fitted wall-to-wall carpets began to lose popularity for two reasons. First, the notion of nailing down carpets was considered unhygienic as they could not be lifted for regular cleaning. Second, the Arts and Crafts and Aesthetic movements were advocating a return to simpler interiors, which included leaving floors relatively unadorned. A taste for loose carpets or rugs now prevailed. Because these were laid on an otherwise exposed floor, it was easy to remove them for cleaning and they could also be turned or moved to lessen wear and tear. From the 1870s onward many carpets and rugs were being imported from the Far East and soon manufacturers nearer to home were imitating popular Oriental patterns.

Where floors were not carpeted, drafts were excluded by various means. Ordinary floorboards tended to be tongued-and-grooved and a thin layer of parquet – the latter could be purchased in panels and laid directly on top of the boards – gave the impression of an expensive floor. For those who could afford

*F*loors

By the middle of the 19th century mechanized production methods meant that carpets, which had hitherto been something of a luxury, were found in all but the poorest Victorian homes. Until the later years of the Victorian period it was fashionable among the middle and upper classes to have fitted wall-to-wall carpets in all the principal rooms of the house. Often brightly coloured and highly patterned with flowers, swags, festoons, and

also geometric designs, they were popular for not only their decoration but also to eliminate drafts rising from beneath the floorboards. The latter were laid on joists which allowed air to circulate below them, so reducing the risks of damp and rot.

Right: fitted wall-to-wall carpets were a luxury to the early Victorians and motifs were varied (top and bottom). Oil cloth, here stencilled to imitate tiles, was extremely popular for hallway floors.

it, thick hardwood parquet was fashionable and could be laid in a variety of basket or herringbone patterns and embellished using contrasting shades of wood. In contrast, in the humblest households bare boards were generally covered with a plain floor cloth – usually made of coarse canvas and sometimes adapted

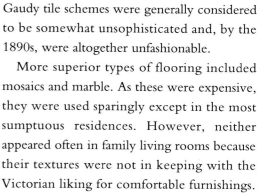

from an old ship's sail. The first linoleums were introduced during the 1860s by the Scottish firm of Michael Nairn and Co. They consisted of compressed cork with a calico or hessian backing covered in linseed oil. The less expensive linoleums were thin, while the better-quality versions were up to $\frac{1}{4}$ in

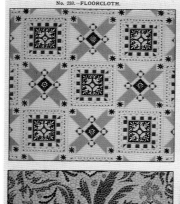

No. 239.—FLOORCLOTH.   No. 1028.—LINOLEUM.   No. 80.—INLAID LINOLEUM.

No. 586.—FLOORCLOTH.   No. 194.—LINOLEUM.   Red.   No. 996.—CORK CARPET.   Blue.

HAMPTON & SONS, Pall Mall East, and Cockspur Street, Charing Cross, London, s.w.

(0.5cm) thick and extremely durable. They had the added advantage of being easy to clean and became the preferred flooring for corridors, bathrooms, nurseries and service areas such as pantries and sculleries in well-to-do homes. Early types of linoleum simulated carpet designs or parquet patterns but later in the period plain brown, green and other so-called "art shades" were more in vogue.

Left from top to bottom: an Italian-crafted inlaid marble floor with naturalistic forms in Leighton House, London, England; encaustic tiles of inalid earthenware were popular for their durability; a 19th-century "welcome" mat; stair rods could be removed to allow the repositioning of stair carpets and so prevent them from wearing out.
Above right: six designs from Hampton & Sons's 1892 catalogue illustrating a variety of simulated floor finishes.

In general, the floors of entrance halls, conservatories and kitchens were tiled. Coloured terra-cotta floor tiles were produced in large quantities by such companies in the "potteries" as Maw and Co. and Mintons. Bathroom, conservatory and entrance hall floors were very often patterned in black and white, and

hall floors were also frequently a colourful, patterned field with a chevron or fretwork border. Kitchen tiles were usually plain red. Gaudy tile schemes were generally considered to be somewhat unsophisticated and, by the 1890s, were altogether unfashionable.

More superior types of flooring included mosaics and marble. As these were expensive, they were used sparingly except in the most sumptuous residences. However, neither appeared often in family living rooms because their textures were not in keeping with the Victorian liking for comfortable furnishings. Instead, they were confined to entrance halls or circulation spaces, making a statement of grandeur. As the 19th century progressed, improved methods of quarrying and polishing meant that granite and other hardstones provided a substitute for marble.

Decorative ELEMENTS

COLOUR

Specifying precise colours for particular periods during the Victorian, or indeed any other, period is something of an inexact science. While it is possible to identify fashionable schemes prevalent during certain decades, such schemes were rarely universal, nor did they preclude other colour schemes, and they did not disappear altogether once their moment had passed. For example, the white and gilt schemes most closely associated with 18th-century French and English drawing rooms enjoyed a number of revivals during the 19th century.

Another factor to be taken into account when prescribing colours for specific periods is the location of the house. For instance, lighter colours tended to be avoided in 19th-century town and city dwellings because the soot and pollution in the air dirtied them fairly quickly. They therefore had to be renewed more often than darker tones. However, in unindustrialized country areas, pollution was not such a problem and consequently a lighter palette was much less impractical.

In an age where the pre-mixed paints we use today were largely unknown, location also often determined the pigments that could be used. In country areas and towns in remoter parts of North America, interior decorations were often carried out by itinerant craftsmen who carried only a limited selection of pigments with them and so had to use locally available ingredients when mixing paints on site. For

Left: in a Victorian artist's town house the light, 18th-century-style moulding or cornicing, dragged in ochre, contrasts with Gothic-style windows.
Right: a room furnished with two French bergère chairs, an English lacquer chest and an Italian mirror, all 18th-century, is given an overall Victorian feel with a backdrop of dragged Ming lacquer-red walls.

example, the blue-green colourwash used on wooden panelled walls in country areas in Britain and North America was derived from the earth pigment *terra verde* (green earth), mixed with egg white and buttermilk. The various coloured limewashes and distempers used on the walls of country houses and cottages were also mixed on site, often using local ingredients.

Given the difficulties of specifying particular colours for particular periods and locations, the best way to choose them today when recreating a Victorian interior is to match paint and fabric swatches (which are available from manufacturers of reproduction period paints and fabrics, *see* The Directory, pages 225-8) against 19th-century paintings of interiors, period treatises, illustrations of decorating and furnishing and, of course, the illustrations and pictures that appear in this book. You should also refer to the chapters in the second half of this book, where colour schemes for the various rooms are described.

It is, nevertheless possible to make some general statements about the use of colour during the 19th century. For example, during the early years of the Victorian era, walls were decorated in predominantly light colours. The exceptions to this were dining rooms and libraries, where darker shades were sometimes used. Writing c.1830 about English drawing-room walls, James Arrowsmith described

them as, "panelled with watered silk of pearl or white, or light tints of pink or lavender". To some degree, such colour schemes were an extension of Regency style, with some Neo-classical and Rococo accents.

Of the darker shades used during the early years, crimson was the most popular, particularly in dining rooms, where John Loudon stated, "few colours look better than a deep crimson paper in flock". Ceilings and ceiling mouldings or cornices would have been tinted to match the colour of the walls, as white, a popular 18th-century shade, was later considered to provide too stark a contrast.

By the second half of the 19th century stronger, darker colours became more fashionable. The high-Victorian palette consisted of warm, rich colours such as vivid bottle greens, blues and golds; wine tones such as clarets, deep burgundies, reds, roses, violets and mahogany browns; and a yellow ivory. Victorian earth tones and other colours from

Left: the inspiration for the walls in this living room came from battered chairs upholstered in dusky pink and a faded lime green. The sofa is by George Smith of London, England.

Below: pale blue and white serve to lighten the heaviness of dark Victorian furniture. Here floral bedcoverings and a ticking-upholstered chair combine happily in a converted attic bedroom.

*Above: comfortable clutter in a semi-circular living room: the white day bed and foliage motifs complement the green scheme of the room.
Below right: a warm yellow and cream scheme.*

Above: a colour-washed plaster paint finish provides a warm background for a 19th-century Venetian mirror and a chaise longue.

Below: the master bedroom in Cedar Grove, Vicksburg, Mississippi, is decorated in fashionable 1840s lilac and yellow. All the furniture was made by Mallard of New Orleans in the 1840s. The large armoire avoided the need for several smaller closets which were taxable in Vicksburg at the time as additional rooms.

Right: due to the introduction of aniline chemical dyes in the middle of the 19th century, bright yellow became a popular colour. In this 1860s row or terraced house in Brook Green, West London, England, the upstairs living room has been recreated by the Marshalls in bold Victorian style. The glowing yellow walls provide a splendid back-drop for a Napoleon III day bed, c.1890. The bed is covered in striped Watts & Co. fabric which is a mixture of silk and cotton.

Nature included ochre, terra-cotta, and a soft stone-green. During this period, the general feeling was that deep, rich colours enhanced the importance of a room, whereas conversely lighter colours diminished it. For instance, a pale-walled Victorian dining room was considered cold and bare, and therefore not conducive to entertaining guests and eating.

This is not to say that white and lighter tones were not used during the high-Victorian era. Indeed, throughout the 19th century, lighter colours, such as pinks, sea-greens, light blues

The vivacity of freshly applied colours during the high-Victorian period was partly due to the invention of aniline dyes during the middle of the 19th century. The aesthetic consequence of this technological advance was the creation of a fashion for sharp yellows, vivid blues and acid greens of a chemical intensity that had not been seen before. Even when earthy reds or deep browns were used, they were brightened with gold or bright yellows. First used in textiles and wallpapers, the new colours were eventually incorporated into

shades of white – from ivory to pale gray – were quite common. Toward the end of the Victorian period, similar muted shades such as whites, greens, lilacs, purples and black, were also popular in Art Nouveau-inspired schemes.

Despite the occasional garish "mistake" associated with some of the excesses of the high-Victorian period, it is safe to say that colours, particularly darker tones, were used in a more sophisticated way during the second half of the 19th century than ever before. This was, in part, due to a greater understand-

Right: a late 19th-century dining room recreated in a home in Melbourne, Australia, by designer Suzie Forge. The deep red-brown colour scheme evokes the Victorian fondness of dark interiors. The gold embossed wallpaper up to dado level and the wide decorative border with a scrolling foliage pattern

below the intricate moulding or cornicing are also typical of the era. Other details in the room are in keeping with the period, including the heavy gilt picture frames, overhanging ceiling lamp and the imposing black marble fire surround. The ebonized gilt mirror over the fireplace is topped by a Wedgwood cameo.

and grays, tended to be used in bedrooms. Pale colours were also employed in French-inspired drawing rooms: the use of ivory with gold or blue was particularly popular.

It is often assumed today that richly coloured high-Victorian schemes were sombre and muddy in hue. However, such assumptions are, on the whole, based on 20th-century examinations of surviving interiors that failed to take into account the effects of coal dust, pollution, fumes from gas lighting and sunlight on fugitive or unstable pigments and dyes. When new, these colours were in fact rich, possibly dark, but almost always vivid.

paints. Some experiments with these new shades resulted in a number of somewhat lurid colour combinations, with tones such as purple and mustard, being used.

Partly as a reaction to this, more muted colours were employed by followers of the Arts and Crafts movement. "Greenery-yallery", a muted olive-green favoured by Aesthetic designers, particularly for woodwork, and burgundy, old rose and hyacinth-blue for walls, were prime examples. However, in Aesthetic-inspired rooms which were used during the day, light colours were also employed and schemes based on several

ing of the nature of colour; achieved by what amounted to a scientific study by architects of the Gothic Revival and, more particularly, by the architect and theorist of colour and ornament, Owen Jones. (Jones made the first systematic study of Moorish ornament at the Alhambra in Granada, Spain, and published *The Grammar of Ornament* in 1856, a handbook for design in the 19th century.) These ideas and discoveries were rapidly taken up by commercial decorators, who initially adapted them for the production of textiles and wallpapers.

The basis of Jones's theories on the use of colour was that it was aesthetically "correct"

The formal parlour in the Garth Woodside Mansion, Hannibal, Missouri, has deep-coloured walls and an intricate wallpaper border which are typical of the Victorian period. The furniture is Eastlake style, c.1870.

A paint-effect stone fire surround is the focal point in this 19th-century Gothic-style hallway. The joinery has been dragged and the walls are ragged and spattered. The moulding or cornicing has a trompe l'oeil effect.

Many city and town-house interiors in the late 19th-century were painted in dark greens and blues to minimize the effects of pollution and coal dust as well as the staining caused by gas and oil lamps.

The walls of this handsome American Empire dining room are decorated in panel and frieze "Morning Glory" paper depicting stylized foliage forms. Such decorative effects could also be achieved by hand-stencilling.

to use a complex pattern consisting of one main colour and many subsidiary colours, often tonally the same and juxtaposed with various shades of the main colour. Generally speaking, no primary colour was used, unless it had been moderated to make a deeper or softer shade and was juxtaposed with a secondary colour. For example, a poppy-red could be used with old gold, amber, hyacinth-blue or gray-blue, but not with a primary yellow or blue. Some tertiary colours, such as maroon, purple, olive green and ochre could also be used. The Victorians also favoured a wide choice of deep neutral shades, such as cream, slate, drab (a mixture of raw umber, ochre and Indian red), buff, sandstone and various grays.

Considerable thought was given to creating the right balance of both colour and texture between walls, mouldings or cornices, ceilings and woodwork. This was particularly the case when a tripartite dado-field-frieze combination was used, with different coloured papers or paints applied to each section. Some manufacturers even supplied "matching" papers for all three sections.

The greater understanding of colour applied to the design, manufacture and the application of textiles, wallpapers and paints was also seen in the use of specialist paint finishes. For example, simple as well as highly elaborate stencilled borders and friezes were successfully used to complement colours and patterns on other sections of walls. Woodwork and joinery were also sometimes stencilled, designs often being taken from textiles and papers used elsewhere in the room. The architect William Burges and decorator John Crace, for instance, went so far as to use stencilling as an overall wall pattern.

Where wallpapers were not used, broken colour finishes such as colourwashing, ragging, sponging, stippling and spattering were often employed on walls, woodwork and moulding or cornicing. The essence of the technique involved distressing a semi-translucent paint or glaze, applied on top of a contrasting or complementary coloured groundcoat, to produce subtle patterns over the surface.

All manner of specialist paint finishes, for example woodgraining, staining, waxing and marbling were also much in evidence, particularly during the latter years of the 19th century. The simulation of various kinds of woodgrain, for instance oak, mahogany, rose wood, walnut, satinwood and bird's eye maple, on doors, architraves and other architectural joinery, complemented the rich, deep colours which were often used to decorate walls and made use of aesthetically pleasing combinations of colours found in Nature. Similarly, the simulation of various types of marble, such as Sienna, Breche, white, black and gold, porphyry and verd-antique, utilized

naturally occurring colour combinations – which could also be adapted to complement colours used elsewhere in the room.

When choosing colours for the recreation of a Victorian interior today, the effects of modern lighting should not be overlooked. Electric light, particularly the fluorescent type, casts a much harsher light than the gentle glow of gaslight, oil lamps or candlelight, which were prevalent during the 19th century. Electric light can make Victorian colours appear more vivid or garish, less dusky and muted, than they would originally have looked. The solution is to tone down the original colours on the walls, or to use low lighting or else adopt candlelight where possible.

Left: this muted green was a popular colour throughout the high-Victorian period and was especially favoured by Aesthetic designers in the later part of the period.

Below: rich red walls were often found in houses of the American Empire period. The colour remained in evidence throughout the 19th century on both sides of the Atlantic, particularly in living rooms.

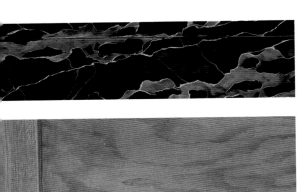

Above: inspired by rosewood, the red and black graining on this door in Christophe Gollut's apartment or flat imitates the dramatic figuring characteristic of the natural wood. The architrave and baseboard or skirting have been marbled.

Above: in this country kitchen the door, walls and ceiling have been dry-brushed to simulate the texture and discolouration of aged paint. The ceiling has also been naturally blackened by candles, which accentuates the overall aged effect.

Above, from top to bottom: all sorts of decorative paint finishes are available to the interior decorator today and can lend a stylish period effect. For example, black and gold marbling; oak graining; mahogany graining; stone blocking and gilding techniques are some of the more popular finishes you can apply to doors, mouldings or cornices, architraves, walls, picture frames and furniture.

Above: in an American Empire-style room in Richard Jenrette's carefully restored house on the Hudson River in New York State, the walls have been painted to resemble stone. The dark gray marbled baseboard or skirting complements the pair of columns which flank the arched doorway. The Classical influence in this interior is strong and is accentuated by urns and busts.

Above: distressed lacquer-red walls contrast with a marble fireplace displaying a collection of mainly American 19th-century pressed glass candlesticks. Right: the walls in a recreated period interior have been ragged in shades of yellow, simulating the "streaking" efffect caused by unstable pigments found in many traditional paints. The moulding or cornicing adds Gothic-style detail.

Far left: in a mid 19th-century bedroom the ornate plaster-panelled walls have been embellished with grisaille – a three-dimensional effect using tones of gray and brown. The fruit and flowers motif was copied from an original French fabric, c.1850, and was applied with stencils and also, in parts, by hand.
Left: the late 18th-century fashion for decorating rooms with prints pasted onto pale wallpapers or painted walls survived into the early Victorian era. Here a trompe l'oeil effect in a corridor depicts a common theme of animals and reptiles.
Above: during the restoration of this cottage near Houston, Texas, layers of paint were carefully removed to reveal a repeat-pattern stencil frieze.
Below: in a house in Devon, England, the walls have been copied from the stencilled bedroom at the American Museum in Bath. Stencilling once provided an inexpensive alternative to wallpaper.

FABRICS & WALLPAPERS

*T*here was considerable growth in the textile industry during the Victorian era. Most of the output was fuelled by technical developments such as power-loom weaving and machine-printing from engraved metal rollers; mass-production helped to keep costs down and so made products more affordable to the rapidly expanding middle classes. However, traditional methods of production – wood-block printing with alum, iron mordants and vegetable dyes such as madder (red), indigo (blue) and quercitron (yellow) – did remain in use for the manufacture of high-quality fabrics, such as floral chintzes, and among the followers of the Aesthetic and Arts and Crafts movements during the second half of the century.

Various other technological advances had a major impact on the appearance of Victorian textiles. Among these was the discovery, during the first quarter of the 19th century, of various new mineral colours, such as manganeze bronze, antimony orange and a solid green (instead of indigo "pencilled over yellow"). The development of vividly coloured, coal-tar and aniline dyes in the mid 1850s served to further accentuate the contrast between Victorian fabrics and those from previous centuries. Although, ironically it was to previous centuries, and other countries, that most of the leading Victorian designers looked for inspiration.

Left: in a Jacobean mansion in North Wales the walls are covered in Regency pink and gold striped brocade. The chaise longue is on an Aubusson carpet. Right: the walls of this Victorian-style room have colour-washed Lincrusta below dado level and a subtle sage-green and blue reproduction paper above. The mixed fabrics include deep velvets, flocks and colourful Persian rugs.

At the beginning of the Victorian era favoured furnishing fabrics for the top end of the market included glazed chintzes and silk damasks, patterned with formalized flowers and leaves in predominantly light colours. However, as general demand increased, particularly from the newly prosperous but not exceptionally wealthy middle classes, power-loom fabrics woven in a mixture of cotton and worsted wool, or silk or wool, came to constitute the main output of textile manufacturers. Colours also became darker and patterns more complex and exuberant – shaded architectural and *trompe l'oeil* motifs and ever more naturalistic flowers proving to be the most popular. Heavier materials such as velvets and brocatelles also came into vogue and in combination with the darker colours produced a richer, more sombre effect.

The use of richer colours within elaborate *trompe l'oeil* patterns could be seen in, for example, Rococo-style fabrics (also known as Louis Quatorze), which featured scrolls and cartouches, shaded to create the appearance of relief and incorporated into "realistic" floral designs. Similarly, Elizabethan style, which emerged during the mid 1830s but became particularly popular during the 1840s and early 1850s, was characterized by either abstract designs made up of bands of strapwork, cartouches and brackets, or flowers with strapwork shaded in order to create a three-dimensional effect.

However, the pictorial, three-dimensional designs showing, for example, scenes of children and animals such as dogs, railway stations, and the Crystal Palace surrounded by elaborate floral wreaths, which were on display at the Great Exhibition of 1851 prompted a reaction from design reformers who believed that their "three-dimensional" effects were dishonest, in poor taste and did not actually constitute a pattern. Instead, they advocated a return to the use of simpler, flat patterns that were based on geometric or historic ornament, and a more restrained and stylized form of floral design.

Gothic style was one of the first historical-revival styles to find favour with the leading design reformers around the middle of the century. It was based on the formal patterns of 15th- and 16th-century damasks and velvets and some of the most notable examples were designed by the English architect A.W.N. Pugin as early as the 1840s. Most of these flat-pattern fabrics had a basic ogival structure incorporating stylized scrolling leaves and heraldic motifs such as *fleur-de-lys*. (Pugin was a purist who believed in strictly adhering to original and authentic prototypes for designs. He deplored the use of shaded architectural motifs, and the imitation of one material by another, such as printed chintz

Left: some documented 19th-century fabrics. Above: animal skins were popular with the Victorians. Here a "panther velour" print bedspread complements a brown and cream room.

shades or blinds designed to imitate a row of stained-glass windows.

The adaptation of Moorish-style flat patterns was primarily inspired by the publication of Owen Jones's *Plans, Elevations, Sections and Details of the Alhambra*, in 1842. Some of the designs consisted of intricate, interlaced patterns of delicately carved stonework and were copied in woven textiles, usually in primary colours. Geometric designs representing tilework were also employed, as were vertical

stripes of Moorish ornament which were integrated into floral patterns. In addition to using Moorish designs in his flat-pattern fabrics, Jones also created woven silks based on Classical ornament, with anthemion and palmette motifs and patterns derived from Indian decoration. His influential *Grammar of Ornament*, published in 1856, also illustrated European ornament from prehistoric times up to the Renaissance, as well as patterns from Egypt, Assyria, Persia and China.

The fabrics produced by followers of the Aesthetic and Arts and Crafts movements during the second half of the century were inspired not only by Classical, Medieval, Gothic, Renaissance and Middle-Eastern flat patterns, but also by Japanese principles of art and design. For example, in the fabrics he designed for Warner & Sons in the early 1870s, the English architect E.W. Godwin incorporated patterns with a rigid geometrical structure, enclosing highly conventionalized flowers reduced to a flat, circular form, all set against a background of Japanese ornament. He also produced textiles (and wallpapers) that included birds such as sparrows, kingfishers and peacocks, that were treated in a Japanese manner.

Other leading textile designers of the Aesthetic movement included Bruce Talbert, Christopher Dresser and Walter Crane. In addition to the Medieval and Japanese patterns and motifs employed by Godwin, they also produced Renaissance-style patterns incorporating motifs such as *putti*, dolphins, grotesques and scrollwork and designs based on Turkish, Persian and Cretan embroideries. Favoured colours were subtle and subdued and included, for example, soft olive- and gray-greens (called "greenery-yallery"), as well as blue-green and pale turquoise.

Like E.W. Godwin, Bruce Talbert particularly favoured sunflowers as a central motif in many of the floral fabrics that he designed. These were sometimes depicted in a highly stylized form, but in other examples were drawn with an almost botanical accuracy.

Oscar Wilde believed that both the sunflower and the lily were, "the two most perfect models of design, the most naturally adapted for decorative art" and, together with peacock's feathers, they became in many respects the symbols of the Aesthetic movement.

However, from the 1870s to the 1890s the most fashionable textiles were designed and produced by William Morris and his assistant J.H. Dearle. A founder of the Arts and Crafts movement, Morris created more than 50 flat-pattern designs for printed and woven textiles, as well as a large number of embroideries, carpets and tapestries. Most of them were hand-blocked using traditional vegetable, rather than chemical dyes and typical designs depicted stylized but recognizable flowers and birds within a Medieval- or Gothic-style pattern structure. Although they accorded with the same principles of design, Morris's textiles had a rhythmical, sensuous quality largely absent in the relatively static flat patterns produced earlier by Pugin and Jones.

Because Morris's textiles were made using traditional techniques they were relatively expensive and so beyond the pocket of the middle and lower-middle classes. However, during the latter part of the century numerous machine-printed copies were made and mass-production made them more affordable. Although in most cases the use of chemical dyes rendered the colours in these copies less subtle than in the originals.

During the last two decades of the 19th century, Liberty & Co. began to import silks from the East that were either plain or printed with Indian- or Japanese-style designs. In the 1880s they also introduced a selection of "Art Fabrics", which incorporated Art Nouveau elements into Aesthetic designs. Many of the fabrics were commissioned from leading designers such as Christopher Dresser, Walter Crane, Lindsay Butterfield and C.F.A Voysey. Voysey's designs, for instance, were highly stylized floral patterns featuring precisely drawn, sinuous, undulating lines and flat colours without any shading. Typical subjects

Left: the smoking room in Cedar Grove, Vicksburg, Mississippi, has deep red drapes fringed with gold, a style popular in the 1860s. Above: the dress drapes in the French Empire-style bedroom in the Morris Jumel Mansion, New York are purely decorative and do not draw.

included anemones, irises, poppies, tulips, lotus flowers and scrolling, acanthus-like leaves. Stylized birds, either in flight or perched on branches were also depicted.

During the last decade of the century, Liberty & Co. also commissioned a number of designs from the Silver Studio. Those by Arthur Silver himself tended to display swirling, sinuous lines and a marked discrepancy of scale between motifs such as flowers and leaves. Those designed by Harry Napper, just after the turn of the century, incorporated more formalized motifs, such as Glasgow-style roses, spade- or heart-shaped leaves, trees and berries or grapes with squared-up leaves.

The manner in which the enormous choice of furnishing fabrics available throughout the Victorian era were utilized in and around the home varied both from room to room and at different periods during the century. For example, in more opulent reception rooms, particularly during the mid- and high-Victorian periods, the tops of windows were dressed with scrolled, scalloped or gilded lambrequins. Flat-fabric cornices or pelmets were a fashionable alternative, especially later in the century. Drapes were invariably hung from brass or wooden poles flanked with elaborate finials. And where the poles were not concealed by a cornice or pelmet or a valance, they were held on brackets embellished with decorative rosettes.

During the winter months, the drapes in reception rooms were made of luxurious fabrics such as velvet, mohair, brocade and silk and augmented with tassels, ribbons and festoons. When drawn back, they were secured with ropes or flat tie-backs of ormolu, rosette-headed pins or leaf- or scroll-shaped fitments on either side of the window.

During the summer months, and in hotter climates, lighter fabrics such as muslin, chintz or cretonne, lace and white batiste tended to be used. In many households, these lighter fabrics were also used all-year-around in bedrooms. And toward the end of the century, the fairly widespread belief that it was unhygienic to use fabrics that retained the smell of food led to a fashion for hanging lighter-weight, swagged cretonnes in dining rooms. Lighter fabrics were also easier to clean.

Above: inexpensive African cloth hung on the walls of a bedroom create a warm period feel.
Right: in this light dining room the authentic green colour of the walls is given added emphasis by a minimalist window treatment reminiscent of the purely decorative drapes of the Federal period.
Below left: heavy damask drapes hung from a cornice in the Old Merchant's House, New York.
Below right: drapes made from generous swathes of fabric are true to Victorian style.

For much of the century, particularly during the high-Victorian period, drapes were invariably made up into very full pleats and folds, partly for aesthetic reasons and partly to improve insulation against drafts from the windows. The drapes also served the useful function of shielding other fabrics in the room from sunlight which, over a period of time, caused colours to fade.

Various contemporary authorities on 19th-century interior design were critical of the "elaborate confections" used to dress windows. Some believed such fashions were encouraged by upholsterers seeking to boost their income from increasingly complex and therefore costly designs. Others, such as J.C. Loudon, considered these French-inspired "enormous folds" were just "abominable in taste". However, Loudon did admit that "window drapes give the mistress of the house an excellent opportunity for exercising her taste in their arrangement". Charles Eastlake, in his *Hints on Household Taste*, argued for simpler treatments in which drapes should simply hang from brass rings attached to stout metal

rods – a fashion that became increasingly popular toward the end of the 19th century.

Net or "insertion" drapes were often hung in both large and small Victorian homes during the second half of the 19th century and were used to cover either the entire window or just the bottom section of it. In grander dwellings, "insertions" were made of either silk, satin, patterned muslin or Swiss lace on a voile backing, while in most middle- and lower middle-class homes, plain muslin or sometimes relatively inexpensive, machine-made Nottingham lace was used.

During the mid- and high-Victorian periods, fabrics such as velvets, serges, damasks and tapestries were made up into elaborate *portières*. Tied back with braided and tasselled silk ropes, they were used to sound- and draft-proof doorways and were also draped from decorative arches in hallways. However, the high cost of the typical heavy-weight fabrics used for making *portières* meant that they were rarely found in poorer homes. From the 1870s

Left: the dining-room walls in Christophe Gollut's home are covered in a German striped damask. Below the dado is a small cut-velvet design. The sofa has a typically Victorian double layer of tassels and is upholstered in cut chenille. The pillows or cushions show a mix of 19th-century fabrics.

Above: rich drapes and fabric on the walls of this Parisian apartment or flat lend a refined 19th-century feel. The Victorian side chair has padded upholstery and is embellished with tassels on the skirt and shoulders. Below left: a traditional chair given a feminine Victorian touch with a loose white linen cover.

Below middle: it is easy to disguise a table made of inferior wood or one with a damaged surface by simply draping a piece of 19th-century fabric such as a Paisley shawl over it, as has been done in this home in Los Angeles, California. Below right: a Victorian chair covered with red and white ticking.

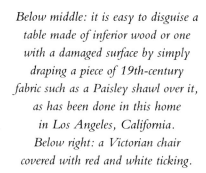

to the 1890s *portières* became so fashionable that they were even used instead of doors in some houses.

By the middle of the 19th century, a wide selection of floor coverings were available to the Victorian householder: at one end of the scale were the relatively inexpensive mattings and oil-cloths, at the other, costly Wilton and tapestry carpets. Factory-produced oil-cloth was made from canvas, smoothed and sized and covered with two or three coats of oil-paint and a layer of varnish. Hard-wearing and easy to wipe clean, it was used in halls, parlours and kitchens. Decorations included printed tiles, flagstones and wooden floors, stencilled patterns and motifs taken from Persian or Turkish carpets.

Matting, generally imported from India and the Far East, was used in most rooms in the house, but particularly in front parlours and bedrooms. Carpets and rugs were usually placed on top of it, both for aesthetic reasons and to increase the warmth and sense of comfort in a room.

During the middle of the century pile carpets became more readily available and they gradually began to replace the flat-woven varieties popular during the early part of the Victorian era. Staple types included level-looped Brussels carpet, cut-pile Wilton and tapestry carpet, the latter woven with preprinted threads and often featuring, according to Muthesius, "strident flower patterns, naturalistic animals and landscapes, and imitations of Rococo gilt borders and other monstrosities".

By the middle of the 1870s fitted wall-to-wall carpets became unfashionable, partly on the grounds of hygiene, and stained or polished wooden boards, or parquet flooring, combined with loose-lay rugs and carpets came into vogue. These could be taken up and beaten and cleaned more easily than fitted wall-to-wall carpets. The most popular rugs were Oriental, either Persian or Turkish in origin, while rugs and loose-lay carpets designed by such as William Morris, C.F.A. Voysey or Walter Crane also became fashionable, if expensive.

Velvet, repp and glazed cotton or chintz were the standard materials for covering upholstered furniture during the Victorian era and were invariably embellished with elaborate trimmings, buttons, ruching, cords, fringes and tassels. However, it was also fashionable to drape sofas and chairs with kelims and Paisley-pattern shawls, particularly during the high-Victorian period. The development of the Jacquard loom made it possible to manufacture Paisley shawls with complex all-over patterns in rich, dark colours. Many examples had a central motif surrounded by scrolling patterns filled with Indian-inspired floral and leaf ornament.

Paisley shawls and many other original 19th-century furnishing fabrics and carpets have survived and can be bought today either at auction or else from antique dealers. Alternatively, there are a large number of specialist manufacturers and suppliers who produce high-quality reproductions of 19th-century fabrics (see The Directory, pages 225-6). A huge selection is available. Many of them are screen-printed examples of patterns that were originally hand-blocked and have been copied from the original documents. Although they do not quite match the colour and crispness of line of the originals, they have the advantage of being far more affordable. Hand-blocked fabrics are available, but are obviously that much more expensive.

Right: a Louis XV sofa draped with Oriental and European fabrics. Pillows or cushions were popular accessories to Victorian furniture because of the comfort and decoration they afforded. These are an eclectic mix of fabrics and needlework.

Right: antique Oriental carpets and Persian rugs were a usual feature of Victorian interiors from the 1860s onward. Kelims from the Balkans were used as floor coverings and for drapes and upholstery. Ottomans were also sometimes carpet-covered.

Wallpapers

In England, during the early years of the 19th century, the State imposed a high tax levy on wallpaper. Indeed, in 1806 the wallpaper industry was regarded as such an important source of revenue for the government that the falsification of wallpaper stamps was added to the list of offences which were punishable by death. The consequences of this were two-fold. On the one hand, in an attempt to increase their sales and profits, British manufacturers began to concentrate on producing simple, inexpensive designs that would appeal to a larger market, in particular the rapidly expanding middle classes. On the other hand, most of the elaborately patterned scenic papers which were used in the reception rooms and main bedrooms of wealthier houses were imported from France.

By the 1830s, the quality of French wallpapers was such that many commentators on interior decoration felt that it was now almost wasteful to use silk on the walls, the new papers having an equally pleasing look. Many of them, in particular those incorporating sophisticated *trompe l'oeil* effects, were in fact simulations of draped and swagged fabrics, such as silk damask, and proved popular on both sides of the Atlantic.

However, the eventual lifting of taxation on wallpaper in 1836 encouraged British designers and manufacturers to once again produce colourful and complicated patterns.

The subsequent increase in production was further fuelled by technological advances, which included increased mechanization and the ability to apply papers directly onto improved smooth plaster surfaces, rather than paste them onto canvas stretched over a series of battens fixed to the wall.

One of the most influential designers of wallpaper during the first half of the 19th century was the renowned British architect A.W.N. Pugin. Like many other leading architects of the day he produced a number of designs to commission and the papers he created for the new Palace of Westminster in London, England for example, were particularly admired. Working with the decorating firm J.G. Grace & Company, he also produced several commercial designs, including a number of variations based on a popular repeat diaper, or diamond, motif.

Many of the most fashionable papers produced during the 1850s and 1860s, including those imported from France, sported pictorial patterns incorporating three-dimensional depictions of animals, flowers and plants. Other representational designs included landscapes, panoramic views and simulations of architectural features such as mouldings or cornices, friezes, statuary, windows, doors and wood carvings.

Nevertheless, A.W.N. Pugin, and artists and wallpaper designers such as Owen Jones and Richard Redgrave, criticized such fashionable

pictorial papers on aesthetic grounds. Jones, who mostly worked to commission, and who decorated the home of novelist George Eliot, in Regent's Park, London, England, published his hugely influential *Grammar of Ornament* in 1856. In this he argued the principle that wallpaper patterns should be flat, and justified it by pointing out that walls were flat, and that three-dimensional patterns and motifs created the false and inappropriate illusion of an uneven surface. He also believed that supposedly accurate, three-dimensional replicas of images occurring in Nature did not, in fact, constitute a pattern, and were therefore dishonest. Instead he felt that patterns should be formalized and stylized interpretations of Nature.

Another influential figure in the mid 19th-century debate as to what designs constituted aesthetically acceptable patterns and colours in wallpapers was Henry Cole. Superintendent of the Great Exhibition of 1851, and a friend and colleague of Jones, Cole published his *Journal of Design and Manufactures* in 1849. In this he encouraged the use of "full tones in general", such as reds and greens, to create a comfortable feeling in a room. Flock papers were also recommended as they added to the richness of the effect.

However, the most authoritative and influential designer of wallpapers and fabrics during the 19th century was William Morris, architect, designer and a founder of the Arts

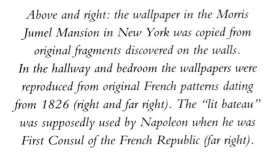

Above and right: the wallpaper in the Morris Jumel Mansion in New York was copied from original fragments discovered on the walls. In the hallway and bedroom the wallpapers were reproduced from original French patterns dating from 1826 (right and far right). The "lit bateau" was supposedly used by Napoleon when he was First Consul of the French Republic (far right).

and Crafts movement. Writing in *Das Englische Haus* at the end of the century, the German commentator Muthesius described Morris as "the father of modern wallpaper", and believed that his flat-pattern designs had a "light but sure touch" that "one can almost regard as the English national style".

While the wallpaper designs of Pugin and Jones had consisted of relatively static repeats of heraldic devices or Medieval motifs, Morris's patterns, inspired by Medieval and Gothic tapestries, were far more rhythmical and representational. His genius for mixing strong, pure colours to harmonious effect and his ability to give a flat pattern a narrative quality were unsurpassed.

Most of Morris's wallpapers were produced using the traditional hand-blocked method and so were fairly expensive. However, his designs were widely copied by other manufacturers such as Jeffrey &

Company, and their tasteful mass-produced, machine-printed versions proved both popular with, and affordable to, the middle classes during the second half of the 19th century.

The last two decades of the century witnessed a reaction to the richly coloured and elaborately patterned wallpapers that were in vogue during the mid- and high-Victorian periods. The architect C.F.A. Voysey, for example, rejected Morris's patterns as too "sensuous" and in the late 1880s he produced a selection of formal, urban patterns inspired, in part, by the ideals of the Aesthetic movement. In the mid 1890s Voysey's patterns became even sparser and his colours paler; the overall effect was a precursor of the aesthetics of Modernism that came to the fore after the turn of the century.

Throughout the 19th century wallpapers were used in a far more sophisticated way than they usually are today. (For a more detailed

description of the application of papers during specific periods in different rooms in the house, see the individual rooms chapters in the second half of this book.) Several patterned papers were often applied in the space in-between the baseboard or skirting and the ceiling. The dado, for instance, was usually covered with a patent "leather" or embossed paper, such as Anaglypta or the slightly more expensive Lincrusta. Produced in a variety of patterns and widths, embossed papers were initially imitations of stamped Spanish leather, which had first been used as a wallcovering in the 17th century. Typical stamped patterns included strap-work motifs in the "Jacobethan" style. At first these papers were painted a dull brown colour, with a stippled, darker brown glaze applied on top, in order to create an effect of imitation leather. However, during the second half of the 19th century they were painted in a variety of rich

colours, such as dark reds and greens, or in a tint of the dominant colour in the room. All sorts of embossed patterns, such as simulations of plaster mouldings, were also made. One of the main advantages of using embossed papers on the dado was their durability and the fact that the application of a hard-wearing varnish made them easy to clean – useful qualities, particularly in high-traffic areas such as hall-ways, where accidental knocks and scrapes were almost inevitable. The fact that they could be painted in plain colours also made them an ideal background against which to set richly coloured and patterned upholstered furniture. Also, embossed papers were often

Above: colour and pattern had dominant roles in interior decoration during the second half of the 19th century. The colour-washed Lincrusta below the dado and the gilt wallpaper above are typical of the high-Victorian period.
Right and below: inside the Eastlake-style Durfee House in Los Angeles, California, built c.1880, the walls are papered with all sorts of Bradbury & Bradbury patterns, including friezes and panels on the ceilings. In the entrance hall "Fenwick" paper represents land, water, plants and the sky. The woodwork and shutters have been typically woodgrained.

used on ceilings and friezes in order to counterbalance intricately patterned and coloured papers adorning the walls below.

By the 1870s, when the tripartite division of the wall into dado-field-frieze became fashionable, various designers, such as Walter Crane, E.W. Godwin, William Burges and Charles Eastlake produced co-ordinating papers for all three sections and angled versions were also made for staircase walls. Special ceiling papers were also produced, some of which featured circular repeats and were intended to cover the entire ceiling, while others were made to be set inside plaster frames. Complementary borders, which ran below the moulding or cornice were also often supplied.

During the last two decades of the 19th century, strip papers designed specifically for the frieze – often a dominant feature of late-Victorian interiors – were manufactured in a variety of patterns and colours. Repeat stencilled patterns and murals were particularly popular, the latter recommended by R.W. Edis in his *Decoration and Furniture of Town Houses*, published in 1890.

However, the application of different coloured and patterned wallpapers on the various divisions of a wall was not without its critics. Successfully combining papers required a good eye for both pattern and colour, and sometimes the overall effect could be far from harmonious. Muthesius, for example, was alarmed by it, and warned that it was, "easy to decorate and patternize to excess".

A wide selection of Victorian wallpapers is still available today from specialist manufacturers and suppliers (see The Directory, pages 227-9). Some companies, such as Osborne & Little, Watts & Co. (founded in 1874), Warner & Sons (founded in 1870) and Arthur Sanderson & Sons Ltd (founded in 1860), produce papers using original 19th-century wooden printing blocks, or very accurate reproductions of them. Sanderson, for example, took over the printing of original Morris & Co. papers before the company went into liquidation in the early 1940s.

FURNITURE

*O*f all the economic, social and cultural developments that had an impact on the design of furniture during the 19th century, the most significant was the expansion of the prosperous middle classes. The desire to furnish their houses in a manner that reflected their new-found wealth and status was reflected throughout the Victorian era in the revival of styles of furniture that had in previous centuries been the preserve of only the upper classes and a cultural elite. The "Louis", "Fat classical", Neo-gothic, Elizabethan, Neo-renaissance and near-Eastern styles – fashionable either throughout or for specific periods during the century – were already tried and tested and so provided an aesthetically uncertain middle class with reassurance through familiarity. However, the desire of an upwardly mobile section of society to display its affluence resulted in the embellishment of many of these original styles not only to make them somehow "better", but also to enhance their sense of value. In many cases the results, particularly toward the end of the 19th century, were no more than a pastiche of the original style.

Furniture design was also influenced by notable improvements in the technology of furniture making. New mechanical methods of production facilitated an enormous increase in the number of pieces being produced, many of which were inexpensive reproductions of

Left: Brazilian glass and animals, English and Italian candlesticks and tortoiseshell boxes adorn a 19th-century exotic table with camel-head legs.
Right: a German mahogany desk with ivory key holes in a Parisian apartment or flat. A drawing of Cocteau and 19th-century bronze pieces stand on the desk. The leather chair carries the inscription "Combat de coq".

previously hand-made and costly items. The invention of the coil spring and improved methods of laminating and shaping wood allowed for the design and construction of entirely new items of furniture, bentwood chairs and brass beds being but two examples.

A further influence on the various types of furniture considered fashionable was the new phenomenon of collecting antiques. For instance, George IV's purchase of 17th- and 18th-century furniture from France during the Revolution encouraged a fashion for "Neo-Louis" styles that survived to the end of the 19th century. Similarly, the admiration that members of the Arts and Crafts movement had for traditional craftsmanship filtered

in middle-class homes by the last two decades of the 19th century. The second development was the increasing influence that women were able to exert on the furnishing of the home. As a result greater attention was paid to the comfort of furniture, the coil-sprung, deep-buttoned, upholstered sofa being a prime example.

Of all the revival furniture manufactured during the 19th century, the 17th- and 18th-century French "Louis" styles, particularly Neo-rococo, were the most popular. By the 1840s virtually all the leading furniture manufacturers were making Neo-rococo pieces. For instance, in 1840, William Smee &

as the drawing room or boudoir, where the female influence was strongest, considerable quantities of "carcase" furniture, such as wardrobes, chests of drawers and commodes, were also made.

By the end of the 19th century, Louis-style furniture was being produced to meet two quite different demands. On the one hand, companies such as Gillows were making copies for the upper end of the market virtually indistinguishable from the originals. On the other hand, a fashion for "fussiness" and "spindliness" at the lower end of the market gave rise to numerous pieces bearing little relation to

An early Victorian English sarcophagus-shaped mahogany wine cooler with lion-mask handles.

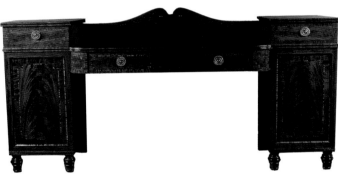

An early 19th-century English mahogany pedestal sideboard with turned feet.

A Wedgwood-mounted side cabinet, c.1870, made in the Neo-classical manner in amboyna.

through to the upper-middle classes from the 1870s and produced a generation of collectors of pre-industrial pieces.

The fashion for collecting furniture from previous centuries was, during the latter part of the 19th century, given added impetus by an increasing sense of national pride. The political ideology of nationalism thus gave birth to the adoption of "national" styles of furniture: 18th-century in England, Colonial in America, and Renaissance and Biedermeier in Germany.

Two other significant cultural developments of the era had a major impact. The first was the establishment in 1854 of trade links with the Far East. Japanese designs were taken up by the Arts and Crafts movement and had filtered down to items of occasional furniture

Sons advertised typical chairs with sprung, deep-buttoned upholstery. Durable, stylish and comfortable, but not too quirky, these were just the sort of seating middle-class families were looking for. Indeed, the curved shapes augmented with scrolls and volutes of the Neo-rococo style afforded that ideal combination of being luxurious to look at and easy to make, even using mechanical carving techniques.

Other French Revival styles which came into vogue during the second half of the 19th century included Louis Quinze and the panel-back side-chairs from this period were the basis for the popular "balloon-back". Louis Seize was more rectilinear than Neo-rococo and also found favour. While most of the Louis styles tended to be used in rooms such

the French originals. For instance, any item with cabriole legs, a curved shape or "Rococo-style" fretwork was passed off as "Louis", or simply described as "fancy".

In North America the vogue for Louis styles followed a similar pattern to that in Britain. Prior to the Civil War Neo-rococo parlour and bedroom suites, chairs and tables were available from manufacturers such as John Henry Belter. Belter's perfection of lamination techniques allowed him to produce the sweeping curves characteristic of Neo-rococo, which could then be elaborately carved, and his rosewood furniture was much imitated by other makers. Post Civil War, mechanical production replaced traditional craftsmanship and tastes, as in Britain, moved toward the more rectilinear Louis-Seize style. The fashion for ebonizing wood and emphasizing shapes with ormolu mouldings and gilt-incised lines was also much in evidence.

Throughout the 19th century the vast increase in trade in-between countries also saw the dissemination of Louis styles across the globe. From the 1850s to the 1870s suites of Neo-rococo parlour and dining-room furniture made in London were exported to Australia and New Zealand. To make storage easier and reduce shipping costs, some of them had removable arms and legs.

From the 1850s onwards, many new items of furniture, for example *étagères*, whatnots, occasional-, work- and sewing-tables, screens

century, a wide variety of other styles became fashionable at different periods. "Fat-classical" was essentially Neo-classical in form, but had more flowing lines and was "fattened" by carved, naturalistic ornamentation. In North America the style took on a simpler and more practical form than in Britain. Some of the pieces, particularly carcase furniture, were enormous. These often featured a minimal amount of carving and were sometimes embellished with stencilling. On both sides of the Atlantic Fat-classical was fashionable up to the 1860s. However, less showy and more functional pieces were still available at the end of the century.

Elizabethan styles were popular mainly in England during the first half of the 19th century. The term Elizabethan was used loosely to describe pieces that were neither Gothic nor Classical, and manufacturers often made use of Jacobean and Carolean motifs, such as bobbin or corkscrew-turned legs and footrails or stretchers. Usually installed in formal rooms such as dining rooms, halls and libraries, this "Old Englyshe" style found favour with the middle classes, who felt that some instant ancestry would give greater credence to their new-found status.

A fine-qualtiy large Gothic Revival oak library table, c.1850 with trestle supports.

Above left: a satinwood and marquetry étagère. *Above right: a mahogany capstan table, c.1830.*

A high-quality walnut balloon-back chair, c.1860 with French-style cabriole legs.

and footstools, were introduced in order to supplement the basic furnishings. Most were produced in one or other of the popular Louis styles and together they contributed to a gradual breakdown of the symmetrical arrangement of furniture around a room that had been almost universally adopted in previous centuries. The new practice of arranging drawing-room furniture in small groups or vignettes became most fashionable during the high-Victorian period and was facilitated by the practice of attaching casters to tables and chairs and by the appearance of the *chaise volante* or "flying chair". Made of lightweight wood or *papier mâché*, it could be easily picked up and moved around the room.

While Neo-Louis furniture was the most consistently popular throughout the 19th

Neo-gothic style originated in England in the late 18th century, notably in the pieces commissioned by George IV and made by the young designer Augustus Pugin. Most early 19th-century pieces consisted of Gothic architectural details and ornaments simply grafted onto quite basic furniture shapes. For instance, ogee, or S-shaped arches, were added to brace table legs and spiky fragile fretwork was inserted into chair-backs to give something of a "fancy-dress" look. Neo-gothic never really became popular in North America and appealed mainly to aesthetes and eccentrics. However, during the second half of the 19th century, the Neo-medieval origins of the style did find a more practical outlet in the works of Bruce Talbert, Charles Eastlake and other members of the Arts and Crafts movement.

By the early 1870s Neo-renaissance style had become more widely popular than the various Neo-Louis styles. Also known as free-Renaissance in England, it was characterized by very large, weighty pieces with rectangular outlines and 16th- and 17th-century-style ornamentation which typically took the form of rich carving, turnery and contrasting inlays. Some pieces were also painted. In North America, after the Civil War, Alexander Roux and other makers produced opulent and massive variants of the style, featuring combinations of rosewood, burr-walnut and other contrasting veneers, with ebonizing, gilded linear patterns, porcelain plaques and ormolu mounts. Plainer versions, often made of oiled oak rather than French-polished darker hardwoods also became popular with the wealthier

end of the market. Known collectively as Eastlake-style, these were also often ebonized and embellished with Japanese-style gilded stencilling and inlays.

Neo-renaissance furniture made for the middle and lower ends of the market were, particularly by the 1880s, bastardized versions. The carcase furniture, for example, incorporated a profusion of shelves and brackets, as well as panels of bevelled glass. The fact that such pieces were overly fussy and flimsy contributed to the decline in popularity of the style by the end of the 19th century.

Near-Eastern-style furniture, also known as Moorish, Turkish or Arab style, was fashionable throughout the Victorian era, especially after the 1860s. Typical pieces included ottomans and over-stuffed divans and couches of undefined shape and usually covered with pillows or cushions. In wealthier households, smoking and billiard rooms as well as corners of large reception rooms were sometimes furnished entirely in this style.

While Japanese art and ceramics became popular in Britain and North America around the middle of the century, it was not until the 1880s and 1890s that native manufacturers, such as Nimura & Sato of Brooklyn, New

York, began to produce large quantities of Japanese-influenced occasional furniture. Typical pieces incorporated legs and frames that were made of real bamboo or sometimes simulated in paint, woven-grass door panels and tabletops.

Just as the period from 1880 to 1914 saw an influx of Japanese-inspired designs, so an increasing nationalism in Europe and North America resulted in a vogue for national revival styles of furniture. In Britain this meant collecting original antique pieces or else high-quality reproductions of Chippendale, Adam, Hepplewhite and Sheraton furniture produced by firms such as Gillows for the top end of the market. However, copies made for the lower end of the market were not always true to scale. A similar trend took place in North America with manufacturers turning out accurate and not so accurate reproductions of 18th-century, American Colonial furniture.

Just as technological advances in the manufacture of furniture had a major impact on both the quantity of pieces being produced and their style and appearance, so they gave rise to entirely new products. *Papier mâché* was first made in England around 1830 and was used initially in chairbacks and as tabletops and decorative elements on carcase furniture. Later occasional chairs, cabinets, tip-top tables, firescreens and even some suites of furniture were made from it. The curvaceous lines of Neo-rococo style lent themselves to this new material which could be moulded into virtually any shape and the most popular form of decoration was black japanning embellished with mother-of-pearl inlay, hand-painted flowers or landscapes, and stencil gilding.

By the 1840s new metal furniture had become quite commonplace. Cast iron, for instance, was combined with wooden slatted seats and marble table tops in the construction of garden and conservatory furniture, as well as hall and umbrella stands and fenders. Cast iron and brass was also used for the first time in the construction of beds during the latter part of the century, largely as a response to an

increasingly widespread desire to improve standards of hygiene in the bedroom (*see* Bedrooms, pages 188-99).

The most notable technical development was the invention of bentwood furniture. Invented by Michael Thonet and first shown at the Great Exhibition of 1851 in London, England, bentwood was being manufactured in vast quantities by the 1860s. Thonet's perfection of a technique for bending solid wood into curved and circular shapes resulted in a style that bore some relation to Neo-rococo, but was also classless in its simplicity. That, together with the fact that it was lightweight and therefore easily transportable to colonies such as Australia and New Zealand, did much to explain its popularity around the globe.

Improvements in technology made possible the mass-production of furniture to meet the growing demand during the latter half of the 19th century. However, the furniture produced by members of the Arts and Crafts and, to a lesser degree, the Art Nouveau movement at the end of the century, can be seen as a reaction to the increasing ugliness and poor design of pieces produced in the various neo-revival styles. Arts and Crafts and Art Nouveau furniture, like most other 19th-century styles, drew its inspiration from the styles of previous centuries – broadly, Neo-gothic and Elizabethan for the former and Italian Renaissance and Queen Anne for the latter – the result was, in both cases, a return to traditional methods of construction, the use of high-quality materials and the dispensing with "unnecessary" ornamentation. As William Morris wrote in 1880: "Have nothing in your house that you do not know to be useful or believe to be beautiful."

Above left: a Rococo Revival chair restored with silk damask, based on its original upholstery. Right: the front bedroom of the Old Merchant's House in New York is dominated by an American Classical mahogany armoire, c.1830. The armoire has unusual doors built in to both sides which house book shelves.

Before you buy a costly set of dining chairs measure them against the following checklist, which will help you to recognize authentic Victorian chairs and choose the best examples:

1. Look for signs of wear and tear. The most commonly damaged areas are where the legs meet the seat, where the vertical or back supports meet the seat, and the feet. A certain degree of wear, particularly to the feet, should be expected and indicates that the chair is of a certain age. Avoid damaged or poorly repaired chairs.

2. Look for weaknesses such as signs of breaks or splits: these must be expertly repaired to keep the chair intact.

3. Make sure that there is no evidence of small, irregular holes in the wooden parts – these indicate woodworm.

4. Check the rungs, spindles, legs and arms. These may become loose with age and joints may have been repaired with nails or screws. Joints should only be repaired with glue, as nails and screws split and damage the wood. Any loose or creaking joints will weaken the chair and make it rickety.

5. Make sure that rungs and spindles are well-fitted and that joints do not look disturbed. (This indicates that a replacement part may have been added.) Replacement parts are often made from a different type of wood to the rest of the chair and lack the darker shading which builds up in the crevices and around the joints.

6. The patina or sheen on period chairs will often fade to a golden colour on the arms, seat and wherever the chair has been rubbed. Look out for signs of artificial staining which try to disguise this natural ageing effect.

7. Examine the colour and grain of the wood of all parts of the chair to ascertain that it is original throughout. The colouring of the wood should not vary, although the grain may run in different directions.

8. Check the footrails or stretcher rails: if they are too close to the floor this my indicate that the chair has been lowered.

Dining room Chairs

1. Today balloon-back chairs are popular in dining rooms, although originally they belonged in the parlour and came in sets of four or six with a "loo" card table.

1

2. Made by G.J. Morant of New Bond Street, London, England, this is an early Victorian oak and holly chair. Fine single chairs are valuable; but a set of six will often be worth double the value of a set of four and a set of eight is a premium.

2

Left: a set of antique chairs is a key investment for a Victorian-style dining room. Here, a dining room decorated in a dark colour scheme is given a Victorian feel with late 19th-century copies of 18th-century chairs and a Paisley tablecloth.

3

3. The taste for Gothic furniture lasted throughout the 19th century period. This is a rosewood chair in the Gothic style, c.1840.

5

6. An English Victorian oak Gothic elbow chair, c.1845. The toprail is carved with acanthus leaves.

6

4

4. During the 19th century many styles of 18th-century chairs were reproduced. The frame of this late-Victorian Italian example is embellished with paintwork.

5. A mid 19th-century gray-painted and parcel-gilt chair with a panelled back carved with scrolls and foliage. The buttoned seat and back are upholstered in gray damask.

7

7. A robust William IV mahogany balloon-back open chair with heavily scrolled arms and circular tapering fluted legs. This example shows elements of the more restrained Regency style combined with the decorative Victorian style. An authentic period mahogany chair is likely to be heavier than an equivalent reproduction chair.

Occasional Seating

1

1. Dating from the late-Victorian period, this mahogany elbow or armchair with drop-in seat is embellished with brass stars and stylized bellflowers of inlaid ebony and was made by Edwards & Roberts of Oxford Street, London, England.

2

2. An early Victorian walnut throne in Renaissance style with deep-buttoned velvet upholstery. In the middle of the typically arched back is a female mask flanked by scrolling foliage and a female and a blackamoor bust. The frieze is carved with dragons and vases of fruit.

3. The Victorians admired the craftsmanship of late 18th-century furniture design, as this George III Sheraton-style elbow or armchair shows. Made c.1885, the satinwood frame is painted with Prince of Wales feathers, flowers and drapes. The Prince married in 1863 and was very much in the public eye.

3

5. This oak elbow or armchair is very similar to a set of chairs designed c.1837 by A.W.N. Pugin, the leading Gothic revivalist and renowned English architect.

6. The exuberant carving on this Anglo-Indian rosewood chair, with the dolphins on the scrolling arms and the claw and ball feet, is typical of mid- to late-Victorian taste.

6

4

4. In the second half of the 19th century papier mâché was widely used for making chairs, trays and boxes. This typical japanned chair is decorated with gilt and mother-of-pearl flowers and exotic birds.

5

7. Carrying the stamp of Bell & Coupland, this early Victorian elbow or armchair has a U-shaped toprail carved with scrolled foliage and inset with bone and ebony "compass medallions".

Right: a fine bergère library chair with nailed leather upholstery and cane sides next to a French Empire marble-topped commode. The deep red colour scheme of this living room has the womb-like atmosphere so favoured by the Victorians.

CHECKLIST

In order to help you identify genuine Victorian occasional chairs and choose the best examples use the checklist below as a guide:

1. Assess the type of wood and carving. Most 19th-century occasional chairs were made of walnut, rosewood or mahogany. They are characteristically bold and shapely in design and often display ornate carving. The quality of carving will be a major factor in the value of the chair.

2. Make sure that there are no splits in the wooden frame, or cracks if the chair is made of papier mâché.

3. Make sure that the chair appears to be constructed of the same wood throughout and check for consistency in colour, grain and general wear and tear. Any replacement parts, for instance, feet, legs, stretcher rails or footrails, will detract from the value.

4. Examine the legs for signs that they have been adjusted, as this will lower the chair's value. Look for a visible joint low down on each leg and make sure that legs which have been lengthened in this way have been firmly spliced so that the chair is stable.

5. Make sure that the upholstery is not too worn, torn or frayed. Old chairs may no longer have their original upholstery and if they have been reupholstered this should have been done using traditional tacks (not with a modern staplegun) and with traditional stuffing (not using foam or other synthetic materials).

7

Sofas and Chaises

1. Part of a suite of Spanish giltwood seat furniture dating from the second quarter of the 19th century. The curved "serpentine" seat is upholstered in brown leather painted with flowers on a trellis ground. The cartouche-shaped back is framed with serpents and crested with eagles.

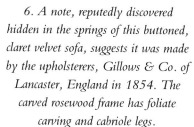

1

2

2. This pale satin-ash padded sofa is typical of Biedermeier furniture. Dating from the second quarter of the 19th century, scroll arms and feet complement the undulating back.

3

3. A reproduction 19th-century "conversation piece" designed to seat four people and made by George Smith (see Directory, page 229).
4. A Victorian walnut three seater sofa with a pierced and scrolled "surmount" in the middle of the back.

6

4

6. A note, reputedly discovered hidden in the springs of this buttoned, claret velvet sofa, suggests it was made by the upholsterers, Gillows & Co. of Lancaster, England in 1854. The carved rosewood frame has foliate carving and cabriole legs.

7. Dating from the mid 19th century, the toprail of this American mahogany scroll-end sofa is carved with a ribbon-tied laurel leaf motif.

5. The lion throne of Edward, Prince of Wales, made in India, c.1875. Such ornate pieces with royal feathers, coats of arms and dragon arms typify the extravagance of some high-Victorian furniture.
Left: a late 1830s mahogany American Classical settee in the Old Merchant's House, New York. Upholstered in black horsehair, the arms are a pair of massive scrolls.

5

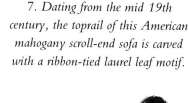

7

Dining Tables

1. An early Victorian circular oak extending dining table, c.1840. The moulded top has four clip-on leaves on reeded tapering legs.

2. Perched on carved cabriole or gently curving S-shaped legs, the moulded top of this fine satinwood octagonal table, c.1850, is supported on a central baluster and four subsidiary fluted columns. Satinwood furniture was highly favoured but rarely used in the solid as it was very expensive.

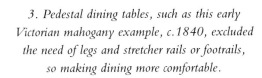

3. Pedestal dining tables, such as this early Victorian mahogany example, c.1840, excluded the need of legs and stretcher rails or footrails, so making dining more comfortable.

4. This D-ended mahogany dining table, c.1860, has a cranking mechanism enabling the surface to be extended without the need for extra legs – the additional leaves rest on extended bearers. Here the moulded top rests on six lotus-carved and turned legs on ceramic casters.

5. A mahogany dining table made in 1840 by J. Kendell & Co. Also known as a tea table it has a swivelling fold-over top and two frieze drawers.

6. Extending to over 17ft (5m) this multi-purpose mahogany dining table made by Gillington of Dublin, Ireland c.1840, has two oblong end sections which can be removed to reduce the overall size of the table and serve as an additional pair of occasional tables.

CHECKLIST

The following checklist will help you to evaluate Victorian dining tables and select authentic examples:

1. Check that the table is not a "marriage" of a separate top and base. The table should be made from the same wood throughout and the colour and patina of all parts should correspond. Both the top and the base should show similar signs of wear and tear.

2. Remove the table top from the base and look for an exact outline of the base on the underside of the top. Any discrepancy in the markings where the underside of the top rests on the base may indicate a replacement part.

3. Expect to find uneven areas of fading and a certain amount of scratching and knocks on authentic 19th-century dining tables.

4. Examine the end-sections of D-end tables carefully. Although large, multi-pedestal tables with extending D ends were found in the Victorian era, many were dismantled early in the 20th century. Today, some have been elongated again with "married" end sections.

5. Inspect the underside of the dining table and check that there is at least a 2in (5cm) overhang between the tops of the legs and the outer edge of the table top. So-called "improvements" were made to dining tables by cutting a round or an oval shape from an originally square top.

6. Look for replaced leaves. The colour and grain of the wood of each leaf should match. These are best examined from the underside as the fixed part of the table top is likely to be more faded through greater use. Leaves should be of equal thickness and also match the thickness of the table top.

7. Make sure that there are no signs of open or plugged screw holes. These suggest that the original parts of the table are not intact.

Right: the pedestal table, chairs and display secretaire in the dining room of the Belvedere Mansion in Galena, Illinois, have furnished the room since its completion in 1857.

CHECKLIST

If you wish to obtain an authentic Victorian occasional table, the following checklist will be a useful guide:

1. Most table legs have to support a comparatively heavy top and therefore are susceptible to the effects of wear and tear. Inspect the legs carefully, particularly cabriole-type or S-shaped legs which tend to break just above the feet. Watch out for disguised repairs.

2. Look for a finial or decorative turned knob where the stretcher rails or footrails meet under a card table; this is a particularly Victorian feature.

3. Always examine the underside of the table to verify that the top belongs with the base: there should be no obvious signs of alterations and no marks on one part that do not correspond with markings elsewhere on the piece.

4. When acquiring a dumb waiter – a piece of occasional furniture which has two or more tiers of trays around a central column – make sure that it is not composed of "married" sections. For instance, the column section may not be consistently turned so a careful inspection is necessary. Two-tier examples command a premium, but they may either have been cut down from three-tier pieces, or else constructed from unrelated parts.

5. The whatnot – defined as a mobile stand with open shelves – evolved from the 18th-century étagère and was popular from 1805 to 1910. It is a symbol of the Victorian era and was used to display all manner of ornaments. Most whatnots had three or four tiers and were made from solid mahogany, commonly veneered with walnut or calamander. After 1845 many examples became more elaborate, having scrolled supports and pierced galleries.

Left: in a five-story house in Greenwich Village, New York, this fine pedestal table with a marble top is the focus of a room full of work produced by various master craftsmen of the American Gothic period, from the 1830s to the 1850s.

1

1. An early 19th-century mahogany butler's tray with hinged sides and a folding stand. Along with knife and plate boxes, these were popular pieces of dining-room furniture and they are much sought-after today.

2

3. A mid 19th-century mahogany, ebonized and gilt iron German corner console table. The frieze – or framework directly below the table top – is carved with lotus leaves and the bowed green marble top is supported by triple-eagle legs.

3

4

2. An early Victorian brass-mounted three-tier étagère, c.1840. Made of amboyna it has leaf-scroll feet and pierced galleries.

4. The dumb waiter, usually made of mahogany, was defined in the Cabinet Dictionary of 1803 as, "a useful piece of furniture, to serve in some respects the place of a waiter, whence it is so named." It was used for holding plates, glasses and so on.

5

5. This mid 19th-century German rosewood and marquetry work table inlaid with scrolling foliage still contains its original fitted interior and sewing equipment, so increasing the value of the piece. The top is decorated with a chinoiserie scene.

6

6. The Victorians favoured exotic woods. This thuyawood, maplewood banded and ebonized table has a central Classical urn finial.

7

7. A pedestal card or games table. This English example, c.1840, is made of rosewood and features a swivelling baize-lined top.

8

8. This Italian carved giltwood pier or console table, c.1830, depicts a female figure with a sheaf of corn, representing summer.

Side cabinets and Desks

1. A marquetry side cabinet, c.1850, in the French manner. The piece is inlaid with birds, vases and flowers on a walnut ground.

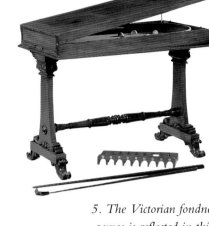

1

2. Made by Maples of London, England, c.1900, this fine cylinder desk is inlaid with boxwood and sycamore foliage; the interior is fitted with satinwood drawers. The main lock is stamped "J.T. Needs 128 Piccadilly". Locks can help to authenticate antique pieces.

2

3. An early Victorian kidney-shaped desk, made of fine figured walnut, c.1840. Although not original, the three panels of inset black tooled leather are in keeping.

3

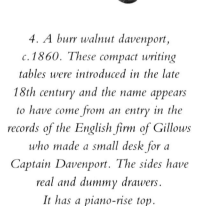

5

5. The Victorian fondness for indoor games is reflected in this mahogany bagatelle table, c.1850. The cues, nine ivory balls and scorers are all original. This piece is after a design published in 1850 by the British firm of W. Smee & Sons.

4

4. A burr walnut davenport, c.1860. These compact writing tables were introduced in the late 18th century and the name appears to have come from an entry in the records of the English firm of Gillows who made a small desk for a Captain Davenport. The sides have real and dummy drawers. It has a piano-rise top.

6

6. A mid-Victorian walnut drop-flap writing table, which is inlaid with boxwood, ebony and tulipwood bands.

7

7. Large Victorian partners' pedestal desks are mainly found in mahogany and are often veneered. On this 1840s example the rear of the pedestals contain panelled cabinets.

CHECKLIST

To help you recognize Victorian desks, davenports and side cabinets and choose the best examples, use the following checklist as a guide:

1. Make sure that the feet of the piece are original. They should match the rest of the body and mouldings may be echoed around the edge of the body. Old feet will naturally show signs of knocks and scrapes.

2. Inspect inlay or decoration for damage. For example, a composition of semi-precious stones, called **pietra dura**, was a popular form of 19th-century furniture decoration. This can come away from the main piece and so detracts from the overall value. Check that decorative inlays match and complement each other in colour and design, be suspicious if they do not correspond.

3. Look at the top of the door of a side cabinet, or at the central top drawer of a desk for the maker's stamp; this is a sign of a good example and adds to the value of a piece.

4. The wood in all parts of a piece should match in colour and grain; check the sides in particular. Examine the drawers, which should correspond in colour, and make sure they have not been stained to look old. Replacement drawers devalue a piece.

5. Examine any panels of veneer, as large sections are prone to splitting. Check the piece for modern veneers: for example, a split inside a drawer where the exterior appears undamaged indicates reveneering.

6. Do not reject a piece on the grounds that it has a replacement baize or leather writing surface. These are common and do not greatly affect the value of the rest of the piece.

7. Check the wood around any locks: it should be undisturbed if the lock is original. Locks may be stamped with a date and the maker's name which can help to authenticate the piece.

Right: a French side cabinet ebonized with brass and mother-of-pearl inlay, c.1860, beneath a Victorian gilt mirror.

COLLECTIONS

In a letter in 1851, Charlotte Brontë wrote of the Great Exhibition held that year in the Crystal Palace in London, England: "Its grandeur does not consist in one thing, but in the unique assemblage of all things. Whatever human industry has created you find here ... it seems as if only magic could have gathered this mass of wealth from all the ends of the earth." The Great Exhibition was the first and largest of a series of local, national and international exhibitions held during the second half of the 19th century, in Britain, the Colonies, North America and on the Continent of Europe.

The thousands of exhibits were testament not only to the major advances in technology, manufacturing and the arts and crafts that were taking place during the 19th century, but also to the fact that designers and manufacturers, artists and craftsmen were increasingly drawing on the ideas, experiences and products of previous centuries and other countries for inspiration. Such developments were given additional and considerable impetus by the increase in international trade, foreign travel, the publication of periodicals on interior design and decoration and, of course, the exhibitions themselves.

To the Victorian public attending these exhibitions, which they did in vast numbers, was as much an educational outing as an opportunity for "window shopping". For example, the numerous items of pottery

Left: pressed glass scent bottles from a 19th-century American collection displayed on a Renaissance Revival marble-topped dressing table.
Right: a collection of North American shell boxes – these were often made by Victorian ladies – including a scallop shell inkwell from Niagara Falls and a basket-weave tray from Brewerton, New York.

and ceramics, sculpture, glass, silver and metalware on display showed the new middle classes not only what was aesthetically fashionable, but also offered them the material means through which they could furnish and ornament their homes. And just as the Great Exhibition, and the others that followed it, were collections of objects that attested to the economic and cultural advances of Victorian society, so the assemblage and display of those objects by its citizens in their own homes reflected and confirmed their prosperity, social standing and aesthetic and cultural interests to both themselves and others.

During the high-Victorian period the accumulation and display of collections of numerous useful and decorative wares in the typical Victorian home had reached the point where, notably in the drawing and dining room, every available surface and display cabinet was virtually crammed full. To followers of the Aesthetic and Arts and Crafts movements, the sum total of all this was nothing more than clutter. However, to most Victorians bareness and insufficient ornamentation in a room was in poor taste. They believed that the presence of such objects provided fertile topics for conversation, and that the "massing" of them – the positioning of pieces so that no one item dominated the grouping at the expense of another – was almost an art form in itself.

In Britain, one consequence of an expanding middle class was an increase in the popularity of drinking tea, and so the production of tea services and table wares. The development of bone china, which was less expensive to make than 18th-century hard-and-soft paste porcelain, also made such wares more affordable. During the early part of the Victorian era most porcelain echoed the Baroque and Rococo fantasies prevalent during the reigns of George IV and William IV. And at the Great Exhibition in London, England even quite ordinary domestic wares were extravagantly decorated with beautifully crafted Baroque- and Rococo-style figures, grotesques, animals and floral swathes.

Above left: Victorian linen and British royal memorabilia displayed in a bamboo-style étagère.
Above middle: Scots who emigrated to the United States during the 19th century often collected tartanware.

Above right: an interesting collection of Victorian glass on an Italian specimen marble-topped table.
Left: two 19th-century blackamoor busts with a group of fine Victorian silver photograph frames.

However, during the second half of the century there was a reaction to such excesses. For example, ceramics produced by the Arts and Crafts movement were much simpler in design. Form and function were harmonized, and inspiration was drawn from Nature and other motifs from the pre-industrial age. Companies such as Minton, Derby, Worcester and Copeland produced porcelain table wares in various historical-revival styles; copies of pieces made at Vincennes and Sèvres during the reign of Louis XVI were popular with the wealthy upper classes. The influence of the Gothic Revival was evident in wares produced by Charles Meigh, Derby and Davenport produced a wide selection of

colourful Japan wares and considerable quantities of Chinese blue-and-white porcelain were imported.

Numerous useful and decorative wares were collected by the Victorians. For instance, Staffordshire portrait figures were being mass-produced as early as 1845. Subjects included royalty, military and sporting heroes, animals, actors and even murderers. Today the most collectable military subjects are those that commemorate the Crimean War. Pastille burners and miniature rustic cottages were also popular items.

Relief-moulded stoneware jugs, coloured dark and pale green, buff, white and gray, were also collected. Many early versions were

Gothic in form, and popular decorations included Classical subjects and scenes from the Bible and popular novels. (The vast numbers of relief-moulded jugs that were produced during the early part of the Victorian era can be partly explained by the passing of the Registration Act of 1842, which allowed makers to register their designs, thereby preventing other manufacturers from copying them for a period of three years.)

Worcester figural wares were also very sought-after. Some were inspired by drawings of children by the English illustrator, Kate Greenaway; others by figures from classical Greece, India and Japan.

Parian ware, originally known as statuary

Above left: a cameo of a Chinese jar and figure, an English lustre jug and blue candle lustres capture the Victorian love of things Far Eastern. Above middle: a camel collection evokes the exoticism of Egypt.

Above right: hats hung on a wall create a country mood. Left: because tea was a luxury many tea caddies such as these tortoiseshell examples have locks. Afternoon tea was often mixed by the hostess.

Above: Staffordshire figures standing in front of a papier mâché *tray decorated with butterflies.*
Left: pottery figures and animals were collectable items.

porcelain and developed as a substitute for the white biscuit figures popularized at Sèvres and elsewhere in the 18th and early 19th centuries, was made by firms such as Minton, Coalport, Worcester, Belleek, Wedgwood and, in North America, by the United States Pottery Company. The most collectable pieces were statuettes of military and literary figures, and nudes; but Parian tablewares and wall fittings were also produced.

Majolica, a form of earthenware painted to look like the colourful glazes of 16th-century Italian majolica, was fashionable during the latter part of the Victorian era. Minton, Wedgwood and, in the United States, Edwin Bennett and Griffen, and Smith and Hill, led the market. They produced a variety of wares, including figural pieces and statuettes of birds and animals. Most wares were moulded in

high relief with a palette of ochres, browns, whites, turquoises, pinks and greens. Sculptural elements were either Classical, Renaissance or Japanese. In the United States a selection of "Etruscan" majolica from Phoenixville, which was reminiscent of early 19th-century Wedgwood, proved popular. Similarly, Rookwood art pottery, again inspired by European and Japanese originals, featured Japanese flora and fauna in coloured slips under bright, clear glazes. At the end of the 19th century, Rookwood also produced all kinds of vases depicting American Indians.

In Britain, Minton art pottery, featuring partially clad children in Classical settings and mythological scenes, was much in demand, as were Bretby figural pieces, such as gypsy children, black cats and monkeys. Burmantoft art pottery was also collectable; earthenwares

Right: a group of Victorian majolica pieces each characterized by a thick coloured glaze, including plates, jugs and, on the left of the picture, a large cheese bell with a cow finial.

were produced by William de Morgan, best-known for his decorative tiles, chargers, plates, dishes and vases – many of which were inspired by Iznik and Persian patterns and designs. Similarly, Linthorpe and Ault produced a selection of innovative colourful pieces inspired by mystical views of Nature as well as Celtic, Egyptian, Classical, Islamic, pre-Columbian and Aztec designs.

During the first half of the 19th century the work of sculptors such as Mathew Digby Wyatt and E.W. Wyon was influenced by the Neo-classical tastes popular during the reigns of William IV and George IV. Sculpture was also invariably life-size, expensive and so very much the preserve of the rich. However, the invention of the Cheverton reduction machine made it possible to produce small-scale, identically proportioned and relatively inexpensive copies of life-size pieces. As a consequence, the demand for sculpture increased dramatically during the second half of the Victorian period. Subject matter and style varied. For example, James Wyatt II's sentimental work "Lila" (1838) – a portrait of his daughter asleep on a pillow or cushion – inspired a profusion of sleeping children and babes-in-woods. Queen Victoria's patronage of Sir Edgar Boehm's sentimental sculptures promoted a similar demand, while her fondness for the romantic paintings of the English artist Edwin Landseer resulted in several of the subjects he depicted being transformed into three-dimensional sculptures rendered in marble, bronze, terra-cotta and Parian ware.

The work of French and German *animaliers* also became highly collectable. Pierre Jule Mene's hunting scenes were much sought-after; farm animals sculpted by the Bonheurs were also in demand, as were German *animalier* Christophe Fratin's sculptures of monkeys, retrievers and his bears in human postures.

During the 1870s popular "New Sculpture" began to oust Neo-classical-inspired pieces; Lord Leighton's treatment of an athlete wrestling with a python conveyed

included vases, *jardinières*, bottles and jars resembling Japanese and African gourds, and pilgrim bottles. A vast number of motto wares and knick-knacks produced by the Torquay potteries were also widely collected.

Ornamental Doulton wares were also popular. These included vases, jugs and tankards, and small models of mice and frogs. Useful and ornamental Wemyss wares included jugs painted to resemble sailors or Scottish

personalities, wall plaques, dressing-table sets, mugs, various commemorative souvenirs, and moulded pigs, cats and rabbits.

The influence of the Aesthetic and Arts and Crafts movements during the second half of the 19th century could be seen in the output of a number of small manufacturers. Most of their wares displayed the highest standards of craftsmanship and were affordable by only the wealthy. Some of the most desirable items a sense of movement largely absent in Neo-classical subjects. The use of the *cire perdue* (lost wax) method of casting also lent his work a greater sense of spontaneity than had been possible with the more clinically precise sand-cast pieces.

Other influential sculptors working in the new style included Sir Alfred Gilbert, whose subjects included mythical, allegorical, religious and contemporary figures. Numerous miniature versions were made of many of his best-known works, including "Eros", "Icarus" and a "Tribute to Hymen". Copies of American Hiram Power's sculptures, notably his "Greek Slave", were also in demand, as were, particularly in Australia, Bertram Mackennal's mythologically inspired works. The latter's "Circe", which was mounted on a base depicting a melee of naked male and female figures, caused a storm when it was first exhibited at the Royal Academy in London, England in 1894, and the base had to be covered with red baize so as not to "deprave or corrupt" the viewing public.

In Britain there was a marked revival in the glass industry during the Victorian era. In the early years the hand-blown, clear glass shapes favoured in the Georgian period remained in vogue, although they were now often embellished with various types of cutting work. However, the repeal of the Glass Act in 1845, which had made British glass very expensive to produce, fuelled a fashion for ornate engraved glassware, much of which was inspired by the output of French firms such as Baccarat and Saint Denis.

Similarly, after the Great Exhibition of 1851 at Crystal Palace in London, England, the increased importation of mass-produced Bohemian colour-flashed and engraved glassware stimulated a demand for coloured glass. Among the most popular items were vases, liqueur sets, goblets and candelabra engraved with stags in woodland settings, civic buildings or views of German towns and spas. Some pieces featured engraved panels, gilding and enamelled portrait medallions.

During the second half of the 19th century French opaline glass became fashionable. Popular pieces were decorated with sprays of flora trailed over bands of gilt flowers and leaves. Liqueur sets, decanters, lamps and drinking glasses from makers such as Emile Galle also reflected the French influence; many of the designs were either Medieval or naturalistic plant and insect forms.

The Italian influence was marked mainly by the importation of contrasting and strongly coloured Venetian glassware, and by the "fancy" coloured glass made, for example, by the London manufacturer James Powell. Powell's pieces featured tones of colours and applied fruits, flowers and ferns, and were popular in both Britain and North America.

Dark brown or green enamelled Nailsea glassware, which was produced in Bristol, was also in demand. Popular items included rolling pins, ornamental shoes and bells, and flasks. Spun-glass ornaments, such as birds and ships displayed under glass domes, were also produced in considerable numbers, as were coloured ornamental flower stands or *épergnes*.

For the top end of the market, cameo wares were produced by English companies such as Thomas Webb & Sons and Richardsons. Mostly Neo-classical in style, they were purely decorative and incorporated multiple layers of colour. Webb & Sons also made Rock Crystal wares of polished and engraved coloured glass, and coloured Burmese glass – the latter using a technique developed by the Mount Washington Company in North America. The best examples were gilt-enamelled and typical decorative motifs included

Above left: a wonderful 19th-century oval display cabinet. The wood is painted black and the pierced surround is picked out in gold. Designed to be hung on a wall, the dark background shows up the individual collectables to good effect.

Left: a grouping of 19th-century political and Royal commemorative ware, including a large Disraeli stoneware jug (1881), a Gladstone plate, a shell-framed portrait of Queen Victoria (1887) and a Prince Albert memorial plate (1861).

fish, flora and fauna and Egyptian imagery. After the Centennial Exhibition in Philadelphia in 1876, the Mount Washington Company also produced large quantities of art glass which was inspired by Venetian craftsmen, Classical civilizations, the European Renaissance and the Near East. Table wares, chandeliers and paperweights were among the most common items. Paperweights were also made by the New England Glass Company and the Boston and Sandwich Glass Company

designed to imitate more expensive cut glass. Pressed-glass commemorative wares were also popular; Henry Greener, for example, produced many pieces for Queen Victoria's Jubilee of 1887.

The English manufacturer, Sowerby, manufactured many high-quality pieces in vitro-porcelain, including spill holders, wall pockets, small baskets and candlesticks. Some pieces incorporated various Aesthetic designs, including imitations of carved ivory – reveal-

and parallel demand for less ornate pieces emerged. Some of the best examples were made by Christopher Dresser, who was particularly inspired by his knowledge of plants and a trip to Japan. His revolutionary designs for tea services and other useful domestic wares combined form and function and were largely devoid of decoration.

The most revolutionary development in the manufacture of silverware was the invention of a technique for electroplating silver over

Right: an array of late 19th-century toys and games, including a doll's house, alphabet blocks, pub skittles (1860s), a painted cast-iron terrier (1890), a boxer rebellion Chinaman ball game (c.1900), a wooden puzzle and a Victorian Noah's ark with animals.

Right: a delightful period doll's house stands in the hallway of designer Tessa Kennedy's Victorian home in Surrey, England. She furnished the miniature rooms with great attention to detail and even made tapestry carpets with 40 stitches to the inch.

in North America, and Baccarat in Europe.

Undoubtedly the most significant technical innovation in glass-making during the 19th century was the development of a technique for press-moulding glass by mechanical means. As a consequence, manufacturers were able to mass-produce affordable glassware that met the needs and pockets of the expanding middle and lower-middle classses. Much of the output of leading manufacturers such as George Davidson, Mount Washington and the Boston and Sandwich Glassworks consisted of domestic items such as cups, mugs, bowls, dishes, vases and other table wares. Made of clear or coloured glass, they were

ing the Japanese influence – while others were derived from children's book illustrations by artists such as Walter Crane. High-quality pressed glass was also produced by Webb & Co., Molineaux and John Derbyshire, the latter manufactured figures of Britannia and Punch and Judy.

In Britain, Classical- and Renaissance-style silverware remained fashionable throughout the 19th century. Leading silversmiths such as R. & S. Garrard, Hunt & Roskill, Storr & Mortimer and Charles and George Fox produced functional and decorative items that were large-scale, elaborate and expensive. However, after the Great Exhibition a new

copper or nickel alloy. Stamped E.P.N.S. silver plate was mass-producable, and relatively inexpensive and so met the requirements of the expanding middle classes. Elkington, Mason and Co. dominated the industry, and produced high-quality items, such as snuff boxes, candelabra, fruit dishes, tea urns and coffee pots, at low prices. Other leading manufacturers included James Deaking & Son, James Yates and Walker & Hall.

Toward the end of the 19th century various craft guilds began to make exquisite handmade silver in accordance with the ideals of the Medieval guilds. Prohibitively expensive, these pieces, from makers such as C.R.

Ashbee, were beyond the pocket of all but the very rich. On the other hand, selections of Cymric silver and Tudric pewter available from Liberty, in London, England, were far more affordable: they were hand-finished, but mass-produced.

In North America leading silversmiths included the Rhode Island firm of Gorham. Many of their wares were executed in various Rococo styles, while others incorporated native American and Japanese motifs. Silverware from Louis Comfort Tiffany was also much in demand. Early pieces included Rococo Revival flatware, while later wares were in Pharonic, Louis XVI, French Second Empire, Etruscan and Renaissance styles. Tiffany also copied Islamic and Moorish designs and used native American and motifs such as flora and fauna, fishes and shells.

In addition to useful and decorative table wares, 19th-century silversmiths produced a vast number of small artefacts and novelty objects, particularly during the high-Victorian period. Among these were nursery items such as children's rattles, christening mugs, doll's house furniture, miniature tea services and dining-room items such as nutmeg graters, wine labels and vinaigrettes. Novelty items included snuff boxes, pin trays and caddy spoons made in the shape of hands, and cruets in the form of birds such as owls.

Throughout the Victorian era collections of fine art formed an essential part of the decor in many homes, particularly in drawing and dining rooms. Subject matter varied enormously, and included portraits of the family, royalty and famous figures of the day, landscapes, topographical views, still lifes, hunting scenes, architectural studies, sentimental studies of children, episodes from the Bible and classical Greece and Rome, and Japanese characters and motifs.

During the early years, brightly coloured oils in gilt frames were grouped with prints, portrait drawings and silhouettes, and clusters of black-framed miniatures were often hung in-between them. Similarly, during the high-Victorian period gilt-framed oils, watercolours and prints were arranged in dense and symmetrical patterns, although in many Aesthetic and Arts and Crafts interiors one large canvas or drawing dominated a wall, while lesser works, such as prints and etchings were grouped at random around it.

In addition to ceramics, sculpture, glass, silverware, fine art and many other decorative objects were to be found in the typical

Left: a papier mâché writing slope, c.1880, with an inlaid watercolour picture and mother-of-pearl stands in front of a hand-painted tray on a heavy, carved pedestal table.
Right: a collection of 19th-century boxes and a star-shaped shell souvenir picture.
Below: tin hat boxes and a Victorian tri-fold screen, c.1880s, decorated with découpage.

Victorian home. While some were not originally displayed as collections, they often are today. And displays of "Victoriana" are an effective way to help recreate the atmosphere of a Victorian interior.

So-called "shades" – displays of imitation flowers, stuffed birds, shells or miniature figures under glass domes – could be found on tables and mantel shelves in many Victorian homes. Popular subjects included religious figures, children, animals, domestic scenes, exotic fruits crafted in wax, and realistic "flowers" made also of wax or else from feathers or hair. Chinese ivory fans, decorated with mother-of-pearl, as well as French-made copies, also made fashionable displays.

Examples of decalcomania, a type of glassware decorated at home by glueing scraps of colourful paper – images either cut out from magazines or sold in sets by craft shops – to the inside of clear glass vessels and then coating them with enamel or whitewash were also sought-after. *Pot-au-cheminee* (vases) and "witches balls" incorporating mirrored glass were particularly popular, and scraps of decorative paper were also collected in their own right, as well as being used to decorate screens. Typical subject matter included heroes of the day, children and animals.

Novelty "pop-up" cards known as "mechanicals" came into vogue during the latter part of the 19th century and, like

Left: the Victorians were avid sculpture collectors, as reflected by this 19th-century blackamoor chandelier in the Belvedere Mansion, Galena, Illinois.

Below: a perfect American Gothic interior complete with "hatbox" wallpaper, a massive Roux mirror, fine chairs and parian figures.

Valentine cards and sailor's valentines, are now highly collectable. The latter were octagonal-shaped wooden boxes rather than cards and were decorated with shells arranged in mosaic patterns, dried leaves or paper lace, set under protective glass covers. The maritime theme was also prevalent in scrimshaw, and nautical images were engraved onto whalebone, narwhal tusks or shells.

Collections of miniature portraits depicting relatives and loved ones were in vogue throughout the 19th century. However, after the 1840s they were gradually replaced by the Daguerreotype and the Ambrotype – precursors of the modern photograph. Popular images included portraits, family groups, still lifes, topographical studies and, in North America, Civil War subjects.

Toward the end of the century, following the perfection of techniques for developing photographic images on paper or card, and then making several copies from one exposure, photographs became available for sale in shops. Subjects collected included members of the Royal Family, famous actors and architectural studies.

Above: the Victorians did not go along with the dictum that "less is more", and no wall was left bare. Here a collection of oils, watercolours and miniatures give an authentic period backdrop.
Below left: designed by Jonathan Hudson, this room was inspired by the paintings of the Victorian artist, Sir Lawrence Alma-Tadema. It is interesting to note that Victorian pictures were hung so that they could be lit from below.
Below right: late 19th- and early 20th-century paintings in a fine American Gothic interior.
Right: an excellent collection of 19th-century glass paintings of the same village in maple frames.

As today, toys were collected by both children and adults during the Victorian era. Lead soldiers, or "flats", and all manner of wooden toys such as miniature shops, houses, theatres and boats were the most common. Tin cars, ships and animals were manufactured in large quantities in the United States and in Germany and were exported all over the world; Ernst Paul Lehmann was one of the best-known makers. Automata were also displayed, as well as played with.

During the second half of the 19th century there was a substantial increase in the manufacture of dolls, notably in Germany and France; the best examples were made by Bru Jeune and Jumeu. Dolls made from *papier mâché*, wax composition, cloth and china gradually superseded the traditional wooden examples. Among the most sought-after were "Bisques", which had faces made from unglazed china; "Parisiennes", or "fashion dolls", which depicted adults or adolescents wearing detailed copies of contemporary fashions; and "character" dolls, which were usually made of wax and had realistic rather than idealized facial expressions.

Above: interior designer Christophe Gollut's dining room, situated on the piano nobile of an 1850s house in Knightsbridge, London, England, has a generous display of closely-hung paintings, reflecting the way that pictures were often exhibited in Victorian homes. Behind a pair of well-disguised doors lies the kitchen which was converted from spacious wall cupboards. The doors and walls of the room blend cleverly together and are covered with striped German fabric in dusky lime green and pink. Below the dado is a small cut-velvet design which complements the original cut-velvet covers of the chairs.

Above: decorative porcelain can be displayed in all sorts of configurations on the wall – either hung or else standing on unobtrusive brackets.
Below left: a collection of etched, painted, gilded, jewelled and cut glass and a massive bronze horse displayed on an étagère.
Below middle: a 19th-century display cabinet filled with cranberry, vaseline and irridescent Victorian glass in the Steamboat House, Galena, Illinois.

Above: in a utility room a collection of earthenware pots, decoy birds and gardening implements is displayed against walls of a suitably earthy colour.
Below right: this massive piece of early Victorian furniture has a ground-level mirror for ladies to check that it wasn't "snowing down south", in other words that they were not revealing their petticoats! The built-in mirrors serve to magnify the effect of the French vaseline glass on display.

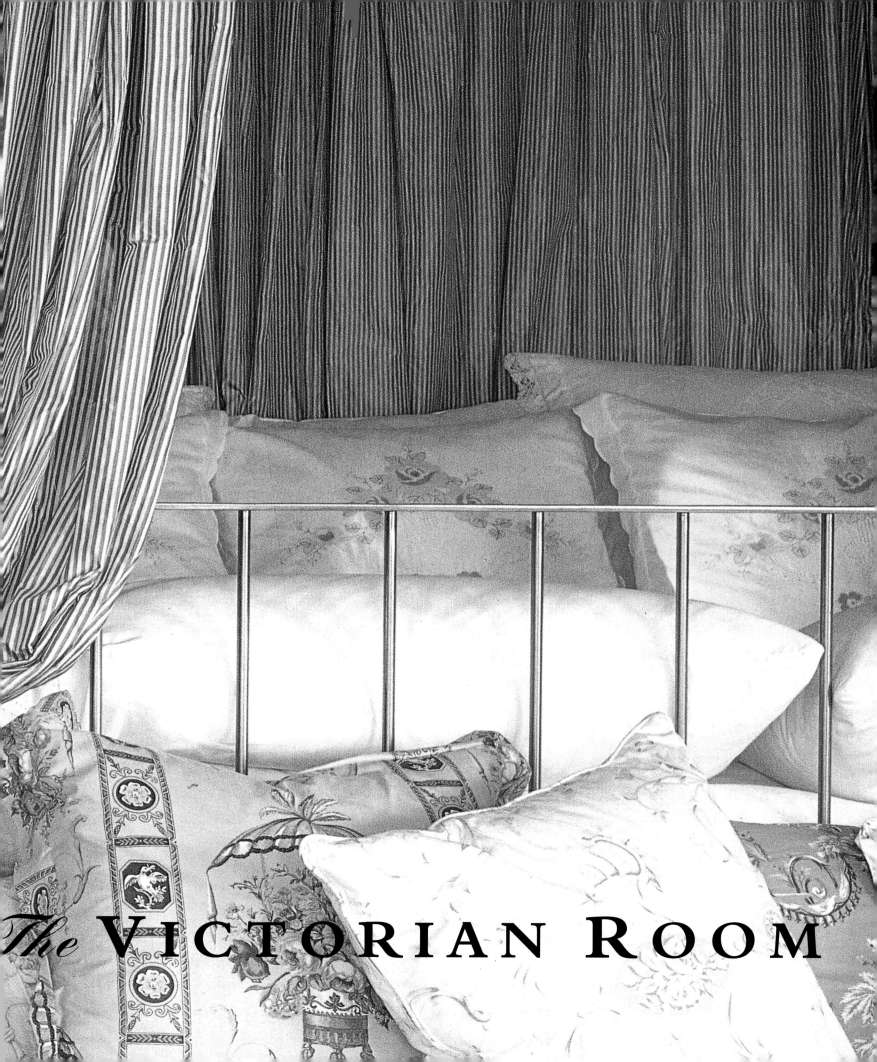

The Victorian Room

ENTRANCE HALLS

*I*n terms of both design and function, entrance halls in Victorian houses can be broadly divided into two basic types. Most prevalent throughout the 19th century was what was essentially a corridor leading, usually off a small lobby or vestibule, from the front door to important reception rooms on the entrance floor and, via a staircase, to a landing and additional reception rooms on the upper floor. In addition to serving as a thoroughfare, the purpose of these often long and relatively narrow areas was to provide a *cordon sanitaire* in-between the noise, dirt, heat or cold, and hustle and bustle of the world outside and the comfortable seclusion indoors. The entrance hall also served as a reception and waiting area for visitors prior to their admittance into the heart of the home and also as a repository for coats, hats, umbrellas, letters and parcels.

The other type of entrance area found in Victorian houses was the "living-hall". Conceived by architects building houses in the Neogothic style during the 1830s and 1840s, it was a throwback to the "great hall" of Medieval times. This large room served not only as a transitional area for occupants of, and visitors to, the home, but also as a principal room of the house in which the owner could entertain on special occasions such as Christmas, the New Year and during the summer. Initially confined to only the largest of houses, these living-halls

Left: red drawing-room drapes in a house in London, England, contrast with the tiled floor and the black, white and gold wallpaper in the hallway.
Right: stone-blocked walls in the entrance hall of a Mediterranean home help to keep the room cool. The flooring is reminiscent of India matting, popular in the 19th century because it could be taken up and beaten regularly.

were often built through two stories and incorporated a gallery on the first floor. By the 1870s they were reduced in scale and became an adjunct to the main living room in many larger residences and smaller country houses.

Because both types of entrance hall were the first "room" visitors encountered when entering a house, the Victorians bestowed as much care and attention on their design, decoration and furnishings as they did with the other principal rooms. The entrance hall was treated as an emblem for the rest of the house, and the first impressions it offered instantly communicated the status and lifestyle of the occupants.

Having been let in through the front door by a maid, both visitors and occupants would enter a lobby, or vestibule, which was often partitioned off from the main hallway with glass-panelled double doors. The purpose of this area was to improve the architectural proportions of what, in most houses, would otherwise have been a long and perhaps visually unwelcoming corridor. In addition to providing a space for coat, hat and umbrella stands, the lobby or vestibule also acted as a draft-excluder as the double doors were hung with heavy drapes during the winter months.

In houses where the entrance hall beyond the lobby or vestibule was a long corridor, architects used scrolled plasterwork brackets at intervals to visually "break up" the monotony of narrow walls, as well as bridges of ornamental fretwork, particularly in Italianate and Neogothic style houses. Such attempts to make the hallway more visually interesting were also reflected in the decorations and furnishings, although always with an eye to the practical in what was a high-traffic area. Thus, many ceilings were embellished with applied ornamental plasterwork. Floors were either made of marble, tiles or wood, the latter was stained or grained and varnished and parquet was commonly used in larger hallways. Authorities such as Charles Eastlake recommended encaustic tiles for hall floors because they were aesthetically pleasing and hard-wearing. Medieval- and geometric- patterned tiles,

made by companies such as Minton, were the most popular, and for the less well-off linoleums became available toward the end of the 19th century. Floors were also augmented with rugs, runners, narrow strips of dark green or brown oilcloth and India matting – all of which "broke up" the length of the hall visually and could be regularly turned, beaten and, when necessary, washed.

For most of the 19th century, hallway walls were usually divided into three horizontal sections: the classic arrangement of a dado from the top of the baseboard or skirting to a dado rail which measured approximately 3ft 6in (1m) from the floor, a field from dado to picture rail, and a frieze from picture rail to ceiling moulding or cornice. Generally, strong, dark colours and bold patterns were favoured both for their decoration, and for their durability and ease of cleaning.

During the early part of the 19th century the dado was often covered with marbled slabs of paper, which were easily replaced if they became damaged. While Charles Eastlake's recommendation of washable and hard-wearing encaustic tiles as an alternative proved popular, less-expensive oil-painted leather-paper, Lincrusta and embossed Anaglypta were more widely used during the second half of the Victorian era. Mahogany, oak and grained softwood panelling or wainscotting was also used up to dado height, notably in North America and Arts and Crafts houses in Britain.

For the field, designers and manufacturers, notably William Morris, produced block-printed wallpapers and chintzes and dense organic patterns depicting stylized flowers and foliage were particularly popular during the 1880s and 1890s. For those who could not afford them, machine-printed wallpapers and textiles provided a less expensive alternative. Printed with engraved copper rollers, so-called "sanitary" papers were available in a wide selection of patterns with popular designs based on chrysanthemums, peonies, acanthus leaves and 18th-century French scrollwork. Smooth-surfaced, these wallpapers were also rendered washable after varnishing. For the frieze around the top of the walls,

Opposite: the hallway of a high-Victorian Gothic "domestic palace" built by Sir Gilbert Scott's associates. Now a private home, Hall Place in Hampstead, London, England, was famous for its musical soirées during the 19th century.
Left: early 19th-century furniture, made in the Shenendoah Valley, in the hallway of a home in Sheperdstown, Virginia.
Right: preserved in its original condition, the hallway floor in this 1830s house in Galena, Illinois, remains painted to resemble tiles. The walnut banister is made locally. The table is an American interpretation of Regency style, c.1820, and the side chairs are comparable to Hitchcock chairs which were mass-produced after the 1830s.

the most common form of decoration was stencilling or wallpaper, with the design based on a motif picked up from the field below.

Joinery in hallways was almost invariably made of dark hardwoods, such as mahogany, or softwoods, such as pine, the latter usually stained dark or grained to resemble hardwoods. In many North American houses joinery was often lighter-coloured than that found in most English homes due to the influence of the French and the greater availability of paler hardwoods. In many Victorian hallways, the stairway was a main feature of the decor and as such was often elaborately decorated, even in quite ordinary houses. Wooden staircases – as opposed to stone ones which only appeared in the largest Victorian houses, and in the north and northwest of England and also in Scotland – normally boasted gloss-varnished or French-polished mahogany handrails, prominent newel posts and turned balusters. The sides of the staircase were often decorated with tiles, painted wooden panels, stencilling or squares of white India matting painted to mimic tiles. Mottos of a "homely and instructive nature" were also applied, and "Home Sweet Home" was spelled out beside the stairs as well as over the entrance or on the front doormat. Stair-runners were held in place by twisted cords of braid which were tacked down or by brass carpet rods which echoed the ornamental brass knobs, pulls or handles, escutcheon plates and hinges commonly used to embellish hall doorways. The sumptuous combination of polished hardwoods and brass fixtures and fittings was enhanced by the use of richly coloured and patterned fabrics, such as tapestries, velvets, serges and damasks, made up into *portière* drapes and cornices or pelmets for doors and hung from decorative arches along the length of the hallway.

The amount of furniture in the Victorian entrance hall depended on the space available. Most hallways contained a hall tree, larger versions consisting of a wooden or cast-iron stand with brass or iron hooks for hanging hats and coats, a lidded compartment for holding overshoes, an open-topped compartment for walking sticks and umbrellas, an inset mirror, a glove box and a shelf for newspapers and letters. In smaller, narrower halls, a wall-hung hat and coat rack was often substituted, and antlers were sometimes used. Over and above its function as a receptacle for household paraphernalia, the hall tree also served as a sort of social telegraph for visitors and occupants alike. For example, gentlemen were advised to leave their coats and overshoes in the hall but, unless they were calling on family or close friends, to take their hats and walking sticks into the drawing room, as by leaving the latter in the hall they were signalling their intention to stay in the house for more than 15 minutes – a socially unacceptable duration when visiting a young lady of recent acquaintance.

In the spacious hallway of an 1855 Gothic Revival mansion in Galena,
Illinois, some of the mid-Victorian furniture was made by Mitchell
Romelsburg. The wallpaper is a copy of a mid 19th-century French pattern.

Most entrance areas also housed a grandfather clock and a hall table, the size of the latter again depending on the space available. Used to deposit gloves, parcels, letters and a clothes brush – the latter was kept in a drawer – the table, which was often marble-topped, also bore a salver or tray. Where space allowed, the table was flanked by two chairs or a bench, either of bare wood or covered with tough leather.

The display of artwork in Victorian entrance halls was as much a matter of etiquette as of taste. In *The Decoration of Houses*, Edith Wharton and Ogden Codman Jr advised that sculptures and busts should be displayed on pedestals or recessed in niches, and that family portraits, as well as prints and etchings, were appropriate. However, major works of art were unacceptable: "Where walls are hung with pictures, these should be few in number and colouring. No subject requiring thought and study is suitable in such a position."

To designers and architects such as William Morris and C.F.A. Voysey, the presence of numerous paintings, prints and etchings and items of sculpture only added to the "clutter" of the typical Victorian hallway. The "living-halls" they advocated were spacious and well-lit. In an Arts and Crafts living-hall uncluttered simplicity was the theme: an inglenook and wide hearth were the focus, and the decorations and furniture were elegant but plain. However, to most Victorians such "bareness" was "offensive" and the spacious living-halls found in many houses toward the end of the 19th century were soon filled with antiques, old armour, hunting trophies, curiosities and all manner of relics, much to the disgust of Voysey who complained that the hall had become, once again, so full of "vulgar glitter and display . . . a vast expanse of advertisement" that it reminded him of a railway station.

Left: an impressive Gothic staircase in interior designer Tessa Kennedy's large, rambling country Victorian house.
Right: a high-Victorian hallway in Hall Place, a spectacular Gothic "domestic palace" in North London, England, which can be visited by appointment. During the late 19th century this room was used for musical performances and was fitted with a stage and a trap door for scenic effects. The original 1860s colour scheme of this room remains, broken up by a colonnade of pointed arches rising from marble columns surmounted by floriated capitals which were all crafted by different guilds. The stairs lead to a tower and a large picture gallery, exhibiting watercolours by Alfred Bell.

LIVING ROOMS

The drawing room, also referred to as the parlour, was the most lavishly appointed room in the Victorian home. As a formal reception area it was, unlike the private rooms upstairs, open to the scrutiny and appraisal of guests and visitors. Hence its decor was carefully chosen in order to reflect the prosperity and status, as well as the aesthetic and cultural interests and aspirations of the occupants of the house. Writing at the end of the 19th century, the German commentator Hermann Muthesius observed that: "the aim is to make the room the jewel-casket of the home, in both content and form . . . in many houses it has almost become a museum of old, valuable furniture and art treasures, and is often filled to overflowing in the process."

It is ironic, therefore, that the drawing room was for most Victorians the least used room in the house – being largely reserved for the formal receiving of guests, especially on Sunday afternoons, parties and family gatherings on festive occasions. In *The Effects of the Factory System* (1899) Allen Clarke noted that: "It is shut up for six days a week, and is only kept for brag; ostentatious superfluity in the idea of the artisan's wife is, as with those in higher grades of society, a sign of superiority." Although not a strictly accurate observation – many middle and lower middle-class parlours also doubled up as sitting, music and sewing rooms – Clarke's observation provides an insight into the correlation

Left: a high-Victorian interior in a 1930s London mews house. There is a blend of fabrics, paintings, old Chinese ceramics and two reproduction sofas.
Right: designer Christophe Gollut has recreated a characteristic Victorian colour scheme from the aubergine cotton fabric on the walls to the terra-cotta marble paint finish on the moulding or cornice.

between the display of wealth and culture in the home and social standing in Victorian society.

While many lower middle-class houses had only one parlour, which was usually at the front on the entrance floor, most middle- and upper middle-class homes had a front and a back parlour. Often divided by folding doors, they served different purposes: the front room being used as a reception area for visitors; the back as a family sitting room, which in some cases also doubled up as a dining room. The popular American women's journal *Godey's* noted that in houses with both front and back parlours, "many prefer to use the back room as a library [while] others again, station a piano back there and call it a music room on that solitary claim". Some larger houses, such as Beckwith House in Mitchell, South Dakota in the United States, had triple parlours. Running the whole depth of the house, they were again divided by folding doors and allotted specific functions, such as formal reception room, sitting room and music or sewing room. In the grandest houses, there was often a fourth reception room, which was usually furnished as a study or a smoking room for men.

Whether or not it served more than one purpose, the drawing room or parlour, used for entertaining guests and visitors, was invariably the most spacious room in the house. It also boasted the highest ceilings, the most elaborate and ornamental architectural fixtures and fittings, and the most sumptuous decorations and furnishings. Styles of decor varied considerably throughout the Victorian era: Neo-rococo and Louis XIV, French- and Italian-Renaissance, Elizabethan and Gothic, Aesthetic and Arts and Crafts, Oriental, Art Nouveau and Queen Anne Revival were all popular at one time or another. However, the historicizing decorative schemes among them could not, for the most part, be described as accurate recreations of earlier eras. Rather, they might best be considered as inspired by them. For instance, John Loudon's *Encyclopedia* (1833) was divided into the following historical sections: "Grecian", "Italianate", "Gothic" and "Fat Classical". Similarly, it wasn't unusual to find Victorian chairs described as Regency incorporating elements of Gothic detailing.

Despite the vagaries of fashion, the one influence that remained virtually constant in the decor of the Victorian drawing room was the feminine touch. First and foremost the parlour was the domain of the women of the house. While fathers and grown-up sons spent their working lives and much of their leisure time outside the home, wives and daughters lived most of theirs inside it. And the products of "suitable" female occupations such as beadwork, embroidery, crocheting, needlepoint and other gentle arts and crafts naturally found their way into the parlour, giving it a comfortable, feminine air. Muthesius summed up the decor of the English drawing room as "dainty". However, in the high-Victorian parlour, the luxurious combination of plump, stuffed upholstery – suggestive to some of the ampler female form – and gently rustling layers of fabric – echoing the subtle rustling

Left: the drawing room in the Belvedere Mansion built in 1857 in Galena, Illinois, is full of fine Victorian furniture and artefacts, overlooked by an impressive oil painting of General Rawlings. The Belcher chairs on the right have the heads of presidents carved in the backs.

Above: a Victorian-style parlour in the Steamboat House, Galena, Illinois. There is a fine reproduction suite of mid-Victorian chairs and the portraits almost obscure the wallpaper which is a recreated 19th-century pattern.

Below: a view through the double pocket doors of the intimate parlour in the Belle of the Bends inn in Vicksburg, Mississippi. The walnut love seat is an 1850's original and the gasolier is 1880s.

of silk petticoats – draped at windows and over pieces of furniture, could be described as conveying a subtle, albeit repressed, female sensuality. As the commentator Hermann Muthesius observed, "the decor is designed to create comforts that make it agreeable to linger there".

Drawing-room walls during the early decades of the Victorian period were often without a dado. Fabric, for example damask, or paper wall-coverings consequently covered a large expanse from the moulding or cornice down to the top of the baseboard or skirting, the latter was often relatively high and had a complex profile. However, Charles Eastlake believed that a single drop of wallpaper running from the baseboard or skirting to the ceiling was "a most dreary method" of decoration. Favoured patterns incorporated scrolls, vines, birds and gilded traceries and were generally small-scale and finely detailed. Popular colours included cream, pale blues and greens, lavender and pearly gray. For instance, the drawing-room walls at the Marmillion Plantation in Lousiana, in North America were pale lavender, as was the ceiling, and augmented with a frieze of decoration including painted scrolls, flowers, birds and jewels. In grand houses the wallpaper was also often finished at the top and bottom, and sometimes in the corners, with a gilt wooden or metal fillet; in smaller houses a printed paper border, usually of French manufacture, would have been used instead.

During the middle- and high-Victorian period an ever-wider selection of patterned wallpapers became available via mass-production. Simple floral patterns, found for example in Thomas Carlyle's house in Chelsea, London, England, were particularly popular. However, as the

Right: the parlour at Cedar Grove, Vicksburg, Mississippi, which dates from the 1840s. The suite of furniture includes a courting couch – designed to seat three – on which the courting couple would sit on either side of a chaperone. The long drapes which "puddle" on the floor are copies from a popular 1860s design and the windows are separated by a central gilded pier mirror, which was shipped from France during the mid 1840s. Pier mirrors were a popular 19th-century device which created the illusion of an additional window.
Left: an 1840s marble fireplace which was shipped from Italy to Vicksburg, Mississippi, up the Mississippi river, especially for the parlour at Cedar Grove. The chairs are Victorian Southern style and the kerosene or paraffin lamps are fine examples of the popular French Empire style.

century wore on more grandiose and geometric papers found favour, such as those produced by Watts & Co. Embossed and painted Lincrustas and Anaglyptas were increasingly used for dados and ceilings, usually darker shades for the former and mid-tones for the latter, and colours generally became richer than they had been previously. Rusty reds, deep browns and terra-cottas were popular, and were frequently enhanced with black, yellow and gold outlining and stencilling. In the grandest houses, imperial purple and a variety of blues from indigo to Prussian to deep azure were used, while wallpapers and fabrics manufactured with new chemical-based dyes, such as sharp yellows, brilliant crimsons, saturated blues and virulent greens, began to appear in middle-class homes. Sometimes fabrics were stretched

Throughout the Victorian era drawing-room ceilings and mouldings or cornices tended to be painted or papered in the lighter tones picked up from the main wall colour. However, and this was particularly so in the grander houses of the high-Victorian period, ceiling mouldings or cornices, elaborately carved to depict garlands of hothouse flowers and fruits, were often picked out in rich, naturalistic colours. When this was done, the field or surface of the ceiling might also be embellished with applied decorations, which were either hand-painted or stencilled in gold and rich polychromy.

While the drawing-room woodwork during the early years of Queen Victoria's reign was often painted in pale colours, typically ivory, and the mouldings were picked out in gold, during the high-Victorian years it tended to be painted in richer colours harmonizing with those elsewhere in the decor. Rose, plum, sage-green, ochre and gold were especially favoured. Black was also used, either as paint or as stain and was often combined with gold leaf on relief mouldings.

Throughout the 19th century, drawing-room floorboards in most houses tended to be stained, varnished, polished and also painted in dark brown natural wood colours. Parquet was much in evidence in larger houses, and fitted wall-to-wall carpets were also widely used. *Cassell's Household Guide* recommended Axminster or velvet pile with elaborate patterns such as acanthus scrolls and cabbage roses. During the increasingly hygiene-conscious 1880s and 1890s fitted wall-to-wall carpets were falling out of favour and, being easier to beat and clean regularly, loose carpets and rugs were considered a healthier and more practical alternative. The most popular types, particularly during the 1870s and 1880s, were machine-woven and patterned in French or

over battens to substitute hand-blocked or machine-printed papers and stencilled plasterwork, often incorporating motifs picked up from the ceiling, and provided an alternative way of decorating walls.

During the latter part of the 19th century, when the decor was influenced by the designs of the Aesthetic and Arts and Crafts movements, drawing-room walls were usually decorated in the traditional tripartite manner, and such as Walter Crane manufactured matching papers for the dado, field and frieze. Textiles such as chintz, cretonne and Japanese grass paper were also commonly used for the dado, particularly in the 1880s and 1890s, while lush-looking organic papers were applied to the field above. In many cases, colours were inspired by the paintings of such artists as Sir Edward Burne-Jones, Dante Gabriel Rossetti and J. A. Whistler, notably the paler ones such as hyacinth-blues, soft olive-greens, lemon-yellows, ivories and grays.

In Art Nouveau-inspired interiors wall colours tended toward the off-beat or quirky, such as olive, sage and mustard, and friezes featured deep bands of stencilled long-stemmed flowers and stylized birds. By the end of the 19th century, Muthesius observed that in most ordinary homes flower-patterned papers, or, more usually, machine-printed copies of them by William Morris, remained the popular choice, any wood panelling tended to be painted white, while the frieze often carried a delicate repeat pattern faintly echoed in the ceiling above.

Left: a collection of Victorian furniture including a Boulle table, c.1850
and a set of William IV deep button-back salon chairs.
Above: modern fabrics used to recreate a Rococo Revival-style living room.
Right: a perfect American Gothic-style parlour in the Village, New York.

Right and opposite page: in a piano nobile of an 1850s house in Knightsbridge, London, England, there is a comfortable mix of 18th- and 19th-century European furniture, although the overall feel of the room is French. The pink, lilac and green colour scheme of the walls is characteristically Victorian. The ceiling paper is by Cole & Son and the shades or blinds are silk damask.

Below left: this dramatic room in a North London, England apartment or flat gives a strong impression of a French 19th-century interior. Key features are the chairs, marble-topped tables, festoon shades or blinds and blackamoor figures. Below right: a countryfied 19th-century style informal living room with furniture upholstered in Waverly's "Sweet Violets" fabric.

Oriental styles. In the case of the latter, blood-red and blue were favoured colours, while Aubusson- and Savonnerie-type patterns in pale colours were considered by many writers as "ideal" for the drawing room. The increasing use of chemical dyes resulted in brilliant colours appearing in ever denser and more naturalistic ornamentation during the high-Victorian period. Carpets from the Arts and Crafts movement typically featured shades such as soft blues, deep reds and ivory, or moss-green, gold and brown. However, although they were widely admired, even William Morris baulked at the considerable cost and tended, like many others, to use Turkish and Persian tribal carpets as less expensive and perfectly acceptable alternatives.

While the central table became the focus of many early- and mid-19th century parlours, in most houses the fireplace remained the

feature that usually first caught the eye on entering the room. One writer referred to it as, "the sacred family altar", while Lucy Orrinsmith in *The Drawing Room, Its Decoration and Furniture* (1877) described it as a, "rallying spot, to collect around it the richest rugs, the softest sofas, the cosiest chairs, the prettiest treasures". Great black and white edifices made of marble were the most common, although wood, often elaborately carved, was also used. The arch-topped register grate was virtually universal, and bellows – sometimes embroidered and painted – tongs, brushes and coal scuttles became more ornate as the 19th century wore on, as did the large brass fenders that were drawn up around the fireplace to stop coals from falling out of the hearth and long dresses from accidentally catching alight as women passed by, unfortunately a fairly common occurrence. Firescreens, which were either painted,

embroidered, inlaid with marquetry or lacquered *papier mâché*, were also considered a necessity for protecting carpets and drapes from renegade sparks as well as guarding female complexions from the heat of the fire. A hearth rug was also sometimes placed over the edge of the carpet to protect it. During the summer months in country houses, fireboards painted with landscapes, and baskets of fruit and flowers were used to fill

in the bare hearth, while in city houses parasols, fans and arrangements of pine cones, ferns, mosses and bouquets of flowers were used instead.

As the Victorian era progressed, mantel shelves grew deeper to accommodate ever-more elaborate garnitures, and a draped lambrequin, made of velvet, serge, plush or lace became a fashionable essential. During the first half of the 19th century, large gilt pier glasses were a standard feature above the chimneypiece. However, these were gradually replaced by mirrored overmantels, often made of mahogany and walnut and featuring numerous shelves and niches for displaying ornaments on either side of the glass. And later fire surrounds were sometimes flanked with built-in cabinets for books. The darker colour schemes of late-Victorian drawing rooms were made brighter by artificial and natural light reflecting off both the overmantel mirror and large, silver mirrors hung around the room. The effect of the latter was to create expansive double views, and in many town houses pier mirrors were positioned in-between two windows to create the effect of a third window.

Window drapery was also a significant feature of the Victorian drawing room. Lace or net drapes were almost universally used during the second half of the 19th century; either Swiss lace on a voile backing, or machine-made Nottingham lace or, by the more design-conscious, patterned muslin. Many rooms also had Venetian shades or blinds, made of iron and japanned in bright colours, as well as drapes.

Scrolled, scalloped or gilded lambrequins spanned the tops of windows in many homes, flat fabric cornices or pelmets in others. Drapes were almost always hung from heavy brass or wooden poles. When not covered by a cornice or pelmet these were often grained rosewood or painted gold, and supported on brackets finished with decorative rosettes, the latter echoing "cloak-pin" tie-backs and elaborate finials. The drapes that descended from them were invariably made of white muslin during the summer months and sumptuous fabrics such as velvet, brocade, mohair and silk during the winter. Folded and held back with ropes or flat tie-backs attached to ormolu, rosette-headed pins or

Below: because the Victorian bedroom was a private sanctuary, a parlour area was sometimes incorporated, as in this house in Los Angeles, California.
Right: a warm, 19th-century feel has been achieved by a mix of fabrics.
The wallpaper is by Colefax & Fowler and the drapes by Pallu & Lake.

leaf- or scroll-shaped fitments, they were usually embellished with tassels, ribbons and festoons. Styles tended to echo prevailing women's fashions. For example, in 1880 *Godey's* suggested combining fabrics in two or three shades of the same contrasting colours – the results bearing more than a passing resemblance to the under- and over-skirtings women wore toward the end of the 19th century.

In addition to providing insulation against drafts, window drapes also shielded the drawing room from sunlight, causing fabrics to fade, which was regarded as "unfashionable". Elaborate *portières* tied back with braided silk ropes were also used extensively to sound- and draft-proof doorways in many houses, and from the 1870s to 1890s these became so fashionable that they often replaced doors altogether. Little wonder that Scarlett O'Hara was able to fashion her green velvet dress, embellished with tassels, braid and trim, from her mother's *portières!*

began to use unmatched pieces once again, often incorporating exotic elements such as Oriental tables, arranged asymmetrically.

Although such arrangements were asymmetrical, they were not random. The fact that high- and late-Victorian drawing rooms were filled with all manner of sofas, chairs, footstools and tables – the tops of the latter draped with fabrics and laden with ornaments and collectables – meant that they had to be carefully positioned to allow ease of passage through the room, particularly that of women wearing wide skirts and sleeves and long trains. The furniture was also aligned to facilitate conversation, the best arrangement for this being small groupings or vignettes in which chairs were juxtapositioned with tables displaying memorabilia, the latter providing inspiration for all manner of small talk. The aesthetics of these conversational groupings revolved around the "massing" of objects – furniture, ornaments and plants – in order

Left: a collection of 19th-century pillows or cushions, including patchwork, bead and needlework designs, some are bordered with tassels. Pillows or cushions are useful additions to seating, lending a period feel and a touch of comfort.

Left: the bold Paisley-style upholstery, fake leopard pillow or cushion and exotic pictures in this corner of a drawing room in Los Angeles, California, neatly convey the Victorian fascination with the Orient.

Judged by the standards of interior decoration today, the typical Victorian drawing room was over-furnished and unrestrainedly cluttered. However, for much of the 19th century, and particularly during the high-Victorian years, the prevailing view was that an abundance of furniture broke the monotony of too much space. As Harriet Spofford pointed out in her *Art of Decoration Applied to Furniture* (1878): "provided there is enough space to move about without walking over the furniture, there is hardly likely to be too much within the room".

During the first half of the Victorian era, drawing-room furniture was essentially eclectic, while from the middle of the period onward, matching sets or suites, in a variety of historical styles and usually consisting of a sofa, a central table, an *étagère* and assorted parlour chairs, footstools and side tables, became fairly standard in most households. Although by the mid-1870s more fashion-conscious homeowners

to create a visual harmony in which no single item dominated the vignette at the expense of another. "The 'massing' of objects", according to an article entitled "The Art of Furnishing" which appeared in *Harper's Bazaar*, "prevented a 'speckled' appearance within a drawing room, which was something to be avoided when dealing with a full rather than a spare space." Of course, despite the thought and care put into "massing" objects within harmonious vignettes around the drawing room or parlour, many Victorians, in particular the followers of the Aesthetic and the Arts and Crafts movements, believed that the end result was no more or less than clutter.

The largest item of furniture in the Victorian drawing room was the upholstered sofa. After 1850, most examples were coil-sprung and deep-buttoned. Typical examples were often a pair of medallion- and serpentine-backed Queen Anne- or Sheraton-style sofas, with matching

Left: in front of the fireplace in the Old Merchant's House, New York, is a swan rocker c.1850; on the mantel is a mahogany ogee clock 1880-90. Above: a fireplace surrounded by 19th-century bronze and glass lustres and fire implements.

Above: a typical Eastlake-style library fireplace. Below left: an authentic recreation of a Victorian parlour, notice the fabric on the mantel shelf. Below right: a Pugin sofa, Gothic fire surround and Gothic bookcases designed by John Stefanidis.

elbow chairs or armchairs. Toward the end of the 19th century Hepplewhite models, Chesterfields and, particularly during the 1880s and 1890s, circular ottomans upholstered around a padded central post, were also much in evidence.

An enormous variety of upholstered elbow chairs or armchairs were placed around the drawing room throughout the Victorian era: larger ones for men and smaller ones for women, the latter were sometimes without arms to facilitate the decorous arrangement of voluminous, multi-layered skirts. They were rectangular and rounded; compact with low arms or majestic with high arms; fully or partly upholstered, and shaped as *têtes-à-têtes*, which were a pair of joined "conversational" chairs usually facing in opposite directions. Other popular occasional chairs included balloon-backs and ones made of *papier mâché*, the latter were japanned black and elaborately detailed with mother-of-pearl inlay and painted panels depicting royalty, landscapes and castles. Despite the wide range of styles, most English sofas and chairs, as well as those in

Above: this 19th-century English marble fireplace with a French inset acts as a display-piece for numerous Victorian collectables: a pair of French rouge marble ormolu-mounted urns; a pair of English Regency stag and doe two-branch candelabra with lustres; two French bronze figures of a blacksmith and a miner and a Napoleon III bronze sphinx, and a recumbent lion.

Overleaf: in a South Kensington house in London, England, the grand piano nobile *successfully evokes the mood of a light Victorian interior.*
The walls have been painted in distressed drags of buttery yellow and the drapes are made from ivory silk. The generally pale shades of the room and numerous embroidered pillows or cushions add to the femininity of the room.

North America, Australia and New Zealand were, unlike their European equivalents, low-seated. As Muthesius noted at the end of the 19th century, these were considered conducive to intimate chats.

Sofas and elbow chairs or armchairs were usually upholstered in horsehair, covered in patterned velvet or silk. Where horsehair was used, protective "loose" covers of glazed chintz were often applied and could be easily removed for cleaning, as coal dust was an ever-present problem during the 19th century. William Morris produced beautiful, hand-printed, washable chintzes, but most households made do with cheaper, machine-printed copies. Patterns and colours were usually chosen to match other fabrics, such as drapes. A homely air of domestic intimacy was provided by the white antimacassars, also known as "tidies" that were draped over the arms and backs of all upholstered furniture. Found in even the grandest parlours, these crocheted or knitted doilies were used to protect furniture from the greasy stains of Macassar oil, a popular hair dressing for men during the 19th century. From the 1870s onward, antimacassars were replaced in some households with draped and patterned chair scarves.

While the fireplace was the visual focus of most drawing rooms, a large circular or loo table was the central piece of furniture, at least up until the 1870s. Usually standing on a single architectural column supported on a flat base with either bun feet or lion's paws, they were commonly made of mahogany, walnut or rosewood, or grained to simulate them. In wealthier households, many tables had inlaid or white marble tops and were embellished with intricate carvings. However, the custom of draping tables with fringed fabrics – Paisley-pattern shawls were very fashionable during the high-Victorian era – meant that the lower-middle classes could disguise ordinary pine tables.

During the early and middle years of the 19th century, the central table in the parlour was, in many households, the focal point of family life. In middle-class homes the family Bible usually occupied pride of place on top of it, and father, mother and children would pray, read, talk, sew and play around it under the light of a table lamp. However, in the second half of the 19th century it became less functional and more decorative – a place to display prized ornaments, memorabilia and collectables. In some households it was even replaced altogether with a variety of pier tables, side tables that were often two-tiered, consoles and credenzas, all grouped together with sofas and chairs in a series of vignettes around the room.

Another item of furniture commonly found in Victorian parlours, particularly in North America, was the *étagère*. A large, tiered piece, it was designed to be placed against a wall and was used, like the central table, to display ornaments, although its size often precluded its use in smaller houses, where it was replaced by the "whatnot". This was a triangular-shaped corner piece, either free-standing or hung on the wall, sometimes embellished with ornamental fretwork and invariably over-filled with bric-a-brac.

Left: in a 1920s-30s house in Los Angeles, California, which was built for George Cukor, the chinoiserie living room has been given a lacquer-red distressed paint finish and then dragged with a glaze. The dramatic white and red ceiling, the early Chinese lacquer cabinet with a display of 18th- and 19th-century blue and white porcelain jars along with a successful mix of old and new fabrics, all add to the Oriental feel.
Above: the walls of the library in the same house are lined with books. The old, battered sofas and wing chairs and also the kelim-covered chairs are all in style. The decorative drapes are in fact Paisley shawls that have been draped and gathered to frame the window. And the collection of blue and white porcelain displayed above the cornice or pelmet is another a typical Victorian feature.
Below: the living room in the impressive Jacobean stately home of Plas Teg in North Wales is furnished in Regency simplicity. The fireplace is a 17th-century original, however, this style was much copied during the 19th century. The walls are covered in a rich striped brocade and the carpet is an extremely fine Aubusson.

Above and below: these Tiffany lampshades blend perfectly with a fine collection of American Gothic furniture and artefacts. Tiffany's designs are so derivative that his work has been called, "the last expression of American Gothic". The Tiffany Glass Company was founded in 1885.

Above middle and right: late 19th-century wall and ceiling gas lamps are easily converted to electricity: the hollow pipes incorporate an electrical flex without altering the appearance of the lamp. Right: an authentic late 19th-century gilt and patinated bronze six-light gasolier.

Below: hanging gas lamps were usually suspended some distance from the ceiling in order to prevent fumes from staining the plasterwork above. Below: a Napoleon III rouge marble urn and cover displayed next to an English Regency two-branch ormolu candelabra with glass lustres.

An ornate, late 19th-century French five-light candelabra with rose-petal candle cups, supported by a bronze cherub on a marble base.

One of the original "brand new" electric lamps made c.1880. The lamp base is bronze and the shade is glass with bronze mounts.

Evoking the clutter and cosiness of the Victorian period, a late 19th-century bronze lamp with the shade draped in a light, lacy fabric.

Other items of parlour furniture included footstools, hassocks and ottomans, which were carefully positioned not only for resting the feet, but also to protect the legs of the sitter from drafts. Fabric tubes filled with sawdust were also placed on window ledges and along the bottom of doors to achieve the same effect. Free-standing and wall-hung curio cabinets, tea-trolleys, butler's trays, card tables with folding, green baize-covered leaves, ladies' writing tables, silk and japanned screens, easels and wooden and brass standard lamps were also typical. Where space was not a problem, and the parlour doubled up as a music room, it was quite usual to find a grand piano and an upholstered piano stool with the seat adapted to hold music scores. The Canterbury, a low wooden stand, sometimes mounted on casters and containing a number of vertical partitions, was also a popular piece. Designed to house sheet-music, in many households it served as a repository for papers and other periodicals.

Large areas of drawing-room and parlour walls were given over to displays of art. During the early years of the Victorian period, brightly coloured oils in ornate gilt frames were offset with prints, portrait drawings and silhouettes. Clusters of miniatures, usually displayed in black rectangular frames, were often hung in-between them, as well as around the chimneypiece. The larger paintings were hung on gilt chains from brass picture rods secured at the height of the frieze. Smaller pictures were sometimes hung on little brass rings on nails driven straight into the wall. Similarly, during the high-Victorian period, dense and symmetrical patterns of gilt-framed oils, water colours and also elaborate prints covered the walls, in some cases to such an extent that the wallpaper was barely visible. In Aesthetic and Arts and Crafts interiors, picture hanging was dense, but not symmetrical. Walls were often dominated by a single canvas, drawing or mirror, while lesser works were hung around it in a complex jigsaw puzzle. Narrow, black frames were mostly used for drawings and prints, while oils were generally hung in gilded *gesso* frames.

Classically inspired sculpture, statuary and busts were also favoured. For example, reproductions of Hiram Power's "Greek Slave" – which tasued a sensation at the Great Exhibition of 1851, in London, England – were to be found in many drawing rooms. Despite the Victorians' curious attitude to sexuality and eroticism, nudes were considered acceptable, so long as their faces looked vacant or expressionless.

Although art and sculpture were an important part of the decor of the drawing room, they paled into relative insignificance compared with the often ostentatious displays of possessions accumulated there. Particularly during the high-Victorian period, the drawing room and parlour were, more than any other room in the house, a testament to the current passion for both collecting and making ornaments, decorative knick knacks and artefacts, as great store was placed in such pursuits. As one writer observed during the second half of the

Nothing evokes the atmosphere of a Victorian interior as much as candlelight.
Throughout the 19th century lighting levels were much lower than they are
today and many households relied entirely on illumination afforded by candles
and oil lamps. Rooms look entirely different when viewed by the soft, flickering
flames which also give out a surprising amount of heat. Wax candles were
something of a luxury and poorer homeowners burned less expensive tallow
candles – made from a fatty substance extracted from the suet of sheep and
cattle – which gave off large amounts of smoke and odour. Although early
Victorian candle sticks were extremely simple, later designs became much more
ornate and developed into massive candelabra which could be placed in the
middle of the table for an impressive display of light.

19th century: "what keen pleasure there is in the possession of one new treasure. Where to place it for the best is a fertile topic of conversation".

Mantel shelves, display cabinets and tables were covered or filled with the products of 19th-century female pastimes, such as embroideries, painted fans, feather bouquets, stuffed birds under glass domes, arrangements of ferns and flowers and fruits – both wax and real – and various other domestic bric-a-brac. Collectively they contributed to the predominantly feminine ambience of the room.

As fads and fashions came and went their trappings were enthusiastically acquired and put on show. Similarly, displays of Oriental ceramics, blue and white Chinese export porcelain, decorative glassware, Chinese and Japanese lacquered boxes, and Continental lustres, candelabra and clocks, attested to the increasing prosperity and cosmopolitan taste of most sections of society. The presence of seashells,

fossils and fragments of ancient pottery, usually displayed in glass-fronted cabinets, reflected the Victorian fascination with the seaside and with ancient cultures, while photographs of fathers, sons, mothers and daughters revealed the importance of the family in Victorian society.

Nowhere else in the house did the fashion for uninhibited ornamentation and deep, rich fabrics and colour schemes find better expression. The intention was to create a room which was ostentatious enough to be noticed and comfortable enough to be hospitable. While many contemporary critics condemned such displays of possessions as little better than the accumulation of clutter, they do offer a revealing insight not only into Victorian ideas about decoration in the parlour, but also the personal and cultural interests and aspirations prevalent throughout much of 19th-century society.

Opposite page: wicker furniture and greenery give a Victorian feel to a cool conservatory room.
Above left: a comfortable Ming lacquer interior contrasts with the stone garden statuary outside.
Above right: a typical Victorian grotto created in a country house in Suffolk, England.
Left: Victorian quilts made in Durham, England, thrown over stick back chairs. On the shelf behind is a collection of 19th-century Spongeware.
Right: a quilt made in Gate City, Virginia, c.1880, brightens up an airy garden room.
Overleaf: cascading greenery in the hallway of a Victorian home in Kensington, London, England.

DINING ROOMS

In most Victorian houses the dining room was located on the entrance floor, not far away from the kitchen, the latter being situated either on the same floor or else in the basement below. The exceptions to this normal arrangement were the basement dining rooms found in some North American country homes during the early and middle years of the 19th century. In larger houses the dining room was usually situated at the front of the house, and was set aside almost exclusively for evening meals and dinner parties. Less formal meals, such as breakfast and tea, were taken in a morning room – referred to as the parlour by the middle classes – situated at the back of the house. However, in most smaller houses the drawing room was at the front of the house, while the dining room was a back room: the two were often divided by double doors. Where there wasn't sufficient space for a separate dining room and morning room, their functions were combined.

The Victorian practice of using rooms for more than one purpose was prevalent on both sides of the Atlantic. In North America the colonial custom of eating meals in front of the fire in the kitchen during the winter, and setting up the dining table in a sitting room or hallway, to take advantage of the cooler air, during the summer, survived well into the 19th century, at least in smaller houses. Similarly, in many

Left: the dining room in Richard Jenrette's house has a very early Victorian Classical symmetry. The chairs are by Duncan Phyfe.
Right: the parlour and dining room in the Belle of the Bends inn in Vicksburg, Mississippi, are separated by large double doors, typical of Victorian Italianate architecture. The table is cherry wood, c.1830.

British, American and Australian middle-class homes, the dining room doubled up as a parlour and often also served as a sitting room, study, library or, albeit less commonly, as a schoolroom. However, by the latter part of the 19th century a separate dining room had become a source of prestige, and so an increasingly desirable feature of middle- and upper-middle class housing.

As a "public" room that reflected the status of the homeowner, considerable importance was attached to the decoration and furnishing of the Victorian dining room. Broadly, the ambience of the decor passed through three significant stages during the 19th century. In the early years of Queen Victoria's reign, the Georgian legacy of restrained, dignified decoration was still much in evidence. During the middle of the century and the high-Victorian period the heavier, more masculine style of, for instance, François Premier and Renaissance Revival was

Left: the main dining room of Cedar Grove in Vicksburg, Mississippi, where the credenza on the right conceals a large safe, used to hide valuables during the Civil War. Above: Federal furniture with chairs by Duncan Phyfe in the Morris-Jumel Mansion in New York. Right: plate-warmers were made of tin or cast-iron or in grander houses, of more elaborate brass or copper.

Left: the dining room in the Ullysses S. Grant home in Galena, Illinois, is typical of a middle-class home of the 1860s. The chairs were shown in Frank Leslie's Illustrated Newspaper *of November 14th 1868.*

Above: many houses in the Victorian era retained furniture from an earlier period. Here the dining room in a house in Shepherdstown, West Virginia, has an early 19th-century Virginia table and Philadelphia chairs.

more in vogue. Bulky and elaborate pieces of furniture, dark wooden panelling, heavily carved mouldings or cornices, plush draperies, a surfeit of pattern and the predominant use of sombre colours such as etruscan reds, deep greens and browns, all contributed to an overall feeling of sobriety. Writers such as Robert Kerr recommended that, "the whole appearance of the room ought to be of masculine importance . . . so the decor should be somewhat massive and simple." And the contemporary *Art of Decoration and Applied Furniture* suggested that: "The

first impression which the dining room should make is that of solid comfort. There [should be] no airy trifling with either colour or fabric."

However, by the 1880s and 1890s a reaction to what might be described as the the "Brown Windsor" atmosphere of many high-Victorian dining rooms prompted members of the Arts and Crafts movement to design, and influential writers such as Mrs Panton to advocate, a lighter, brighter and in some respects more feminine style of decoration.

Right: the clever use of a mix of Indian, Chinese and Pailsey shawls draped over the furniture in this dining room in Beverley Hills, Los Angeles, California, creates a Victorian mood. Nineteenth-century Indian paintings reflect the Victorian interest in Oriental art.
Below left: a period pastiche with an eclectic collection of Victoriana, including a set of 19th-century painted gypsy chairs.

Below right: the mood of a Victorian interior can be achieved by eclectic collecting. Here, the old Welsh server or dresser groans with the weight of various types of porcelain ranging from 19th-century Staffordshire printed ware to Majolica. The pillows or cushions are a blend of old and new fabrics and the window treatment has been created by hanging table coverings over poles to act as drapes.

The dining-room walls of grander houses during the high-Victorian era were often wood-panelled, either in their entirety or else up to the dado rail. The panelling was generally dark to complement the furniture, and mahogany, walnut and stained oak were the most popular, although chestnut and maple were also used, particularly in North America. In some wealthier homes, the wood was carved with flowers, fruit and hunting scenes, or, during the last quarter of the century, stencil-gilded with, for example, the geometric designs of members of the Associated Artists such as Louis Comfort Tiffany. (The dining room in Mark Twain's opulent Hartford home, which was completed in 1874, was located at the rear on the darker, north side of the house. The lustrous walnut panelling and doors were embellished with gilded stencilling, while the walls were decorated with a sumptuous embossed lily pattern in red and gold.) At the end of the century, plain wooden panelling was sometimes simply painted white and where the dado, panelling or wainscotting was not wooden, marble – in the most opulent of homes – paint, tooled Spanish leather or wallpaper was used instead. Embossed Lincrustas and Anaglyptas, stained or painted maroon, dark green, deep bronze or a leather tone, and then varnished for ease of cleaning, were particularly popular and imparted an air of warmth and cosiness.

For the field above the dado level *Cassell's Household Guide* recommended dark silk flock wallpaper, even though it was difficult to keep clean. Patterned papers by William Morris were much in evidence, the most popular designs included mazes of tangled lilies, brambles and vines, and imitations of Medieval tapestries, the latter being thought more "artistic". Tapestries and fabrics, for example damask, were also

Left: the old rose theme abounds on this table covered in layers of old tablecloths and linens. The silverplate coffee and tea service is by Wilcox International Silver Co., 1903.

Below: a collection of 19th-century glass which shows the eclectic nature of Victorian dining. It includes American pressed glass and English and Irish decanters.

used as wallcoverings, and in dining rooms with painted walls and stencilled decoration – commonly gilded chevrons and traceries – was often applied on top. Whether the walls were painted or papered, recommended colours included crimson, for colder north-facing rooms, moss-green for warmer south-facing rooms, as well as dark blues, dull Pompeiian reds, terra-cottas and olives, or, "any of the kindred tints that do not look faded or suggest economy". Crimson and brown were the favoured colours for setting off gilt-framed oil paintings – usually family portraits – and prints of hunting scenes and landscapes that adorned the typical Victorian dining room. The increasingly extensive use of gilded designs and decorations on dining-room walls and ceilings during the latter part of the 19th century, particularly in North America, also had the effect of providing an additional source of light in what were often quite dark and sombre areas – natural and artificial light reflected off the gilding to produce a subtle glimmer that both complemented and to some extent alleviated the dark shadows.

While the frieze was often decorated with stencilled flowers, leaves and fruit, in grander houses the ceiling was either wood-panelled or frescoed, usually in Gothic, Elizabethan or Jacobean Revival styles. Embossed Anaglypta and Lincrusta papers were also available, and were painted, varnished and sometimes gilded. Even in the smallest houses, the Victorian dining-room ceiling was rarely left unadorned and discreet stencilling in the corners was a common form of decoration.

Floors were invariably wooden, and in the early- and mid-Victorian periods they were often covered with carpets patterned with geometric designs, Rococo ornamentation or elaborately realistic flowers. Although a thick, fitted wall-to-wall carpet enabled servants to move about the room noiselessly, stained boards and inlaid parquet covered with rugs gradually became a more popular alternative, partly because rugs were easier to clean regularly. Oak, walnut, cherry and Southern pine were the most popular woods in North America. Hardwood trim borders were often used to frame the rugs and their colours either

picked up the tones of the wallpaper, or consisted of reds, blues and greens common to real or imitation Turkish patterns. In North America, crumb cloths designed to catch accidental spillages were often used to cover the rugs placed under the table during meals, a custom that dated back to the colonial years.

In the mid- and high-Victorian dining room drapes were usually heavy velvets and often looped back with gold tassels. Opulent patterns as well as plain fabrics appeared in crimson, dark blue, olive and gold. However, the belief, particularly during the latter part of the century, that it was undesirable and in fact unhygienic to use fabrics that retained the smell of food, meant that drapes became simpler than elsewhere in the house. So, while plain, heavy drapes of, for example, mohair, velvet, repp and flet continued to be used – and even hung over doors from wooden or brass poles, and looped back for access (*portières*) – swagged cretonnes, Venetian shades or blinds and screens of stained glass became increasingly popular. In North America dining-room windows were often shuttered as well as draped: both the shutters and the drapes were opened in the morning to let the sun and fresh air in, the drapes were drawn at noon to keep out the sun, thereby keeping the room cool and protecting fabrics from fading, and both were closed at night for insulation.

The late-Victorian obsession with fresh air meant that the dining-room fireplace was not only essential as a source of heat during the colder months of the year, but was equally important as a means of

Left: a country-style Victorian atmosphere is recreated with a fruitwood table, painted chairs and some 19th-century English black and white porcelain. Right: late 18th-century Shendoah Valley furniture in a 19th-century breakfast room and a countryfied sunshine yellow kitchen with rush chairs (below).

ventilating the room and getting rid of the smell of food via the updraft. The fire surround also provided a surface for displaying ornaments such as busts, vases, candelabras and even stuffed birds and fish, as well as shelving arranged around a central mirror for exhibiting chinaware, decanters, snuff boxes and the like.

Artificial lighting in the dining room was provided by chandeliers, wall sconces and, if the room also served as a parlour, ceiling pendants of a sliding type which could be lowered when lit in order to maximize the light cast over the table as well as protecting the diners' eyes from glare. However, even after the introduction of mains-supplied gas and, later, electricity, candles were still used in most households – their soft, warm glow, reflected off large mirrors above the mantel shelf and on the walls, providing an atmospheric light which the Victorians considered the most suitable for relaxed conversation around the table and easy digestion during dinner.

Dining-room furniture from the early-, middle- and high-Victorian era was fairly substantial and generally masculine in appearance. Empire, Gothic and Renaissance Revival styles in mahogany, walnut and rosewood were particularly popular. However, by the late 19th century, lighter and more elegant items of furniture modelled on the Chippendale and Sheraton styles, or designed by followers of the Arts and Crafts movement, which were often in light or green-stained oak, became fashionable.

In the middle of the room was the dining table. The telescopic variety, usually square or curved at each end and rarely less than 4ft (1m) wide, had superseded the draw table of earlier periods, and was favoured

throughout the century. According to the number of guests expected for dinner, it could be extended to double its folded length by turning a pull or handle on a screw thread, opening up the middle and dropping in extra leaves. The advantage it offered over the draw table was that, whatever length it was extended to, the four legs remained at the

corners and so didn't get in the way of the diners. However, its one disadvantage was that the extra leaves had to be stored somewhere when not in use and they were often kept under the sideboard or in another room. Round tables, either of a fixed size on a central column or else of the telescopic variety, were also sometimes used, and were most fashionable in the late 19th century. Nevertheless, some of the more conservative members of Victorian society viewed round tables with suspicion. For example, Archbishop Grantly, in Trollope's *Barchester Towers* insisted that, "there was something democratic and parvenu in a round table". Telescopic tables also came in for criticism from the Arts and Crafts movement and William Morris preferred to use refectory tables with no lengthening mechanism except simple drop leaves, or alternatively several square tables that could be simply butted together as and when necessary.

Dining chairs were an important feature of the decor and Robert Kerr, writing about a typical mid-19th century interior observed: "A substantial aspect in this apartment is the unbroken line of chairs at the wall." He also pointed out that it was fashionable to place some of the chairs around the table. While it was recommended that chairs were low-backed to facilitate serving at table, in practice, they were often high-backed. Sturdy Chippendale-style chairs were a favourite, and were often sold in sets of eight, twelve or twenty, two of which were elbow chairs, armchairs or servers intended for the man and woman of the house sitting at the either end of the table. Balloon-backed chairs were also popular after the 1850s. The fashion in chairs varied almost from decade to decade throughout the century and, according to

Left: a Hammersley breakfast service with a silverplated Elkington tea pot and a Victorian egg cruet. The blue jardinière has a rose garland decoration.
Below left: blue and white transfer china in the well-known willow pattern; a wine glass, jug and goblet are also part of the lunch-time place setting.
Below right: for an evening meal a fine antique cut-work lace tablecloth complements cut glassware and gilt-edged late-Victorian cream china.
Right: this 1830s Staffordshire tea set religiously inscribed, "May we all meet in Heaven", in the Pelham Hotel, London, England, would certainly have been kept for Sunday best. Very often these sets were made not for use but to put in pride of place in a display cabinet.

Left: yellow ranunculus and blue hyacinths arranged informally in a Victorian jug. Circular beaded mats were crafted by ladies of the house. Right: a tall, loose spray of agapanthus, lilies, blue irises, eucalyptus, aspidistra and copper beech leaves in an 18th-century alabaster Roman tazza.

Below left: full-blown roses mixed with fresh herbs such as mint and rosemary in an old metal coffee pot make a sweet-smelling arrangement. Below middle: a silver embossed vase of roses, delphiniums and narcissi reflected in a mirror. Below right: sunflowers in a 19th-century pail.

Mrs Spofford, writing in the late 1870s, "the fashion in chairs varies with the fashions in ladies' dresses. The wide-spreading skirts which were supported by crinolines need a different kind of chair from that which the well 'tied-back' lady of the present day can sit comfortably." Just as the height and width of the chair varied, so did the material with which the seat was upholstered. Leather was often used, as was tapestry which was co-ordinated with other furnishings in the room. And decorative motifs were sometimes picked up from the pattern of the wallpaper. Plain rush seats were also in evidence, notably on many Arts and Crafts oak chairs, although these were often supplemented for comfort with loose pillows or cushions.

Other than the table, the most important piece of furniture in the dining room was the sideboard. Positioned either flat against a wall or in a recess, the classic sideboard of the Victorian era was made of walnut or mahogany and stood on two massive pedestals. It was fitted with

a mirror, shelves, drawers and cabinets – the latter were usually kept locked so that the servants couldn't get at the drink from the bottles and decanters inside! The woodwork was often embellished with carved decorations depicting game, fowl, fish or fruit, in other words, those items of food placed upon it prior to, and during, a meal. Some versions had a brass rail at the back which was hung with gathered silk flounces intended to protect the wall from splashes when cutting a roast and serving food and drink from silverware, silverplate, tureens, domed dishes and decanters. In the latter part of the century, as the fashion for lighter, less bulky furniture caught on, other kinds of sideboards became popular. Among these were Sheraton-style and angular Eastlake sideboards, machine-made oak servers which were fitted with simple shelves and niches, and sideboard cabinets that resembled kitchen servers or dressers.

Whatever the style of sideboard, it served as a repository for silverware, napkins, plates, and various other important utensils used at

Right: a 19th-century American lustreware tea set and (below) some Victorian china, including a blue and white transfer tea pot and cow creamer, a large orange-ground

Ashworth meat platter decorated with Chinese devils, an épergne and an early Victorian soup tureen. Tableware was accompanied by silver cutlery and linen napkins.

A Spode meat plate, c.1860.

A late-Victorian Staffordshire tureen and plate.

A late-Victorian English lustreware teapot.

the dinner table which were not kept in the butler's pantry, if there was one. It was also used, particularly during the high-Victorian years, to display purely decorative silver, silverplate and ceramics such as Sèvres and Limoges. In an age where material wealth equalled moral goodness, such displays ostentatiously conveyed the status and prosperity of the household and the effect was often illuminated by candles and enhanced with a heavy, richly coloured, altar-like cloth, and doubled by a mirror behind.

Among other items of furniture was the wooden dinner-wagon, sometimes a pair of them, which was made up of three shelves held by four vertical corner supports on wheels or casters. This stood in a corner of the room and was used to hold dishes for the meal and so relieve the often over-burdened sideboard. Glass-doored buffets and servers fulfilled a similar role, especially in American households. A small serving table, usually made of mahogany, might also have been positioned in-between two windows and used to carry additional plates and a coffee or tea service, while linen or flatware would have been stored in

its drawers. A wine cooler (*see* page 82) might also have been kept under the sideboard, and brought out just prior to the meal.

A folding screen for protecting diners from both the draft and the heat from the fireplace was also an "essential", particularly in narrow dining rooms. The leaves of such screens were usually covered in leather or painted fabric – Japanese and Chinese motifs were very popular – and the top sections were sometimes glazed. Upholstered chairs, usually a pair and covered in leather, were sometimes placed on either side of the fireplace, provided there was space. However, couches only appeared in smaller houses where the dining room and parlour were combined, and a writing desk, a bookcase and even a piano might also have been installed.

Whatever the style of decor, the focus of the Victorian dining room was always the laid table. With the exception of Arts and Crafts refectory tables, which were commonly laid bare, dining tables were usually covered with a thick wool cloth, which lay underneath the tablecloth itself and was designed to protect the table top and eliminate the noises

A Staffordshire plate and Spode cup and saucer.

A Coalport tea cup and saucer.

An unusual Worcester coffee cup and saucer.

of picking up and putting down dishes, plates, cutlery and glasses. The over tablecloth was usually made of damask, velvet or a more modest chenille, in dark, serviceable colours and edged with a fringe and tassels; white lace was a popular alternative.

Individual place settings usually consisted of a napkin with a bread roll placed on top of it. Plates were only supplied as the food was served, having first been warmed in the kitchen. Two forks and a fish-fork lay to the left of the napkin, while two knives, a fish-knife and a soup spoon lay to the right of it. A spoon and a fork lay across the top, wine glasses were placed at the top right-hand corner, salt and pepper pots were put either in front of each place, or else centrally between two places, and a fruit knife and fork, a cheese knife and a finger bowl were also supplied for each diner.

products from all sections of the community, but notably from the rapidly growing middle classes.)

At Victorian dinner parties most dishes were placed on the sideboard and served from there by servants. This meant that there was plenty of room in the middle of the table to accommodate elaborate arrangements of flowers, fruits and sweets. The German writer Muthesius described a typical display as follows: "The flowers were placed in low silver or crystal bowls" – tall arrangements were avoided so that diners could see each other on opposite sides of the table – "and held upright by lead bands or tubes or wire-netting. Flower bowls stand on runners and grouped around them at intervals are a number of smaller vases containing single specimens or little arrangements in which flowers stand gracefully. . . . The fruit is set out beforehand in bowls.

Right: from left to right, a silver gilt ruby mounted bottle (1857) and coaster. A water jug decorated with engraved grapes and vines; a covered jar engraved with a rustic scene and a pink overlay jug with a grapes and vine motif, all c.1870.

Right: Victorian glass. The ruby épergne is c.1870 and the water jug with applied pink threading and ribbed bands is c.1890. Overleaf: a selection of genuine 19th-century silverware which would have belonged in the dining room.

Even in relatively poor households, the possession of good silver and china was considered a necessity. However ordinary the everyday crockery was, superior sets by notable manufacturers of the day would be available for visitors. While the best china might be more for show than actual use, it was essential for it to be there to be brought out on special occasions such as a birthday, a wedding or a christening. It is also important to remember that, particularly in the wealthier Victorian households, the scale of entertaining was such that even the basic necessities required outnumbered what we would consider normal today. For example, dinner plates and tea cups were counted in dozens rather than half dozens. (The substantial increase in output by 19th-century makers of all manner of useful and decorative tablewares can be largely explained as a response to the considerable increase in demand for such

Dried fruits to be eaten at the end of the meal, together with chocolates, salted almonds, figs and dates, are placed in dainty dishes and dainty forks are provided for eating them. Grapes are always accompanied by grape scissors, and a melon always with a melon knife. . . . With the exception of champagne, wine is served from crystal decanters rather than bottles."

However, toward the end of the 19th century, such displays were considered a "gross vulgarity" by fashionable magazines such as *Vogue*. Instead, silver and glass with a restrained single display of flowers placed in the middle of the table was considered "good taste", a view that has much in common with the opinion of that arbiter of 19th-century taste, Mrs Haweis, who believed that, "the best ornament for a dining room is a well-cooked dinner".

KITCHENS

Given the immense industrial energy and accompanying advances in manufacturing, design and technology that were so much a feature of the Victorian era, improvements in the kitchen were relatively slow to materialize, particularly during the first half of the 19th century. For most households during this period progress was marked by the gradual replacement of traditional open–hearth methods of cooking and heating water with the cast–iron, coal–burning kitchen range. First patented in 1780 by Thomas Robinson, the basic design for this new appliance remained largely unchanged for over a hundred years. Although theoretically more efficient, most ranges, in particular early models, were as labour-intensive to run as previous "systems". Also, they were prone to going out and could make the kitchen insufferably hot during the summer months.

Poor working conditions for the cook and other household servants were exacerbated by the fact that family life in most early Victorian households no longer centered around the hearth, as it had done in previous centuries, and had moved up to the parlour. With the exception of urban working-class and lower middle-class homes, farmhouses and country cottages, in which it still formed the principal living room, the kitchen and its ancillary larders, pantries, sculleries and store rooms were sited in basements. Later, after the passage of new health acts and

Left: most Victorian kitchens did not have built-in storage cabinets.
Open shelving, small cupboards, racks and pots were commonly used to
house and display all manner of crockery, jars, spices and kitchen utensils.
Right: a 19th-century French marble-topped steel table with decorative scrolled
legs provides a useful surface for the preparation of pastry and food.

local bye-laws in Britain during the 1860s, which discouraged the use of basements as habitable rooms, kitchens were frequently located in extensions at the back of the house. The advantage of such an arrangement to the home-owner was that family and guests, not to mention fabrics and furnishings, could be isolated from the heat, grease and smells generated by cooking and cleaning. The disadvantage to the servants was that such kitchens were often poorly lit and inadequately ventilated – the latter contributing to their being too hot or too cold depending on the time of year, and almost certainly always damp.

In Britain and North America – in the case of the latter, especially prior to the Civil War – such kitchens were no more than working rooms, purely functional and bereft of all but the most basic of creature comforts. In these working spaces servants carried out endless strenuous tasks, such as preparing food, scouring pots and skillets or pans, stoking and blacking the cast-iron range, heating water, scrubbing floors and washing and ironing household linen. The fact that the widespread availability of inexpensive servant labour meant that the housewife and other members of the family could keep out of the kitchen goes a long way to explaining why comfort and convenience were slow in coming to this part of the Victorian home.

If lack of progress in kitchen design and technology during the first half of the 19th century was largely due to the kitchen being out of sight and therefore out of mind to the home-owner, improvements from the 1860s onward were stimulated by more than just the return (albeit to a limited extent) of the lady of the house downstairs. Changes in social attitudes toward the role of women and servants, increased

understanding of the importance of hygiene. Technological innovations and fashionable ideas for decoration and design also played their part.

For most of the first half of the 19th century, the lady of the house had confined herself to planning menus for the week with the cook, overseeing the purchase of provisions and, in some cases, keeping the books and instructing new servants on the particular requirements of the household. However, servants became harder to find; in the United States this was partly as a result of the abolition of slavery at the end of the Civil War, and on both sides of the Atlantic there was also the effect of the financial attraction of jobs in the ever-increasing number of new factories. And with the growth of the new middle classes, who could afford fewer servants than the rich, more and more women across society found themselves having to spend time in the kitchen. Although in many cases their activities were initially confined to making bread and training new staff – many of whom, particularly in the United States, were immigrants without English as their mother tongue – as they increasingly began to work alongside their servants, improvements in comfort, convenience and cleanliness soon followed.

Such changes were also introduced as a result of growing concern about the welfare of servants and the conditions under which they worked. This concern was evident in the recommendations of influential writers in England, such as Mrs Beeton, who emphasized the importance of cleanliness in the kitchen – a dirty fire meant a dirty kitchen, as did the presence of mice, rats and cockroaches – and popular women's magazines in the United States, which put forward fashionable notions such as, "the house is not furnished whose kitchen has

Left: a glazed server or dresser top hung on the wall, an Aga stove, wood-panelled kitchen units and stencilled wall decoration combine to provide a country background to a Victorian set of table and chairs.

Below left: in a townhouse in Spitalfields, London, England, the kitchen has a 19th-century country feel; the Aga stove is in the original fireplace. Below: wood-grained doors and panelling lend an authentic backdrop.

not received the same attention as a kitchen that its parlour receives as a parlour". The introduction of mains water under pressure, gas and plumbed-in sinks and boilers, to many houses during the 1860s and 1870s, together with the increasing availability of a variety of proprietary cleaning products, also contributed to the mid-Victorian kitchen becoming a more hygienic and pleasant place to work in than it had been during the previous half-century.

The most notable feature of the Victorian kitchen in upper- and middle-class homes in towns and cities, and the one that distinguished it from most of its predecessors and successors, was that it consisted of not one, but a network of rooms – the ancillary ones leading directly off the main kitchen area. At the heart of the latter was the cast-iron coal- or, in some cases, wood-burning range. When they were first installed, many new owners found them somewhat intimidating. For example, when a range was bought for the White House in the 1850s the cook, used only to working with an open hearth, couldn't operate it. It was reported that as a result President Filmore himself had to cancel several meetings in order to pay a visit to the local patent office to find out how to work the various knobs and pulleys that made the new-fangled appliance function.

Early models consisted of a coal fire contained by the horizontal bars of a grate. Pots, skillets or pans and kettles rested on a hinged tip-bar and hung from a variety of hooks, cranes and trivets over the fire, the latter often being open to the chimney. On one side of the fire was a range for baking, which in more advanced models was surrounded by a flue which hot gases passed through before entering the chimney, thereby providing a more even distribution of heat. The cook could also adjust the temperature in the stove, by opening and closing a selection of dampers and bypass flues. A tank for heating water was positioned on the other side of the fire, the water being obtainable via a faucet or tap in some models and simply via a ladle in others. Toward the end of the 19th century, following the installation of mains water under pressure, many such tanks incorporated a ballcock to allow automatic, rather than manual filling up with cold water.

On the early ranges, the roasting of joints of meat was carried out in the traditional way: on a spit over the fire, with trays placed underneath to catch the melting fat and juices. The more expensive models, installed in wealthier households, featured cheeks at the sides of the grate which could be adjusted to increase the width of radiant heat and so accommodate large joints; vanes within the chimney were turned by the draft in the flue and caused a horizontal spit to rotate via a series of connecting gears and pulleys. On less sophisticated ranges, installed in middle-class suburban homes, a vertical spit was turned by a bottle jack – a clockwork motor set in a bottle-shaped brass case – usually suspended from the mantel shelf above and semi-circular metal reflectors known as "hasteners" were used to concentrate the heat of the fire on the slowly turning joint.

In this home in Suffolk, England, a central unit houses an assortment of bowls, and pots and skillets or pans are suspended from two overhead hanging rails. Built-in crockery cabinets have been painted to look like an old French armoire.

*Far left: a crowded Colonial-style kitchen with
a rusty red and ochre colour scheme.
Left: this early 19th-century French provincial
armoire provides useful storage space.
Above: an eclectic display of Windsor chairs,
a butcher's block and a vast display of pottery.*

As the 19th century progressed, more sophisticated ranges became available: notably the closed range, or "kitchener", in which the fire was enclosed beneath a hot plate. This arrangement, which required less coal to produce the same amount of effective heat, forced all the hot gases from the fire up through a system of flues to heat the range and the boiler, instead of letting them go straight up the chimney, as with earlier models. The hot plate was mainly used for simmering, and also featured circular holes with removable lids, over which pots and skillets or pans could be placed. Later models featured a separate roasting range in which flues were positioned to provide intense overhead heat and ventilation to allow the meat to brown and the smoke from burning fat to disperse.

Once the initial technical problems had been ironed out, the only major drawbacks to the coal-burning, cast-iron range was the excessive heat it gave off during the summer and the considerable effort required to keep it running and clean – fetching the coal, stoking the fire, clearing soot from the flues, blacking the cast iron and polishing the nickel-plate ornamentation being some of the most arduous and menial of daily household duties. Gas ranges, which were first displayed to the public at the Great Exhibition of 1851, in London, England, provided a cleaner and less labour-intensive alternative. However, high fuel costs made them prohibitively expensive to run for any length of

time and, together with electric stoves, they only began to supplant their coal-burning predecessors as gas and electricity became more widely available and economical toward the end of the 19th century.

Unlike modern kitchens today, the main kitchen area in Victorian households had no built-in work counters. Instead, food was prepared on a large, centrally positioned wooden table, usually made of deal, which was scrubbed clean every day. Shallow drawers for utensils and measuring cups were incorporated underneath it, and being lower than a modern work surface, it was better suited to strenuous activities such as kneading dough. Because the servants ate all their meals at this table, an assortment of chairs were sited around it. Other tables often placed in the main kitchen area included a small, marble-topped one for rolling out pastry and a long wooden one positioned next to the sink (provided the latter was not installed in the scullery, as was usually the case in larger houses) for draining washed dishes.

Unlike today there were few, if any, built-in storage cabinets in the Victorian kitchen. In both Britain and North America, open shelving was almost always augmented with a free-standing wooden server or dresser, often set alongside the range in the recess created by the chimney breast. Featuring shallow, grooved shelves and hooks for storing and displaying chinaware, jars and containers not kept in ancillary rooms, a deep shelf for the breadbin, drawers for table linen and base

Above: the potters, Hinchcliffe and Barber, have taken designs from their work to create a period-style kitchen. Pottery is displayed on open shelves.

cabinets for various utensils not hung over the range, the server or dresser remained a prominent feature of the Victorian kitchen even after increasing concern about standards of hygiene and cleanliness saw open shelving fall out of fashion.

The main advantage of open shelving was that it promoted efficient household management, as virtually everything necessary for the orderly running of the kitchen was visible and easily to hand. The disadvantage was that chinaware, pots, skillets or pans and kitchen utensils were at the same time exposed to moisture, grease and dust. The solution to this dilemma was the glass-fronted cabinet, which became increasingly popular, especially in the United States, toward the end of the Victorian era. The fact that the contents of these cabinets remained on show contributed to the increasingly decorative appearance

of the boxes, tins and packets that became available via the fast-developing advertising industry during the last two decades of the 19th century.

Other furniture to be found in the main kitchen area of many Victorian households included a tall cabinet or linen press which was used in large kitchens for storing table linens and a pie safe – which was a free-standing cabinet with wire windows, used to keep baked food free from flies. Another frequent fixture was an icebox, which in the 1840s was little more than a simple wooden box in which food was placed on a block of ice, but by the 1860s this had evolved into an insulated wooden cabinet featuring porcelain or metal fittings – a

Above: tartan was particularly popular during the early Victorian period. Here checked drapes, tiles, ceramics, upholstery and rugs blend together.

prototype refrigerator – filled with crushed ice. Also common were tubular cast-iron or punched-tin candle holders, designed to keep vermin at bay; numerous patented, labour-saving appliances, such as spice graters, fruit slicers, apple corers and coffee grinders; and a hedgehog (perhaps the most low-tech "appliance" ever used in a kitchen), which slept in a box during the day and scurried around at night catching cockroaches.

The number of ancillary rooms leading directly off the kitchen depended on the size of the house. Almost all homes had a scullery, which contained a sink made of either white or brown glazed stoneware or fireclay, or porcelain-enamelled cast iron; the adjacent wooden draining board often having a large wooden plate rack above it. In houses where there wasn't room for a separate laundry, the scullery also contained a large wash copper (more often than not actually made of cast iron), set into brickwork over a fire, covered with a wooden lid and used for the weekly wash. Some sculleries housed a second stove, which was used for heating water and irons. In addition to washing up, laundering and ironing, the scullery was used for cleaning silver, polishing brass and peeling vegetables, as well as providing storage for larger pots and household cleaning equipment.

In addition to a storeroom or larder (of which there was more than one in larger houses) set off the scullery, many homes had a butler's pantry. Located in-between the kitchen and the dining room, the pantry was usually connected to the latter via a dumb waiter and

provided storage space for tableware, dishes and glasses, in ceiling-high, glass-doored cabinets. It was an additional serving area for making the finishing touches during the preparation of food and also housed the "call box" – a system for summoning servants to other parts of the house: when a cord was pulled or a bell pushed, a number popped up in a box in the pantry informing staff which room required service.

While the appeal of the high-Victorian kitchen today owes much to the functional simplicity of its layout, many of its appliances and much of its furniture, it can also be partly explained by the charm of its architectural details and the style of its decoration. Kitchen floors were either brick, marble or all-tile or hardwood which was varnished, oiled or painted for protection and ease of cleaning, and ceramic tile inserts were often sited beneath the range to guard against fire. Staffordshire quarry tiles, traditionally available in red, blue and buff colours, were commonly used throughout Britain. All floors were either left bare or else covered with washable rag rugs, carpet remnants, decorated oil-cloths or linoleum – the latter floor covering was recommended as hard-wearing and hygienic by Mrs Beeton and became popular toward the end of the 19th century.

Wainscotting encircling the main kitchen area, usually in the form of thin vertical panels, together with simple relief mouldings around windows and doors, added to the character of the room. Like wooden floors, wainscotting was varnished, oiled or painted – bottle-green and chocolate-brown being much-used colours. The presence of a plate rail about a foot below ceiling height not only provided additional storage space, but also, in combination with the wainscot, divided kitchen walls into the dado, wallspace and frieze configuration associated with the late-Victorian parlour.

Again, because of the ease of cleaning, the plaster surfaces of walls in the main kitchen area and ancillary rooms was almost always distempered or painted, usually in unobtrusive tones such as cream, gray, beige and tan, but also, occasionally, in dark red and yellow. Wallpapers were also used, particularly in kitchens that doubled as living rooms, but were always varnished to protect them from the effects of moisture and condensation. Similarly, most kitchen furniture and shelving was painted and it is a popular misconception today that Victorian pine furniture was simply waxed or clear-varnished. However, in some households furniture and joinery made of pine was woodgrained to resemble expensive hardwoods such as mahogany or chestnut.

While lighting in early Victorian kitchens was on the whole limited to candles and oil lamps, the widespread introduction of gas lamps into upper- and middle-class homes by the 1860s helped to improve the gloom below stairs. However, it was only with the advent of electricity

Left and previous page: a selection of mainly late 19th- and early 20th-century kitchen gadgets, many such items are available from antique shops. Culinary implements changed relatively little throughout the Victorian era.

in the 1880s that artificial illumination reached a level commensurate with that found in 20th-century kitchens.

Any reproduction of a Victorian kitchen today will have to be a pastiche rather than an exact copy of the original if modern standards of hygiene and convenience are not to be compromised. Most people would not choose to install a cast-iron, coal-burning kitchen range instead of a modern stove, a scullery instead of a dishwasher or a meat safe instead of a refrigerator. Consequently, "restoration" should revolve around architectural mouldings, decorations and furnishings.

Floors should be waxed or varnished hardwood or all-tile (high-quality reproductions of period-style tiles are widely available from specialist suppliers, *see* The Directory, pages 222–3) and can be supplemented with Oriental-style rugs if a Victorian "parlour look" is desired. Linoleum, which is available from specialist outlets, is also appropriate. Waxed, varnished or painted period-style joinery strikes the right note, as does either open shelving or glass-fronted cabinets. As a broad rule of thumb, keep built-in furniture to a minimum. Displaying period chinaware, storage jars, containers, and period or reproduction utensils on open shelving or on a Victorian server or dresser, is the most effective way of creating the right ambience.

Eye-level open shelving can be supplemented with simple panelled-door cabinets below a work counter. Although a built-in work counter isn't in keeping, it makes ergonomic sense and will not look out of place if it is marbled, tiled or wooden – teak for instance is durable and easy to clean. Tiled splashbacks are also suitable, but a fully tiled dado is only really appropriate for the more functional and less "parlour-like" kitchens that began to appear at the end of the 19th century. If there is space, a centrally positioned table made of pine or oak offers a traditional surface for the preparation of food, as well as a place to eat. Windsor or pressed-back pine or oak chairs provide authentic seating and, again if there is space, a free-standing armoire, linen press or tall cabinet can be used for storage.

Authentic colours for walls and woodwork include white, cream and buff – dark red and bright yellow are lesser-used alternatives – with details picked out in bottle- or apple-green or chocolate-brown. Shelving, cabinets and servers or dressers should be painted to match, and stripped pine is inauthentic. For a "parlour look", windows should be draped with brocaded fabrics or lace or, in less formal town and country kitchens, with netting or muslin. Bare windows, which were recommended by American *Woman's Home* at the end of the 19th century, perhaps bordered with vines, are also acceptable.

Finally, artificial lighting is all-important, and an area which requires some compromise. On the one hand, period or reproduction fixtures and fittings over a table impart a warm glow redolent of the era. On the other hand, task-lighting makes the preparation of food far easier and is visually acceptable if recessed and therefore on its own circuit so that it can be switched off once the meal is served.

BEDROOMS

*T*n the largest Victorian houses, husband and wife slept in separate bedrooms with a connecting door in-between them. In many cases each room would have its own dressing room, and adjoining the lady's bedroom there was often a small sitting room or boudoir which served as a private retreat where she could sew, read and write letters. Lady Barker, writing toward the end of the 19th century, referred to it as, "one's little den". However, in less grand houses, husband and wife shared one bedroom, and there was usually an adjacent dressing room set aside for the man. In an age where large families were commonplace, children rarely had a bedroom to themselves, except in the wealthiest households. Sharing was quite usual, and in smaller properties it was not unknown for the bedrooms of older offspring to double up as private sitting rooms. A nursery for infants and younger children was also a standard feature of upper- and upper-middle-class homes, the former often having the space for separate day and night nurseries. Servants were usually relegated to small bedrooms at the top of the house, often in the attic, although a governess or nanny would invariably occupy a bedroom on the same floor as the children.

Writing in 1844, Webster and Parkes advocated that bedrooms should be, "neat and plain and everything capable of collecting dust should be avoided as much as possible" – a recommendation founded

Left: a selection of Victorian perfume bottles arranged with a pressed silver bowl, a small clear-glass rouge jar and a silver-topped hairpin container.
Right: embroidered white sheets and pillow cases grace the mahogany Empire bed in this Parisian apartment or flat. While original linens can be bought in antique shops or at auction, many companies now produce reproductions.

as much on the Victorian preoccupation with the importance of hygiene in the home as it was on the aesthetics of interior decoration. The desire to create living conditions that were both comfortable and "sanitary" was more noticeably reflected in the design and furnishing of the 19th-century bedroom than in any other room in the house; the kitchen and, toward the end of the 19th century, the bathroom being the only exceptions to this. This is readily understandable if it is remembered that more than a third of one's life was spent in the bedroom. Daily ablutions took place there, until the advent of the separate bathroom, and women, who commonly mothered numerous children, almost invariably gave birth at home in bed, the bedroom serving as a temporary maternity ward. When necessary, the bedroom also doubled up as a sick room, a function it fulfilled with some frequency in an age when antibiotics were unknown and infectious diseases such as cholera and typhoid were all too prevalent.

Today, many Victorian notions regarding health and disease are considered, at best, far-fetched. Servants were instructed to regularly clean bedroom surfaces believed to be contaminated by "emanations" and "effluvia" exuded from the human body while asleep, which Mrs Beeton believed to have, "hung, a viewless vapour in the air, [and] steeped linen and reeked in blankets". Some doctors went so far as to advocate separate bedrooms for men and women because the "emanations" of sleeping females supposedly threatened the "vital forces" of their husbands. However, the conviction that "cleanliness was next to Godliness" led to regular washing and so helped to prevent infection. It was also held that the removal of dust minimized insect infestation, and that a bright and well-ventilated bedroom filled with fresh air promoted better health, sleep and well-being than a dark, damp one that was permeated with stale air. Because these recommendations were

founded on medical fact, they were increasingly accepted and followed by the population at large as the 19th century wore on.

Just as in other rooms, bedroom surfaces did become impregnated with dirt, dust and grime emanating from coal and wood fires, candles and gas and oil lamps. The choice of easy-to-clean decorations and furnishings was therefore a matter of household efficiency and common sense. Unlike the reception rooms of the house, where the decor was open to the scrutiny of visitors and reflected the prosperity and status of the occupants, the bedrooms were for the most part private rooms, upstairs and out of sight. As a consequence, and with the exception of large country and town houses, in which the opulence of the public rooms did sometimes extend to the main bedrooms, there was less social pressure for a show of wealth upstairs.

Many writers on interior decoration discouraged the use of wallpaper for bedroom walls, on the grounds that it provided a refuge for insects such as bed bugs. Stained, varnished or painted panelling, wainscotting or a wood-panelled dado was recommended as it was easy to clean. Distemper was also advocated as a "sanitary" and easily renewable finish and was available in pale, delicate colours such as pearly grays, soft blues and gentle olives for "cooling" brighter and warmer south-facing rooms, or in pale reds, pinks and yellows for "warming" north-facing ones. Pale greens fell out of favour after *Cassell's Household Guide* warned that, "a pale green will impart the cadaverous hue of sickness", while bright greens were avoided altogether once it became known that the pigment used to produce them contained arsenic.

Of course, despite the admonitions of experts, wallpaper was widely used, particularly by the middle classes. During the early and middle years of the 19th century, rich colours and strong patterns were much in evidence, just as they were in the main reception rooms of the house.

The front bedroom in the Old Merchant's House, New York, is an authentic Victorian recreation, the bed drapes are from an 1860s design.

When the four-poster in this 1830s bedroom was reconditioned, enough original fabric was left under the tacks in the frame for accurate restoration.

In the Pelham Hotel, London, England, the bed is given a Victorian feel with period reproduction drapes and fabrics.

Interior designer Tessa Kennedy's "lily of the valley" bedroom is dominated by a four-poster bed, characteristic of the early Victorian period. Made of dark oak and with elaborately turned posts, the heaviness of the wood is alleviated with pale American linen and light bedcovers, drapes and a covered canopy.

In the same house belonging to Tessa Kennedy another dark, Victorian four-poster has a strong Gothic feel, visible in the arched carvings around the top of the canopy. The heavy wooden frame has been lightened with pale colours and white linen. The chest at the foot of the bed adds to the Gothic mood.

Dark drapes are typical of the Federal and early Victorian styles. As the 19th century progressed there was a growing concern with hygiene and it was believed that wallpaper retained unhealthy vapours. Thus papers were often replaced by lightly coloured "tinted" or painted walls.

The striking deep mauve and yellow colour scheme of this bedroom is typical of the American Empire style. The fine Federal bed, Empire chest, églomisé mirror surmounted by an eagle, as well as the relatively simple drapes are all characteristic of the early American Victorian period.

However, an increasing distaste for bold patterns in the bedroom, expressed by writers such as Robert Edis, who believed that, "they might be likely to fix themselves upon a tired brain, suggesting all kinds of weird forms", saw the widespread adoption of lighter and more delicately patterned papers by the 1870s. As with distemper, pale colours were favoured and popular patterns included vertical floral stripings, vines and Japanese-influenced designs by such as William Morris and Arthur Silver.

In the nursery, where the stimulation of young minds during the day was considered just as important as the sedation·of them at night, wallpapers and friezes depicting animals, birds, fairy tales and nursery rhymes, designed by C.F.A. Voysey, Walter Crane and children's book illustrators, were almost universally popular.

Where paint and paper were not used, fabrics such as chintz, or white muslin over silk or batiste, were stretched tightly over wooden panels, which could easily be removed for cleaning. As with wallpapers, pale pastel colours and delicate floral patterns were favoured, and it was also fashionable to use the same fabric for pillow cases and drapes on the windows, mantel shelf and tables.

The most common type of flooring in bedrooms throughout the 19th century was wooden boards or blocks, stained or oiled prior to varnishing, and covered with small rugs which sometimes had a layer of matting placed underneath them for extra warmth. The German writer Hermann Muthesius noted that an alternative treatment for floorboards was to scrub them down with sand and water to achieve a smooth, pale finish. Fitted wall-to-wall carpets were considered unsuitable because, unlike their loose-lay equivalents, or rugs, they couldn't be taken up for regular beating and cleaning. In North America rugs were sometimes strewn with freshly mown grass or moist tea leaves, prior to being beaten, in order to impregnate them with a sweet fragrance. Patterned rugs, such as Aubusson- and Savonnerie-types, were more popular than plain ones, and common colour combinations included blue and pink or red, green and gold. Tiger- and bearskin rugs also appeared in bedrooms where the decor was inspired by the Orient, although they were mainly confined to wealthier households. In less-well-off homes, linoleum was sometimes used in the bedrooms, while in nurseries linoleum or cork matting, often augmented with a thick hearth rug and embellished with suitable patterns such as Voysey's fairytale designs, were popular.

Throughout the 19th century, drapes tended to mirror the decor of the rest of the bedroom. In the wealthiest houses antique brocades, rich velvets and satins trimmed with panels of appliqué and embroidery were much in evidence. However, in the majority of homes drapes were made of lighter fabrics that were easier to clean and allowed light and fresh air into the room – windows were often left open at night, sometimes even during the winter. Festoons of chintz or cretonne, lace and white batiste inset with lace or finished with

Left: a tented bedroom. The quilt on the bed is late 19th century and the fabric is an antique French piece, c.1880.
Above: a Victorian-style bedroom has been recreated with modern Jane Churchill fabric.

Above: the sofa and the footboard of this bed complement the needlework patterned carpet.
Below: a light bedroom is given a feminine air with the addition of old lace and drapes made from an antique wedding veil.

hand-painted borders, were all common, as were better-quality cheese-cloths and striped or dotted muslins. In North America and Australia and New Zealand it was fairly common practice to soften the "glare" from pale pastel drapes by adding a layer of "transparent" muslin or lace over the top of them. These "insertion" or "glass" drapes, as they were called, were adopted by almost all sections of society, and were used to cover either the entire window or just the lower half of it.

In grander homes "insertions" were made of silk or satin, while the middle classes generally used muslin or inexpensive lace. In North America, and in the hotter climates of Australia, New Zealand and India wooden Venetian shades or blinds and shutters which folded back into the window frame were used either in addition to, or instead of, drapes. Some households even dispensed with "dust-trapping" drapes completely, although they were few and far between.

Far left: the New Orleans bedroom in the American Museum in Bath, England. The furniture is made by Prudent Mallard, who left the Duncan Phyfe cabinet shop in New York c.1830. Left: a fine rosewood and walnut half-tester in the Garth Woodside Mansion, Hannibal, Missouri. Below far left: a Renaissance Revival half-tester, c.1875, in the Belle of the Bends inn, Vicksburg, Mississippi. The love seat dates from c.1860. Below left: small-print modern wallpaper provides a suitable background for a 19th-century bed.

Left: a Renaissance Revival dressing table and shaving stand in a bedroom in the Garth Woodside Mansion, Hannibal, Missouri. Below left: made of walnut overlaid with a fine burr veneer, this giant Renaissance Revival bed is over 10ft (2.5m) high. At the foot is a "fainting couch" for the lady of the house to recline on. Below right: also in the Garth Woodside Mansion, the Samuel Clemens room has a walnut and chestnut bed, c.1870, which is a blend of Eastlake and Renaissance Revival styles.

The Victorian belief that beneficial sleep was dependent on frequent changes of air extended beyond leaving the windows open at night or making drapes from lightweight fabrics. Almost all bedrooms contained a fireplace in order to promote a through-draft, and a few were even equipped with patent ventilators. On the other hand, although temperatures in most nurseries were kept reasonably high, and children's clothes were frequently aired on the large brass-mesh or wire-net fender which stood in front of the fire, it is a mistake to think that Victorian bedrooms were warm simply because a fire could be lit in them. In fact they were invariably cold by today's standards, as a heated bedroom was considered to be something of an indulgence.

Prior to 1840, bedroom furniture tended to be somewhat eclectic in style, although subsequently an ever-increasing number of designers and manufacturers began to provide "matching suites" for the

Above: this stripped pine 19th-century dressing table is cluttered with the kind of collections so beloved of Victorian ladies, from scent bottles to baskets.

Right: on the walls of this bedroom by June Ducas is a silk moiré from Colefax & Fowler, while the rose border is from Cole & Son. The vanity unit or dressing table is dressed with lace and the general mix of fabrics and collections combine to give the room a charming 19th-century atmosphere. There are also some fine 18th-century pieces on display.

Below: draping fabric over an ordinary dressing table can give it a Victorian feel. The fabric disguises storage space underneath while allowing space on top for silver boxes, brushes and, in this case, glass lustres converted into lamps.

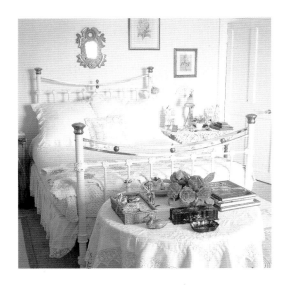

bedroom. These usually consisted of a bed, a wardrobe or an armoire, a washstand and a bureau or dressing table. And in some cases the set included a cheval mirror, which was available in everything from carved and gilded hardwoods to plainer, machine-manufactured soft-woods. For much of the century, dark woods, in particular mahogany, rosewood and walnut, were most fashionable. However, toward the end of the Victorian era, lighter woods such as oak – sometimes stained green by members of the Arts and Crafts movement – satinwood,

bamboo or faux bamboo became increasingly popular. The latter years of the 19th century also saw the appearance of "built-in" furniture. Designed, for example, by C.F.A. Voysey and recommended by archi-tects such as R.W. Edis and writers such as Mrs Panton, it was regarded as being easier to clean and a way of reducing both the clutter and the germ-harbouring dust associated with free-standing furniture. However, the German commentator Muthesius thought that sleeping in a room with built-in furniture was like sleeping in a warehouse.

Above: a quilted bedspread and embroidered pillows conjure up the feel of a Victorian bedroom (left). A 19th-century brass bed with machine-made lace drapes (middle). Old linen and quilts on a 19th-century iron bedstead (right).

Below: a fine brass bed with a 19th-century English quilt and numerous pillows or cushions made from old fabrics (left). A child's room in an attic bedroom with a Victorian brass bed and a rocker (right).

The main feature of the early Victorian bedroom was the canopied four-poster bed. French beds with central supports for drapes and tent beds were also used. However, these were a legacy from the past when houses were built without corridors and occupants had to pass through one room to reach another; such beds providing necessary privacy and warmth. By the middle of the 19th century these models were being condemned on the grounds of both aesthetics and hygiene – as the canopy acted as a trap for dust and inhibited the circulation of air. Consequently, while they remained a status symbol in wealthier house-holds, and were a practical choice in Australia, New Zealand and in the southern states of North America – as cheesecloth or netting could be draped over their bulky frames to protect the sleeper from mosqui-tos – they were gradually replaced with more open styles of bed.

While half-testers became popular for a while, by the last quarter of the 19th century designers such as Charles Eastlake were recommend-ing wooden or metal bedsteads with no hangings at all. The latter, first introduced at the Great Exhibition of 1851 in London, England, where they were presented as the best remedy for vermin, were made of brass, iron or both. Early versions were of simple design, and tended to be restricted to servants' rooms, but later on they were embellished with flowers, scrolls and curlicues and found their way into homeowners' bedrooms. Beds with wooden head- and footboards connected by iron

side bars also became commonplace; popular versions, particularly in North America, included Rococo and Renaissance Revival styles, which featured towering carved headboards and lower, slightly plainer footboards. Spool-turned "Jenny Lind" beds were also common. Favoured woods included mahogany, walnut, oak and also beech which was grained to imitate oak. In the nursery, infants slept in cradles draped with muslin, while young children had metal or wooden beds enclosed by railings and constructed so that the sides could be let down.

For most of the Victorian era, mattresses were laid over long planks of wood which were supported by either the head and foot or else the sides of the bed; wire mesh, which tended to sag after a while, was only introduced toward the end of the 19th century. Mattresses varied in quality: flock or straw-filled ones were considered suitable only for ser-vants; horsehair, goosefeather or a combination of both were widely used, but by the late-Victorian period spring mattresses filled with horsehair sandwiched in-between layers of wool were the most luxu-rious and horsehair-filled bolsters were almost universally used across the width of the mattress as a base for feather pillows.

Where full- and half-testers were used, damask lined with coloured and glazed calico was the preferred choice for bed hangings. Dust ruf-fles or valances, intended in part to stop dust collecting underneath the bed, remained popular in many houses, but were discarded in others

The walls and the ceiling of this bedroom are decorated in French chinoiserie toile. The decoration typifies the way the Victorians confidently mixed styles – here Indian, Persian and Chinese patterns are intermingled.

The Victorian lady would never sit or lie down on a made-up bed, hence the bedroom couch situated at the end of the bed. It was known as a "fainting couch" and a lady could collapse on it if her corset was too tight!

Far left: a common practice in the late 19th century was to decorate furniture with flowers and gilt lines painted onto a black background. Here the bedheads, bedside cabinets and mirror frame have been treated in this way.

Near left: a bedroom in the Ulysses S. Grant home in Galena, Illinois. The "Darling" stove, patented in 1879 by Henderson, Kahn & Co., is a reminder of 19th-century methods of heating.

Far left: early period furniture, such as this Federal bed in a home in Shepherdstown, West Virginia, was considered unfashionable, but pieces often remained in the bedroom. On the wall is a collection of Queen Victoria mementos.

Near left: in a Los Angeles bedroom, a 19th-century feel is evoked with a quantity of antique linen, a fine collection of turquoise vaseline glass and a large tapestry of roses and fruit. Bed linen need not be antique - modern Victorian-style alternatives are produced by numerous companies.

Far left: this amusing bedroom in Christophe Gollut's apartment or flat resembles a French officer's campaign tent during the Crimea. The walls are hung with blue and white American ticking and the floor is covered with Medieval matting. The Swiss campaign bed is early 19th century.

Near left: in a light and airy nursery the walls are decorated with "Pirouette Stripe" and complemented by Laura Ashley crib linens and lace.

Above: pale striped drapes suspended from simple wooden hooks can be drawn to enclose a bed. Right: an early Federal field or campaign bed (c.1800) suitable for a child, in the Old Merchant's House, New York. These beds were simple constructions and so were widely copied during the 19th century.

where it was believed preferable to let air circulate under the mattress. Sheets were usually made from lengths of unbleached muslin or from cotton. Woollen blankets were commonly used for warmth in Britain – quilted eiderdowns only gained acceptance toward the end of the 19th century – and were placed beneath a counterpane made of lace, cotton or chintz. However, in North America, patchwork quilts were the traditional form of bedcover, and were often handed down as family heirlooms. Other recommended fabrics for covers included muslin, silk, batiste, embroidered linen and twilled cotton, all fabrics that were relatively easy to clean.

Apart from the bed, the largest item of furniture was a wardrobe or an armoire. The most popular design, particularly during the middle of the era, was double-fronted with a bevelled central mirror. Most versions contained hanging space, shelves, drawers and racks, and were usually used by women, as men ordinarily had their own cabinets in an adjoining dressing room. Bedroom furniture designed for Victorian men rarely incorporated hanging space, as all their clothes were laid flat when put away. If the wardrobe or armoire was without mirrors, a cheval mirror was usually placed close to it, and smaller versions, known in North America as dressing-case mirrors, were often put on top of

chests of drawers. After the 1880s, built-in wardrobes, which took up a large part of the available wall space, slowly grew in popularity. However, *Cassell's House Guide* recommended hanging clothes from a brass pole across the chimney recess, and protecting them with pretty chintz drapes. This remained a popular and inexpensive alternative to the wardrobe, particularly in country cottages, throughout the second half of the 19th century.

Even after the advent of indoor plumbing and separate bathrooms in the 1880s (see Bathrooms, pages 208–19), the washstand was considered an essential item of furniture in the Victorian bedroom. Usually marble-topped and backed, the latter part to protect the walls from splashes, it was augmented with a sink or basin, as well as various bowls, pitchers and dishes, often decorated with floral patterns, for all the requirements of the daily toilette. Men usually had their own washstand and shaving stand in the adjoining dressing room. A wooden towel horse was usually placed either next to the washstand or else, when there was one, beside a hip bath.

Vanity units or dressing tables and washstands were invariably sold in pairs and the former were typically placed in front of a window, in a bay if there was one, where the light was good. Styles varied from

Below: 19th-century jewellery, including, from left to right: a pavé turquoise bracelet; a silver and gold "tremblant" flower spray, so-called because the flowers move; a Japanese-style bracelet decorated with twisted wire; a large locket commemorating the Queen's Second Regiment; a bracelet by Streeter & Co., inspired by nautical pulleys and rope and engraved, "Ahoy!"; and a pair of French earrings with encrusted turquoise and pearls.

Right: a representation of a typical Victorian lady's vanity unit or dressing table. Displayed on a white embroidered cloth are cut-glass scent bottles and hat pin containers, a feather powder puff and a silver-framed portrait. There is also a matching brush, comb and hand mirror set in embossed silver, a beaded bag, a Royal Worcester hand (1864) and a mother-of-pearl calling card box. A silk bonnet conceals a small hat stand.

plain, machine-made pieces to more elaborate versions with marble tops and inset gaslight brackets. They always incorporated drawers, which were usually lined with fabric such as damask and scented with sachets of lilac or lavender, and some had a central mirror with a tilt mechanism flanked by smaller drawers intended for storing jewellery. Other types had additional pivotal side mirrors for checking the profile. Typical paraphernalia placed on the cloth-covered surface of the dressing table included sets of ivory, tortoiseshell or silver combs and brushes, placed on trays. These "sets" often included matching candlesticks, bottles, bowls, boxes, caskets and ring-holders.

servants removed daily; ottomans with compartments for housing bed linen or shoes; small wall cabinets for storing medicines; framed prints and watercolours; and upright folding screens, made usually of stamped leather, Japanese lacquer, stiff, hand-painted paper or fabric to match the drapes. Such screens were commonly used in lieu of a separate dressing room and, during the summer months, to hide a large wet sponge in a bowl which was brought in to keep the room cool.

Additional furniture peculiar to the nursery included toy cabinets and high-chairs which were often decorated with animals and characters from fairy tales and nursery rhymes. Pictures and prints specifically

Left: the American blue and white ticking on the walls of this bedroom in London, England, is fixed at ceiling level and attached to a pole above the floor to hold it taut. Some of the fabric is pleated to hang as a drape, and can also conceal a door if required.

Left: a typical 19th-century dressing-table set. Overleaf: beside a bed dressed with embroidered linen and a floral Mercella bedcover, c.1850s, a lady's haircomb, ostrich feather and a beaded purse lie on a silk embroidered shawl, c.1900.

Bedroom chairs were often lightweight and made from *papier mâché*, lacquered and embellished with mother-of-pearl. There were also low-bottomed slipper chairs, for tying and untying shoelaces, rockers, in North America, and upholstered elbow chairs or armchairs with high backs to give protection from drafts as they were commonly placed near a window. In a boudoir, or a main bedroom which doubled as a sitting room or where space was no object, a low couch, sometimes known as a "fainting couch" or "reclaimer", was placed at the end of the bed or in a corner or in front of the fire.

Other sundry items found in the typical Victorian bedroom included: large wickerwork baskets for containing soiled linen, which the

painted for the nursery by artists such as Cecil Aldin and John Hassal were also much in evidence. One fashion at the end of the 19th century, particularly among sections of the upper classes, was to furnish the main bedrooms as boudoirs, hence small, occasional tables draped with fabric, elegant writing desks embellished with inlay and marquetry in 18th-century English and French styles, and even pianos were installed. However, such ostentation was in many senses an exception, being at odds not only with the "sensible", hygiene-conscious decor of most late-Victorian bedrooms, but also out of touch with the aesthetic ideals of the Arts and Crafts movement that began to take root toward the end of the 19th century.

BATHROOMS

Up until the last quarter of the 19th century all but the most affluent of homes, on both sides of the Atlantic, were built without bathrooms – that is, internal rooms set aside specifically for the purpose of bathing. Prior to the introduction of mains water piped into houses under pressure, middle- and upper-class Victorians conducted their daily ablutions at a washstand located in the bedroom or dressing room. Commonly in the form of a wooden dresser, the washstand had a marble top upon which were placed various china bowls, ewers and dishes for water, soap, toothbrushes and shaving equipment.

More extensive bathing was carried out either by standing in a shallow tray of water and sponging oneself down, or else by lying in a portable tub or a hip-bath which was normally placed in front of the bedroom fire (or the kitchen stove or in an outhouse in poorer homes). Usually made of tin or cast iron, the latter sometimes painted to resemble marble on the inside, the hip-bath had a high, sloping back designed to support the neck and shoulders and, in some cases, there was also an internal wooden seat. Although the bather's legs hung out over one end, it was possible to immerse most of the body in water – which was by no means an uncomfortable arrangement, particularly if a separate foot-bath was also available. A more invigorating, although less self-indulgent alternative was the portable shower: resembling a small

Left: original Victorian stained glass in Christophe Gollut's apartment or flat in London, England, dictated his choice of wall decoration. The bathroom is painted in faux onyx panels surrounded by black and gold faux portoro marble. The fixtures and fittings are in keeping with 19th-century style. Right: this grand black "marble" bathroom has a Classical Revival feel.

Above: a cool, breezy bathroom in a Mediterranean villa situated in the hills behind Nice, in southern France. The free-standing bathtub and the sink or basin are boxed in with waxed wooden panels (reminiscent of 19th-century bathroom furniture) which match the full-length wall cabinets and the moulding or cornice. White marble reaching dado height protects the walls against splashes. The blue and white gingham-type wall-paper is called "Gannochy Check Blue" and is designed by Colefax & Fowler.

Right: a Victorian Empire-style bathroom created by interior designer Alberto Pinto in his Quai d'Orsay apartment or flat in Paris, France. Dark wood panelling and a bath encased in gray marble lend an air of luxury which is enhanced by an authentic floor rug and a pair of velvet upholstered chairs. The reproduction fixtures and fittings, the towel rail and the hanging ceiling lamp all add to the period feel, although the bathroom is in fact high-tech. The overall effect is doubled by the presence of generous mirrors.

Roman tent. It housed a tank at the top, which cascaded water over the bather at the pull of a cord, and there was a tray at the bottom for standing in and to catch the waste.

All such sinks or basins, bathtubs and showers were filled and emptied by hand; cold and hot water, the latter heated on the kitchen range, was toted up and down the stairs in buckets and hot-water cans by servants. To these servants also fell the even more onerous task of emptying chamber pots or slop bowls, and scalding them with boiling water for disinfecting purposes before putting them back discreetly under the bed or in a bedside commode.

While portable chamber pots were widely used inside the house, fixed sanitary arrangements – which became a legal requirement in England following the Public Health Act of 1848 – were almost always kept out of doors. The inadequate state of the sewerage system in many areas meant that primitive indoor toilets tended to be prone to foul air. Consequently, most households made use of either an earth closet, a toilet, an ash pit or a simple seat over a cesspit located in an outbuilding. (A very early exception to this was the "inside toilet" that Thomas Jefferson installed at Monticello in the United States in the early 1800s, which consisted of an ingenious system of ropes and pulleys that carried his chamber pot from the house along a tunnel to a waste ground outside.) To remove the waste matter from the outside "privies", many towns and cities employed "dustmen" (dust meant excrement during the 19th century).

For wealthy Victorian families, who could afford to retain large numbers of servants to fetch and carry, visits to the "stinking privy" outside the house were unnecessary and labour-intensive methods of bathing were not inconvenient. But to the growing middle and lower-middle classes, who might have only one or two servants, existing sanitary arrangements became increasingly unattractive. And to the poor, whose access to fresh water was often limited, particularly in the cities and towns, and who were more exposed to the inadequate state of the sewerage system, existing arrangements were often the source of disease – there were, for example, two major cholera outbreaks around the middle of the 19th century.

In an age of considerable industrial energy and innovation, the desire to improve standards of hygiene, following a greater awareness of how certain diseases spread, was, for the first time, matched by both the necessary technological innovation and the prosperity to make it possible. The subsequent series of major public and private works during the last half of the century saw the installation of mains drains and other increasingly efficient methods for the disposal of sewage, including the introduction into many homes of mains water under pressure and also gas which provided a means of heating water. Together with improvements in sanitary equipment and methods of heating water, the result was a technological watershed that eventually gave rise to the bathroom in the form that we know it today. Broadly, the installation of mains water under pressure meant that water could be stored in tanks

in the attic or roof spaces of houses, and bathtubs and sinks or basins could be fixed in position, with plumbed-in faucets or taps and plug-holes leading to the drains outside. It also promoted the development of new methods of heating water. These included circulatory hot-water systems, plumbed into and heated by either the kitchen range downstairs or else by boilers which were commonly installed in a bedroom fireplace. An alternative heating method was the application of gas flames directly to the underside of copper-bottomed baths; and, most successful of all, was the gas-fired geyser, which was introduced in the late 1860s and finally perfected in the 1880s, having initially gained a reputation for being noisy, smelly and all too likely to explode. All of these systems obviated the need to fetch and carry quantities of hot (and cold) water up and down stairs by hand. Better drains and an increase in water supply also made technological improvements to the bathroom feasible, which resulted in it being more socially acceptable to install such a room inside the house.

Specific improvements in fixtures and fittings as a result of such advances included the gradual replacement of the marble-topped, wooden washstand with the all-ceramic pedestal sink or basin or, for the less well-off, with sinks or basins made of enamelled metal. Supported on metal legs, suspended from the wall on ornamental brackets or "boxed in" to a vanity unit, the new sinks or basins (which were generally bigger than their present-day counterparts and often embellished with bands of colourful decoration) were easier to clean and therefore more hygienic than their predecessors. Water was supplied, almost universally, via cross-head faucets or taps, which were usually made of brass or nickel plate.

Above left and middle: two bathrooms in the Rockcliffe Mansion in Hannibal, Missouri. Both rooms date from 1898-1900 and are in the Neo-classical style, they have also retained all their original fixtures and fittings.

Above right: in a country house in Suffolk, England, belonging to Keith Skeel, the tiled walls are reminiscent of the Victorian era: tiles were preferred, in particular for floors, because they are durable and easy to clean. The lights and also the sink or basin are high-quality period reproductions.

Right: this wonderful serpentine-fronted, marble-topped washstand stands in the Empire-style bathroom in Alberto Pinto's apartment or flat in Paris, France. Such large-scale washstands are not only impressive to look at but also highly functional, providing ample storage space. They can either be adapted from a Victorian piece or else created from scratch in a 19th-century style.

Below: also in Keith Skeel's home, another bathroom has a fine French double sink or basin and alongside stands a large étagère, used for displaying a collection of old drug or medicine bottles, jars and decanters.

Bathtubs that were fixed to the floor, which had first appeared in North America during the Civil War, were initially made of sheet metal such as lead, copper or zinc, or, in wealthy homes, of glazed fireclay. However, enamelled cast-iron baths, which became widely available during the early 1870s, were soon a standard feature of the Victorian bathroom. Designed with rounded backs, they were often tapered at the faucet or tap end in order to save water, and stood several inches off the floor mounted on feet cast in ball-and-claw shapes, or as scrolls with leaf patterns.

Because early enamels were fairly thin, and therefore tended to chip easily, protective hardwood rails were sometimes fixed to the rim. In some cases the entire tub was encased in wooden panelling. The introduction of pressurized water also led to substantial improvements in the design and efficiency of showers. For example, wealthier home-owners installed expensive combined bathtubs and showers, some of which featured horizontal "needle" sprays in addition to the standard overhead douche.

The improved sewerage system coupled with the ability to store mains water in a tank in the roof space also facilitated a major improvement to the water closet or toilet. For most of the 19th century two basic types of toilet were available. First, the somewhat unreliable hopper-type pan, which was generally installed in lower middle-class homes and featured an inverted cone with a U-bend trap at the bottom designed (but often unfortunately failing to keep out) noxious gases from the sewers. It was flushed with water, let into a hole at the side, which then swirled around the hopper, so sweeping the waste matter through the trap. Second, the Bramah toilet, which was invented by Joseph Bramah in 1777 and was widely used in more affluent households; in this case the pan closed at the bottom by means of a valve or flap. The flushing mechanism was operated by pulling a pull or handle which, via an elaborate system of levers, opened the flap, let in water to sweep away the contents, then closed the valve, and retained a small amount of water in the pan to keep gases at bay.

A marked advance on both of these systems came with a "wash-out" toilet, which was manufactured by Daniel Bostel Bros. and, later, companies such as Twyford, Jennings and Shanks. This model dispensed with the Bramah flap and instead relied on gravity for a powerful rush of water from an overhead cast-iron cistern, operated either by pulling a chain or by lifting the wooden seat, to flush waste matter from the porcelain bowl through an S-bend trap – the latter was a significant improvement on the U-bend.

With regard to plumbing in waste and water pipes, it obviously made ergonomic sense to place most, if not all, of these improved fixtures and fittings into one room – a bathroom. However, the vast majority of houses built prior to the last quarter of the 19th century had not been designed with such a room in mind. Therefore the first bathrooms, in both Europe and in the United States, were installed in what had previously been bedrooms, dressing rooms and store rooms. Partly because of their origins, and partly to allay Victorian fears about the hygienic merits of bringing the outhouse inside, these early bathrooms were furnished as other rooms in the house and sanitary equipment was often "concealed" in furniture-like encasements.

The practice of encasement of the sink or basin, bathtub and toilet was one of the most significant features of Victorian bathrooms from the 1860s through to the 1890s. For example, mirror-backed, marble-topped washstands (available from c.1880 onward) designed for the bathroom were almost identical in appearance to vanity units or dressing tables created for the bedroom – the only significant difference being the addition of a sunken sink or basin with brass or nickel-plated faucets or taps. Built-in, instead of free-standing sink or basin enclosures also became quite common. Similarly, bathtubs were enclosed in hardwood surrounds (mahogany being particularly prevalent), which were gloss-varnished to prevent warping.

Encasement also helped to overcome a natural reticence about installing the toilet inside the house. While many early bathrooms had the toilet segregated in either a small separate room or else inside an adjoining closet, it gradually became more acceptable to incorporate it in the main room, albeit often in an alcove. The toilet was then hung with *portières* or perhaps hidden behind a door with inset panels of etched glass, or located behind a partition wall or a screen in order to preserve privacy. Alternative methods of concealment included installation beneath a built-in mahogany or walnut bench with a panelled front, or within an enclosure which was often designed to look like a chair. For example, at Biltmore, the Vanderbilt estate in North Carolina, in the United States, cane-seated chairs were positioned over the porcelain toilet bowls, and at the actress Lillie Langtry's home in Hampstead, London, England, the elbow chair or armchair custom-built to fit over the toilet bowl was upholstered in blue velvet.

The encasement of sanitary appliances in furniture-like surrounds gave even small early Victorian bathrooms an opulent appearance quite

Above: a free-standing rolltop bathtub and an old-fashioned sink or basin lend a period feel to a modern bathroom built into a loft or attic conversion. Left: this late 19th-/early 20th-century combined bath and shower unit dominate a bathroom in Plas Teg, a Jacobean stately home in North Wales. Below: a fascinating bathroom in Lord and Lady McAlpine's country home in Hampshire sports a bookcase and an eccentric collection of stuffed birds, some perched and others on the wing. All can be viewed from the magnificent Victorian cast-iron bathtub which occupies the middle of the room.

unlike the more functional rooms that emerged during the last ten years of the 19th century. The bedroom- or parlour-like ambience was accentuated by the presence of additional free-standing furniture in keeping with the original purpose of the room. Depending on the space available, it was common to find bureaus, dressers and armoires (that were used to store towels and accessories), small tables, shaving stands, wooden or brass towel racks, and chairs, the latter usually with a cane or rush seat.

Similarly, many early bathroom floors were wooden and covered with rugs which were often Oriental. However, problems with condensation caused by the exposure of hot water to the air (not helped by the fireplace being the only source of ventilation, and only really solved with the invention of the mixer faucet or tap toward the end of the century) encouraged the use of tiled floors that were made of marble, mosaic or terrazzo in wealthier households. For some ceramic floors were too expensive, and figured or marbled linoleum or "cork carpets", supplemented with cork mats in front of the bathtub and sink or basin, provided a less expensive, effective and warmer alternative.

Richly patterned ceramic tiles were also used as "splashbacks" for sinks or basins and bathtubs. However, in all but the wealthiest of homes, they were rarely applied to entire walls until the advent of the purpose-built bathroom during the last decade of the 19th century. Instead, painted tongue-and-groove boarding up to dado height was far more common in middle-class dwellings; painted Anaglypta or Lincrusta wallpaper being a popular alternative. Patterned wallpapers, ornamental friezes and ceiling borders, as used in other rooms in the house, were also much in evidence, the only difference being that sometimes one or two coats of varnish would be applied to protect them from the effects of condensation.

Drapes at windows, pictures, prints and mirrors on the walls, stained or painted glass panels in doors and all manner of potted plants (including bonsai during the "Japanese craze"), together with tumblers, pomades, scents, brushes and all the other paraphernalia of the Victorian toilette, also contributed to the cosy bedroom-like atmosphere of the early Victorian bathroom.

While the opulent-looking bathroom that emerged during the high-Victorian period remained fashionable well into the 20th century, most particularly in North America and Continental Europe, a smaller, more streamlined and lighter-looking room began to appear at the end of the 19th century, notably in Britain, as architects set aside space for bathing in new houses. In *Das Englische Haus* the German writer

This central cast-iron Victorian bathtub is surrounded by rose garlanded arches of Brunschwig et Fils "La Haie" wallpaper panels. These panels conceal large cabinets which run the entire length of two walls of the room. Many companies are now reproducing bathtubs, sinks or basins, toilets and bathroom fixtures and fittings in the late-Victorian style.

Right: washing facilities were often located in the bedroom during the Victorian era. Here, in the Ulysses S. Grant home in Galena, Illinois, a "Warwick china" jug and sink or basin with a full set of slop pail, chamber pot and toilet accessories occupy the corner of a bedroom. The marble-topped washstand is c.1860.

Below left: circular sinks or basins built into Victorian washstands or vanity units are suitable for small bathrooms. Tiles lend a period feel. Below right: late 19th-century painted toilets and sinks or basins are available as modern copies. White-painted tongue-and-grooved boards create a country mood.

Hermann Muthesius described the English bathroom at the turn of the century as a simple, plain room dictated by function, with none of the ostentatious opulence characteristic of many European bathrooms: "A well-equipped bathroom will contain a bath, shower bath, a shelf for towels and a receptacle for used towels". He also praised the hard walls and floors, good hot-water systems and the simple and efficient metal and ceramic fixtures.

This new "simplicity" was based partly upon advances in technology and changes in design, and partly upon a gradual change in social attitudes toward sanitation: namely, an ever-increasing and wider acceptance of the importance of personal hygiene accompanied by a stripping-away of Victorian prudishness about such matters. Thus, wooden floors and wainscots gave way to hygienic tiled floors and

dados (ceramic tiles having become less expensive since the advent of mass-production), giving the room a generally more clinical look. Pipework was exposed instead of being built-in to stop germs breeding in enclosed spaces and, for similar reasons, to make them easier to clean, sinks or basins, toilets and bathtubs emerged from their various kinds of wooden enclosures to stand on sculpted pedestals and ball-and-claw feet. "Low-level" cisterns began to replace high cast-iron ones above toilets, thereby reducing the noise level during flushing. In many cases, drapes at the window were replaced with Venetian shades or blinds, the latter providing both privacy and more light at the same time. Ventilation was improved by the installation of air-inlet tubes, so reducing the effects of condensation. Also central-heating systems became more common, particularly in the homes of the wealthy.

While the overall effect was indeed a simpler, more streamlined look, this was only so by 19th-century standards. Bathrooms at the end of the Victorian era still expressed the decorative spirit of the age: pipework was often cast with leafy vines and floral designs; the facings of cast-iron heaters and cisterns were embellished with elaborate relief work (notably Aesthetic and Arts and Crafts, and Art Nouveau motifs), particularly in North America; toilets and sinks or basins were elaborately decorated on the outside with raised scrollwork and colourful transfer-printed foliage and classical Greek geometrics or landscapes on the inside, the patterns and colours (blue was especially popular) often being "picked up" from the surrounding tiles. Decorative brass hardware – faucets or taps, doorknobs and even door hinges – also remained much in evidence, reflecting the fact that the ornamental spirit of Victorian style even extended to the smallest of details.

Both the earlier bedroom-like and the later more streamlined bathrooms of the Victorian era can be recreated without too much difficulty due to the fact that many original fixtures and fittings can still be found via specialist outlets, and high-quality reproductions have become widely available to meet the growing demand (see The Directory, pages 224–5). Antique brass faucets or taps, sinks or basins and toilets are usually less expensive to purchase than reproduction examples. However, they usually come with non-standard fittings that can make it awkward to plumb them into modern pipework. Original, very large cast-iron, roll-top bathtubs have survived, but the cost of re-enamelling may make smaller reproductions a more attractive alternative. Much the same can be said of combined bathtubs and showers. Of course, the practice of enclosure largely associated with the high-Victorian period, means that modern ceramic sinks or basins, bathtubs, toilets, and also central-heating radiators, can be boxed into hardwood panel surrounds for authentic-looking results. The addition of a reproduction mahogany, walnut or pine toilet seat immediately transforms a plain white, modern bowl.

In larger bathrooms, the introduction of free-standing period furniture – armoires, cabinets, dressers, tables, chairs and towel-rails – accompanied by period pictures, prints and mirrors in antique frames on the walls, is an essential part of a successful recreation of high-Victorian style, as are reproduction (or original) tiles for splashbacks, ornamental dados and flooring. Efficient modern central heating and ventilation via extractor fans also means richly patterned reproduction wallpapers (widely available from specialist suppliers) can be used with a fair degree of confidence, particularly painted Anaglypta or Lincrusta below a dado rail.

While tiled floors strike an authentic note, especially in "simpler" late 19th-century bathrooms, wooden floors, marbled or stained and varnished, are entirely in keeping with bathrooms of the high-Victorian era, particularly when augmented with Oriental rugs and runners, washable rag rugs or cork mats. However, fitted wall-to-wall carpets should be avoided. Similarly, the presence of fabrics such as brocades, damasks, moirés, taffetas, linen and lace, swagged or draped at windows or over small tables, are entirely in keeping, the lighter fabrics being more appropriate for less formal settings and in country houses.

Just as the presence of the correct architectural fixtures and fittings – plaster mouldings, panelled doors, architraves and wainscotting – is essential to recreating the period style, so attention should be paid to small details. For example, brass, crystal and painted porcelain door knobs and light and chain pulls are important elements which are available in reproduction if originals cannot be found.

Finally, as with all other rooms in the house, lighting plays a key role in establishing the right ambience. Period chandeliers and gas and kerosene or paraffin lamps can be successfully converted to run on electricity, and reproductions are available. However, modern spotlights do provide far more efficient illumination and so should be considered acceptable, provided they are recessed.

Below: an original late 19th-century stained oak pannelled toilet with a Gothic niche in an 1850s artist's studio in Kensington, London, England.

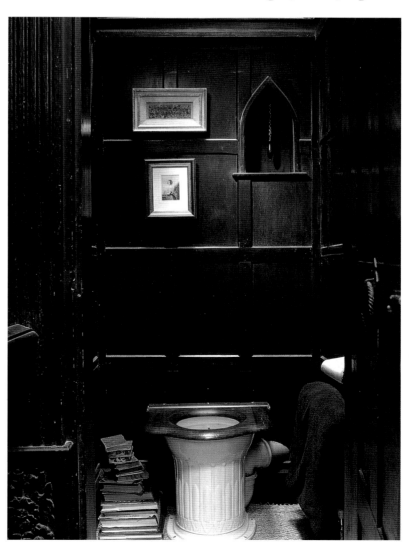

DIRECTORY

REPRODUCTION & ORIGINAL DETAILS

UK

Baileys Architectural Antiques
The Engine Shed
Ashburton Industrial Estate
Ross on Wye
Hereford HR9 7BW
Both antique and reproduction fireplaces, bathroom fittings and door accessories.

Brasstacks
50/54 Clerkenwell Road
London EC1M 5PS
A wide selection of door fittings, including locks, handles and hinges.

Robert Mills
Unit 3
Satellite Business Park
Blackswarth Road
Redfield
Bristol
Avon
Specialist in Gothic architectural details. Carries a wide stock of stained glass, doors, chairs and pieces from deconsecrated churches.

Salvo 91!
County Guide to Britain's Architectural Salvage
PO Box 1295
Bath BA1 6TJ
Guide available by mail order listing more than a thousand dealers and the items they are most likely to specialize in.

Andy Thornton
Architectural Antiques
Marshfield Mills
Elland
Yorks
A constantly changing selection of every type of original and reproduction architectural detail and antique, including doors, fireplaces, stained-glass windows, staircases and all sorts of general bric-à-brac. The company's workshops will reproduce many of the above items to customers' own specifications.

Walcot Reclamation
108 Walcot Street
Bath
Avon BA1 5BG
Period doors, windows, fireplaces and stained glass are just some of the many items constantly in stock.

USA

The Antiques Exchange
715 N Second Street
Philadelphia
Pennsylvania 19123
Doors, entryways, etched and leaded glass, windows and general architectural salvage.

Cumberland Woodcraft Company Inc.
Showroom: 10 Stover Drive
Carlisle
Pennsylvania
Mail to: PO Drawer 609
Carlisle
Pennsylvania 17013
Hundreds of 19th-century pieces recreated in solid oak, including balconies, cornices and gingerbread trim. A comprehensive selection of high-relief wall coverings is also available, as are ceilings and decorative mouldings.

Custom Woodturnings
4000 Telephone Road
1313 Houston
Texas 77087
Specialist suppliers of porches, newel posts, railings, banisters and stair parts.

The Emporium
1800 West Heimer
Houston
Texas 77098
Architectural antiques, doors, stained-glass windows, mantles and gingerbread trim.

San Francisco Victoriana, Inc.
2070 Newcomb Avenue
San Francisco
California 94124
All architectural details, including door and window casings, mouldings, rosettes and wainscotting.

Wooden Nickel
Architectural Antiques
1400–1414 Central Parkway
Cincinnati
Ohio 45210
A wide selection of doors, mantles, leaded and stained glass, furniture and lighting accessories held in stock.

AUSTRALIA

Acco Demolitions
100 Holdsworth Street
Coorparoo
Queensland 4151

Agnews
376 Swan Street
Richmond
Victoria 3121
A particularly large selection of superb-quality reproduction furnishing details, including doors and door fittings, stained glass, tiles, fireplaces and lighting accessories.

All Salvage Sales
1 Pearson Way
Osborne Park
Western Australia 6107

Architectural Heritage
62 Glebe Point Road
Glebe 2037
New South Wales
Stockists of original fireplaces and grates. A range of quality reproduction stained-glass and leaded windows are also available from stock.

Authentic Renovations
283 Canterbury Road
Canterbury
Victoria
Suppliers of period fixtures and fittings.

Bargain Renovators
181 Burwood Road
Hawthorn
Victoria 3123

Exclusive Hardware
1348 Malvern Road
Malvern
Victoria
Suppliers of period-style reproduction hardware.

Federation Trading
127 Weymouth Street
Adelaide
South Australia 7000

S. & L. Holdings Salvage Yards
183 Marmion Street
Palmyra
Western Australia 6157
and: 1 Roper Street
O'Connor
Western Australia 6107

The House of Fretworks
73 High Street
Prahran
Victoria
Stockists and suppliers of period-style woodwork.

Karem Woodcraft
25 Yarra Road
Wonga Park
Victoria
Stockists and suppliers of period-style woodwork.

Melbourne Aluminium and Iron Lacework
452 Heidelberg Road
Fairfield
Victoria
Stockists and suppliers of period-style metalwork.

Mother of Pearl & Sons
574 Willoughby Road
Willoughby
Sydney
Stockists and suppliers of period fixtures and fittings.

Paynter Salvage
441 Canterbury Road
Surrey Hills
Victoria 3127

Period Details
538 Burwood Road
Hawthorn 3122
Victoria
An enormous supplier of interior architectural details – some high-quality reproduction pieces as well as some authentic period pieces.

Recollections
550–554 North Road
Ormond
Melbourne
Stockists and suppliers of period fixtures and fittings.

Regeneration
101 Bay Street
Port Melbourne
Victoria
Suppliers of period-style hardware.

The Renovation Centre
Parramatta Road
Camperdown
Sydney
Major supplier of entrance door leadlights, brassware, timber washstands, tiles and decorated borders. Items made to customers' specifications.

Restoration Station
98 Waterworks Road
Ashgrove
Brisbane
Queensland 4060
Carriers of a comprehensive range of all items required for home restoration.

Rogers, Seller, Myhill
27 City Road
South Melbourne
Victoria
Period-style fixtures.

Sid's Colonial Materials
282 Montague Road
West End
Queensland 4101

Southern Cross Salvage Pty Ltd
6 Pass Road
Mornington
Tasmania 7018

Statewide Salvage
18 Wood Street
Bayswater
Western Australia 6053

Stepney Architectural Traders
71 Magill Road
Stepney
South Australia 5069

Steptoe's Renovation Supplies
112 Rokeby Street
Collingwood
Victoria 3066

T. & S. Recycled Materials
Mathews Way
Devonport
Tasmania 7310

Terrace House Factory Building Materials
Corner Harris & Allen Streets
Ultimo
New South Wales 2007

Timeball Antiques
Period Building Materials
141 Railway Place
Williamstown
Victoria 3016

Uptons Salvage
312 Argyle Street
Hobart
Tasmania 7000

Woolloongabba Demolitions
22 Burke Street
Woolloongabba
Queensland 4102

NEW ZEALAND
Bungalow and Villa Renovation Materials
68 Surrey Crescent
Grey Lynn
Specialist company dealing in new exterior lumber joinery; also mouldings, lacework, doors and windows.

FIREPLACES

UK
The Amazing Grate Trading Company
Unit 7
Avon Gorge Centre
Portview Road
Avonmouth
Bristol
Avon BS11 9LQ
Specialist company dealing in authentic reproductions of traditional period fireplaces, using only the finest selected traditional materials. Solid-brass fenders for fireplaces and reproduction Victorian tiles are also available.

Britain's Heritage
Shaftesbury Hall
3 Holy Bones
Leicester
One of the largest selections of genuine antique and period fireplaces available in the country. The original fireplaces are restored to an extremely high standard. Open seven days a week.

Chapel House Fireplaces
Netherfield House
St George's Road
Scholes Holmfirth
West Yorkshire
Specialist company dealing in good-quality, genuine antique Victorian fireplaces and mantles. More than 400 cast-iron fireplace surrounds and insets held in stock at any one time, with mantle shelves in solid oak, pine and mahogany, as well as in iron and marble. Viewing by appointment only.

Hilton Forge Ltd
Hilton Village
Derbyshire DE6 5SE
*High-quality, reproduction
Victorian cast-iron fireplaces
are made in the company's
own foundry. Solid-fuel coal
or logs, or gas, can be burned.
The "Victorian Classic
Fireplace" collection features
designs taken from the years
1827-1901.*

London Stove Centre
49 Chiltern Street
London W1M 1HQ
*Wood-, coal- or gas-burning
stoves are available from an
extensive range held in stock.
These are in traditional
designs, which are all enamelled and then finished to a
high standard.*

Morely Marketing
P O Box 38
Ware
Herts SG12 7JP
*Stockists and suppliers of
wood- or coal-burning stoves.
There are many designs and
styles from which to choose,
all based on traditional stoves.*

Nostalgia
61 Shaw Heath
Stockport
Cheshire SK3 8BH
*Specialist company dealing in
fully restored Victorian fireplaces. Accessories for fireplaces are also stocked.*

Old Flames
30 Long Street
Easingwold
York
*A range of fully restored and
working Victorian fireplaces
available. Authentic kitchen
ranges also stocked.*

Original Features
155 Tottenham Lane
Crouch End
London N8 9BT
*A good selection of reproduc-
tion fireplaces and accessories
in stock. A full fireplace-
installation service is also
available locally.*

Replicas
262/268 South Road
Walkley
Sheffield
*Specialist suppliers of cast-iron
insets of tiled, arched or keyhole types. Many fireplaces,
surrounds, fenders and fireside
items always in stock.*

Stovay Ltd
Falcon Road
Sowton Industrial Estate
Exeter
Devon EX2 7LF
*A nationwide supplier of
reproduction, cast-iron 19th-
century fireplaces with authentic recreations of Victorian
hearth tiles, surrounds and
fenders. Also suppliers of cast-
iron stoves.*

The Victorian Fireplace
Thanet House
92 Broad Street
Canterbury
Kent
*More than 150 fireplaces on
show and at time, with many
more always held in stock.
Gas fires are also stocked. A
full installation and restoration
service is provided.*

**Wye Valley Stoves &
Fireplaces**
Palma Court
Brookend Street
Ross on Wye
Herefordshire HR9 7EE
*Many cast-iron stoves and
fireplaces, including Victorian
originals always in stock. Also
iron firebacks, fenders, coal
scuttles etc. More than 200
Victorian fireplace tiles held in
stock. Delivery to all parts of
the country.*

USA
**Barnstable Stove Shop
Inc.**
Box 472 Route 149
W Barnstable
Massachusetts 02668
*Antique wood-, coal- and
gas-burning stoves bought,
sold and restored. Other ser-
vices include iron sand blast-
ing, welding and casting.*

Farmham Firecasts
602 S Morton
Okmulgee
Oklahoma 74447
*Stockists and suppliers of tra-
ditional Victorian-style cast-
iron fireplaces with ceramic
tiles. Oak, mahogany and
pine mantles also available.*

Fourth Bay
Box 287
10500 Industrial Drive
Garretsville
Ohio 44231
*Importers of British cast-iron
fireplaces in Victorian styles,
as well as reproduction ceramic
hearth tiles.*

**Good Time Stove
Company**
Route 112 P O Box 306
Goshen
Massachusetts 01032
*Specialist company dealing in
authentic antique heating
stoves, all fully restored and
ready for installation and use.*

**Lehman Hardware &
Appliances**
P O Box 41J
Kidron
Ohio 44636
*Stockists of old-fashioned
appliances, such as Victorian-
style cooking stoves.*

Wendall's Wood Stoves
19964 Inks Drive
Tuolumne
California 05379
*Fully restored and refurbished
antique and classic wood-
burning stoves, as well as gas
kitchen and electric ranges.*

AUSTRALIA
The Antique Garden
438 Chapel Street
South Yarra
Victoria 3141
*Specialists dealing in restored
original fireplaces, all handcrafted and finished in the
company's own workshops.
Fireplaces are made with care
and every attention to detail;
beautiful cast-iron and pewter-
finished grates. Tiled inserts
are also available. Open seven
days a week. Look for other
branches in your locality.*

Lasting Impressions
593 Burrwood Road
Hawthorn
Melbourne
Victoria 3122
*Specialist suppliers and stock-
ists of quality imported
antique and reproduction fireplaces and surrounds.*

**Old Balgowlah
Restorations &
Fireplace Specialists**
377 Sydney Road
Balgowlah
New South Wales 2093
*An extensive and good-
quality selection of both
marble and wooden fireplace
surrounds is available, as well
as cast-iron grates, hearth tiles
and gas-effect log fires. A full
installation service is also provided. Many genuine Vic-
torian fireplaces and spare
parts are stocked.*

DOORS

UK
**The Empire and
Colonial Knocker
Company**
P O Box 1876
Tamworth
Staffordshire B77 4RY
*A unique selection of both
door and cabinet fittings is
held in stock. Each item is
painstakingly handcrafted
from the original patterns
using traditional Victorian
methods and techniques. A
comprehensive mail-order service is also provided.*

Kirkpatrick Ltd
Frederick Street
Walsall WS2 9NF
*A selection of reproduction
ironwork, including door
knockers and other fittings.*

B. Lilly & Sons Ltd
Baltimore Road
Birmingham B42 1DJ
*A large selection of external
door furniture, from patterns
used by the company for more
than a hundred years.*

**The London Door
Company**
165 St Johns Hill
London SW11 1TQ
*Custom-made and fitted,
exact replicas of Victorian
front doors. Internal doors,
room dividers and decorative
glass also available.*

Strippa Door
Victoria House
Higher Bury Street
Stockport SK4 1BJ
*Stockists of a good selection of
doors, shutters, windows and
all accessories.*

Victoria Place
3 Hatton Gardens
Kington
Herefordshire HR5 3RB
*A leading UK manufacturer
of ceramic door furniture. All
products are hand-glazed and
made to traditional patterns
and designs.*

USA
American Home Supply
PO Box 697
Campbell
California 95009
*A large selection of genuine
antique door knobs, locks and
hinges are stocked in a variety
of colours.*

**Blaine Window
Hardware Inc.**
1919 Blaine Drive
RD4
Hagerstown
Maryland 21740
*A manufacturing and distribu-
tion company with a truly
impressive range — more than
20,000 items of replacement
hardware for doors, windows,
closets and more.*

Hardware + Plus Inc.
701 E Kingsley Road
Garland
Texas 75041
*A company specializing in
hard-to-find restoration hardware for all types of antique
furniture, door furniture and
architectural details.*

**Lamson-Taylor Custom
Doors**
Tucker Road
South Acworth
New Hampshire 03607
*A company specializing in
energy-efficient doors made
from native woods to comple-
ment any architectural style.*

**The Old Wagon
Factory**
103 Russell Street
PO Box 1427
Clarksville
Virginia 23927
*Wooden storm and screen
doors, handcrafted in all sizes
to Victorian and traditional
patterns and designs.*

**Jack Wallis Doors and
Stained Glass**
Route 1 Box 22A
Murray
Kentucky 42071
*A complete line of door hard-
ware available. Also hand-
crafted doors and stained glass.*

AUSTRALIA
Knobs and Knockers
736 Hampton Street
Brighton
Victoria
*Hand-forging to customers'
specifications. Will refer inter-
state suppliers.*

Woodlite Joinery
Lot 1 Meyer Road
Lonsdale PO Box 194
Christies Beach 5165
*A company manufacturing
quality wooden windows and
doors. Victorian screen doors
are crafted to the customers'
own design and specifications.*

NEW ZEALAND
Wackrows Joinery Ltd
Gillies Street
Carters Flat
Cambridge
PO Box 150
*Able to reproduce any style of
door required.*

**DECORATIVE
PLASTERWORK**

UK
Allied Guilds
Unit 19
Reddicap Trading Estate
Coleshill Road
Sutton Coldfield
W. Midlands B75 7BU
*Ornamental plasterwork
restored, reproduced and
matched from stock.*

**F.H. Crocker &
Company**
Crozier Road
Mutley
Plymouth
Devon PL4 7LN
*Ornamental and decorative
plasterwork. Repair and
restoration of decorative
mouldings and ornate ceilings.*

Decorative Plasterwork
385 Ladbroke Grove
London W10 5AA
*Specialists in the reproduction,
replacement or repair of decorative plaster mouldings.*

Fibrofix
110 Galbalfa Avenue
Galbalfa
Cardiff
South Glamorgan CF4
2PD
*Specialists in the restora-
tion of all types of antique
and Victorian plasterwork.*

Fine Art Plasterwork
638-640 Streatham High
Road
Norbury
London SW16 3QL
*Manufacturers and suppliers of
quality decorative plaster
mouldings, niches and similar
pieces. A comprehensive
restoration, repair and fixing
service is also provided.*

L. Grandison & Son
Innerleithan Road
Peebles
Borders EH45 8BA
*Ornamental plasterwork,
including repairs to ornamen-
tal ceilings.*

House Proud Decor
29 West Street
Warwick
Warwickshire CV34 6AB
*A company providing a gild-
ing service for ornamental
plaster mouldings, in gold and
bronze leaf.*

London Fine Art Plaster
8 Audrey Street
London E2 8QH
*Undertakes the manufacture,
according to customers' specifications, of mouldings or
cornicings, as well as more
elaborate items. The company
manufactures and fits all types
of fibrous plaster mouldings.*

**Stevensons of Norwich
Ltd**
Roundtree Way
Norwich NR7 8SH
*A company specializing in the
construction of individual
designs in fibrous plaster.
Items made include ceilings,
domes, niches, cornices, arches
and panel mouldings.
Specialist service.*

William Wilson
Unit B
Sidings Road
Fleetwood FY7 6NS
*Fibrous plasterers of reproduc-
tion ceilings and undertakes
the renovation of traditional
plaster ceilings. Heritage selection of hand-crafted ornamental plaster mouldings, cornices,
ceiling medallions or roses and
similar items.*

R. J. Young
15 Station Road East
Ash Vale
Aldershot
Hants GU12 5LT
*The restoration and bespoke
reproduction of plain and
decorative plasterwork and
stucco fascias.*

USA
**Decorators Supply
Corporation**
3610-12 South Morgan
Street
Chicago
Illinois 0609
*Plaster, wood and composition
mouldings, mantles, capitals,
cornices and brackets.*

**Fischer and Jirouch
Company**
4821 Superior Avenue
Cleveland
Ohio 44103

AUSTRALIA
**Hopkins Plaster
Industries**
22 Lincoln Street
Richmond
Victoria 3121

Picton Hopkins
140 Bell Street
Preston
Victoria 3072
*Specialist stockists and suppli-
ers of a range of decorative
plaster mouldings, integrated
ceilings, ceiling medallions or
roses, special mouldings, archways and similar items of
ornamental plasterwork.*

STAIRS

UK
Acorn Antique Doors
The High Street
Twyford
Nr Winchester
Hampshire
*Manufacturers, using old and
reclaimed pine, of staircases,
doors, complete kitchens and
so on.*

R. Bleasdale Co Ltd
301 Caledonian Road
Islington
London N1
*Reproduction Victorian spiral
staircases, straight staircases,
cast railings, balconies etc.*

W. R. & A. Hide
161 Dalling Road
Hammersmith
London W6 OES
*Purpose-made staircases, win-
dows, doors, skirtings, archi-
traves and other mouldings.
No fitting service is provided.*

RGS Joinery
Paldre
Rucklers Lane
Kings Langley
Hemel Hempstead
Hertfordshire WD4 9NB
*Traditional staircases made.
Mouldings and skirtings also
made to order.*

J. & J. Manufacturing
Burrows Lane Farm House
Burrows Lane
Eccleston
Prescot
Merseyside L34 6JQ
*Specialist joiners producing
reproductions as well as restor-
ing existing staircases and fire
surrounds. Also carving,
inlaid work and polishing.*

Monarch Stairways
PO Box 18
Napton
Rugby
*Stockists and suppliers of cast
spiral staircases. A selection of
traditional designs is always
held in stock.*

Safety Stairways Ltd
141 Field Road
Bloxwich
Walsall
West Midlands
*Specialists dealing in cast-iron
reproduction staircases. All
styles, including Victorian,
catered for.*

**Sandleford Products
Ltd**
Old Buildings
Sandleford Farm
Newton Road
Newbury
Berks RG15 9BB
*Manufacturers of spindles,
handrails, newel posts and
similar items. All products are
turned to the customers' own
requirements. A standard
selection is always available
from which to choose.*

Stairrods (UK) Ltd
Unit 6
Park Road
North Industrial Estate
Blackhill
Consett
Co. Durham DH8 5UN
*Items are made to customers'
own specifications, and all
fashioned from solid brass,
which is then polished and
clear coated.*

USA
Heritage Brass
414 East Main Street
Smethport
Pennsylvania 16749
*Specialist company producing
quick and easy to install solid-
brass stair rods in lengths
according to customers' own
specifications. Accessories such
as rods, finials and fastners
are all included.*

**Spiral Manufacturing
Inc.**
17251Jefferson Highway
Baton Rouge
Louisiana 0817
*All-wood spiral and curved
staircases produced in kit form
for home installation. Also
parts for railings, newels and
treads. Metal spiral stairs for
exterior use are also supplied.*

FLOORS

UK
Acquisitions
269 Camden High Street
London NW1 7BX
*Stockists and suppliers of a
wide range of reproduction
tiles for floors, hearths and
fireplaces.*

Candy Tiles Ltd
Heathfield
Newton Abbot
Devon TQ12 6RF
*Manufacturers of traditionally
produced Victorian reproduction floor tiles. Many of their
designs have been influenced
by the work of people such as
William Morris and William
de Morgan.*

Castelnau Tiles
175 Church Road
Barnes
London SW13 9R
*A good selection of reproduc-
tion Victorian tiles is always
held in stock. A complete tile-
fixing service is also available
to customers.*

**Kenneth Clark
Ceramics**
The North Wing
Southover Grange
Southover Road
Lewes
East Sussex BN7 1TP
*Manufacturers and stockists of
an extensive selection of tiles,
all made to a high standard.
Designs are taken from origi-
nal Victorian tiles. Genuine
Victorian tiles are also avail-
able from stock.*

Fired Earth
Twyford Mill
Oxford Road
Adderbury
Oxfordshire OX17 3HP
*Specialist stockists and suppli-
ers of an enormous selection of
both terra-cotta and encaustic
floor tiles.*

**The Hardwood
Flooring Company**
Canada House
Blackwood Road
West Hampstead
London NW6 1RZ
*A company carrying a very
large stock of both new and
reclaimed floors made from
such hardwoods as oak, ash,
beech, maple, teak and
mahogany, as well as pitch
pine floorboards.*

Interior Ceramics
3 York Street
Twickenham
Middlesex TW1 3JZ
*A comprehensive selection of
ceramic tiles, marble, terra-
cotta and slate is held in stock.
Specialists in Victorian reproduction and hand-painted tiles
and panels.*

**H. & R. Johnson Tiles
Ltd**
Highgate Tile Works
Tunstall
Stoke on Trent
Staffordshire T6 4JX
*A specialist company operat-
ing a small encaustic tile
department, which will under-
take commissions to match
and replace worn or damaged
existing tiles.*

Marston and Langinger
192 Ebury Street
London SW1N 8UP
*Stockists of a wide selection of
tiles that are suitable for all
styles of Victorian house.
Traditional floor grilles, of the
type used in underfloor heating, are also available.*

Original Style
Falcon Road
Sowton Industrial Estate
Exeter
Devon EX2 7LF
*All types of tiles are produced,
based on Victorian designs.*

Paris Ceramics
543 Battersea Park Road
London SW11
*A selection of terrazzo tiles
that can create black and white
patterns. Also stocks unglazed
decorated floor tiles.*

Dennis Ruabon Ltd
Hafod Tileries
Ruabon
Wrexam
Clwyd LL14 6ET
*Manufacturers of a wide selec-
tion of tiles, including many
traditional "paver" shapes
such as "bats", "sinters" and
"quoins". These can be
arranged and laid to create an
extensive range of geometric
tiling patterns.*

Scandafloor
Lytham St Annes
Lancashire
*Oak floors fitted to existing
concrete, asphalt or wood sub-
floors. Plank, strip or parquet
designs can be accommodated.*

Victorian Woodworks
139 Church Walk
London N16
*A company specializing in the
laying, sanding, sealing and
polishing of every type of
wooden floor. Also undertakes
the restoration of old floors.*

USA
Designs in Tile
PO Box 358
Mount Chasta
California 96067
*Custom hand-decorated tiles
in traditional historic patterns,
especially English and
American Arts and Crafts
and Victorian transfer.*

**Historic Floors of
Oshkosh**
PO Box 572
Oshkosh
Wisconsin 54902
*Parquetry blocks and floor
borders beautifully crafted from
Wisconsin styles taken from
houses built between 1880
and 1920.*

H. & R. Johnson Tiles
410 West 53rd Street
Apt 728
New York 10019
*Stockists of Victorian wall and
floor tiles. Encaustic and geometric tiles, ideal for restoration work, also supplied.*

Kentucky Wood Floors
4200 Reservoir Avenue
Louisville
Kentucky 40213
*A full line of hardwood floor-
ing available, with an emphasis on custom reproductions.*

**The Victorian
Collection**
North American Sales
190 Highway 18
East Brunswick
New Jersey 08816
*A specialist company carrying
an exclusive collection of
glazed ceramic tiles, as well as
geometric floor tiles.*

AUSTRALIA
Ammolite
18 Grattan Street
Prahran
Victoria
*All types and styles of carpets
made to order*

The City Tiler
252 Moray Street
South Melbourne
Victoria

Classic Ceramics
93 Queensbridge Street
South Melbourne
Victoria

Hawthorn Design & Decor
Corner Auburn Road &
Burwood Road
Hawthorn
Victoria

Olde English Tile Company
73-79 Parramatta Road
Camperdown
New South Wales

St James Furnishings
142 Burwood Road
Hawthorn
Victoria

Tascot Templeton
119 Church Street
Richmond
Victoria

Tesselated and Victorian Tile Centre
18 High Street
Glen Iris
Victoria 3146
Specialist company dealing in Victorian interior and exterior tesselated tiles. Antique wall and border, capping, printed and embossed tiles are also available from stock.

NEW ZEALAND
Morris and James Ltd
Box 77
Matakana
North Auckland
Stockists and suppliers of both wall and bench tiles in a wide range of high-gloss colours. A selection of rich-coloured terracotta floor tiles is also available from stock.

LIGHTING

UK
Christopher Wray Lighting
600 Kings Road
London SW6 2DX
There are at present more than one dozen stores across the country stocking one of the largest selections of lighting equipment and accessories in the UK. The overwhelming majority of the designs are taken from traditional sources, and all are made to an exceptionally high standard of finish and craftsmanship.

Concorde Ceramics
BAF Industries
230 Leigham Court Road
London SW16 2RB
Available through selected shops, these ceramic light switches can be matched with door knobs and finger plates.

End of the Day Lighting Company
44 Parkway
London NW1
Stockists of traditional lighting of all kinds, with a selection of Victorian-style shades and fittings to choose from. The designs include ceiling pendants, wall brackets and table and desk lamps.

Forbes and Lomax Ltd
205b St John's Hill
London SW11 1TH
Suppliers of light switches made of thin bevelled perspex and a brass dolly switch. Ideal to place over wallpaper material or a paint finish. Other mounts are also available.

Fritz Fryer Decorative Antique Lighting
12 Brookend Street
Ross on Wye
Herefordshire HR9 7EG
A shop specializing in decorative antique lighting, especially 1850s-1920s. An advisory planning and fitting service is available.

Kensington Lighting Company
34 and 59 Kensington
Church Street
London W8 4HA
Traditional lighting specialists in handmade lampshades, crystal chandeliers and lamp bases. Restorations and conversions are undertaken.

David Malik and Son Ltd
112 Kensington Church
Street
London W8 4EW
Reproduction chandeliers and antique restoration.

Olivers Lighting Company
6 The Broadway
Crockenhill
Swanley
Kent BR8 8JH
Suppliers of period light switches, in brass, oak or mahogany. Available in single, double or quadruple units.

Stiffkey Lamp Shop
Nells Road
Stiffkey
Townsend
Norfolk NR23 1AJ
This shop specializes in the conversion of original Victorian gas lamps into electrically operating ones. As well, it stocks a wide and completely unique selection of antique lamps. New lights can also be faithfully reproduced from old designs.

Sugg Lighting Ltd
65 Gatwick Road
Crawley
West Sussex RH10 2YU
Manufacturers of both external and internal gas and electric lighting, all in traditional Victorian styles. The company also undertakes the refurbishment of all types of light fittings and mountings.

Victor (UK)
172 Station Road
Westcliffe on Sea
Essex SS0 7SN
Stockists of the the Switchcraft selection of touch-sensitive dimmer switches, which combine a solid brass sensor plate with a wooden back plate in a choice of six finishes.

USA
Aunt Sylvia's Victorian Collections
PO Box 67364
Chestnut Hill
Massachusetts 02167
Makers of Victorian-style lamps, handblown and painted in traditional designs. Reproductions of museum pieces are also undertaken by commission.

Brass 'n Bounty
68 Front Street
Marblehead
Massachusetts 01945
Using genuine antique glass light and lamp shades, this specialist company undertakes the complete restoration of all types of gas and electric chandeliers, as well as wall sconces and floor lamps.

Classic Accents
12869 Eureka
South Gate
Missouri 48195
Manufacturer of a range of reproduction push button light switches, inlaid with mother-of-pearl.

Conant Custom Brass Inc.
270 Pine Street
Burlington
Vermont 05401
Stockists and suppliers of solid-brass light fixtures and fittings. Brass restoration and repair work of old lights is also undertaken.

Fantasy Lighting Inc.
7126 Melrose Avenue
Los Angeles
California 90046
Specialists in Victorian fabric and glass shades with bases. Also floor and table lamps. Shades are available with fringes or beads.

Hexagram Antiques
2247 Rohnerville Road
Fortuna
California 95540
A specialist source of genuine antique lighting fixtures and accessories. A large selection of brass reproduction desk lamps, sconces and chandeliers is also carried. The restoration, rewiring and polishing of old lights is undertaken on behalf of customers.

Historical Lighting Restoration
10341 Jewell Lake City
Fenton
Michigan 48430
This company provides a mail-order service for all types of lighting restoration work. Old gas and electric lights are undertaken, offering brass polishing, lacquering and the electrical conversion of old gas lamps. Handcrafted reproductions are also stocked.

Kings Chandelier Co.
PO Box 667
Eden
North Carolina 27288
Sourced directly from the designers — Swarosky Strass — are original designs of all crystal chandeliers and sconces. Victorian reproductions of solid brass with Venetian crystals can also be supplied.

Old Lamplighter Shop
The Musical Museum
Deansboro
New York 13328
A full restoration service is provided, mainly of old oil lamps of c1880. Painted china shades to match bases are also available.

The Renovator's Supply Inc.
9110 Renovators Old Mill
Millers Falls
Massachusetts 01349
A wide variety of lighting fixtures and switch plates.

Victorian Lighting Works Inc.
251 S. Pennsylvania
Avenue
PO Box 469
Centre Hall
Pennsylvania 16828
Beautiful handcrafted reproductions of Victorian electric- and gas-style chandeliers, wall sconces, pendants.

AUSTRALIA
Antique Decor
899 High Street
Armadale
Victoria

Recollections Solid Brass
Showrooms: 550-554
North Road
Ormond
Melbourne
Victoria
and: 44 Enoggera Terrace
Red Hill
Brisbane
Queensland
Other branches in Perth, Sydney and Cairns.

NEW ZEALAND
ECC Lighting
Showrooms: 39 Nugent
Street
Grafton
Auckland
and: 129 Adelaide Road
Wellington
and: **Accent Lighting**
Christchurch
A wide selection of pendants, brackets, lamps etc.

GLASS

UK
Architectural Antiques
Showroom: 36 New End
Square
Hampstead
London NW3
Shops: 1 Church Street
Marylebone
London NW8
and: 81 Abbey Road
St Johns Wood
London NW8
Specialists in the design and fabrication of stained-glass windows.

Philip Bradbury
83 Blackstock Road
London N4 2JW
Authentic 19th-century designs faithfully etched onto new glass.

The Original Box Sash Window Company
Freepost 28
Windsor
Berkshire SL4 1BR
Any original customer's design can be copied and installed. All units are crafted in solid pine. Single- or double-glazed units can be supplied.

Sashy & Sashy
5 Phoenix Lane
Ashurst Wood
East Grinstead
West Sussex RH19 3RA
Specialist company dealing in sash window restoration and replacements. It is also a suppliers of sash window furniture, such as weights, cords, pulleys and so on.

Stained Glass Supplies
41 Kingsland Road
London E2
Suppliers of both etched and stained glass, using original designs and patterns.

The Victorian Stained Glass Company
83 Stamford Hill
London N16 5TP
This company specializes in the creation of Victorian-style stained, painted and other types of glass decoration for use in windows, screen doors and rooflights.

USA
Delphi Stained Glass
2116 East Michigan
Avenue
Lansing
Missouri 48912
Manufacturers, suppliers and stockists of both stained and bevelled glass, lamp bases, patterns and books.

Golden Age Glassworks
339 Bellvale Road
Warwick
New York 10990
Suppliers of genuine antique and stained-glass windows and doors. It also undertakes the design and manufacture of leaded and stained glass for windows, skylights, doors etc, according to customers' own specifications.

Professional Stained Glass Guild
PO Box 69
Brewster
New York 10509
This organization publishes a full colour magazine every month. Also stockists of Art Glass lamps.

Victorian Stained Glass Illusions
PO Box 931
Marinette
Wisconsin 54143
Specialists in the application of appliqué to the inside of windows A selection of several designs and borders are available, which can be adapted and cut to size to fit different-sized windows.

AUSTRALIA
Aesthetic Leadlight Studio
103 Church Street
Hawthorn
Melbourne
A specialist company providing a service in the matching of designs and original glass. Authentic restorations and repairs are undertaken. The company also buys old glass and leadlight.

Steptoes Renovation Supplies
112 Rokeby Street
Collingwood
Victoria
A specialist company concentrating on the restoration of leaded windows.

COLLECTABLES

Suppliers for this book:
The Antique Traders
357 Upper Street
Camden Passage
London N1
Stockists and suppliers of a wide range of Arts and Crafts furniture and carpets.

Arenski
Stand 107
Grays Antique Market
58 Davies Street
London W1Y 1LB
A fascinating and varied selection of genuine antique glass, commemorative ware of different descriptions and styles and other decorative accessories, including papier mâché, boxes and decorative houseplant pottery containers.

Kate Bannister
The Angel Arcade
Camden Passage
London N1
A fine collection of antique and decorative accessories, including boxes carried in stock.

N. Bloom & Son
40/41 Conduit Street
London W1
A wide-ranging selection of genuine antique decorative accessories. Antique jewellery also available.

Nicolaus Boston
Antique Centre
58-60 Kensington Church Street
London W8 4DB
A specialist collection of decorative houseplant pottery containers and jardinières, including majolica.

Britannia
Grays Antique Market
58 Davies Street
London W1
A selection of china and porcelain spanning many different periods. A collection of majolica and commemorative ware is also stocked.

Cork Brick Antiques
6 Earsham Street
Bungay
Suffolk
A specialist shop concentrating on collecting antique dolls' houses and accessories.

Richard Dennis
144 Kensington Church Street
London W8
Exclusive English studio pottery.

The Dining Room Shop
64 White Hart Lane
Barnes
London SW13
A wide selection of genuine antique dining-room furniture, glassware and other forms of decorative accessories is always held in stock.

Brian Douglas
Vaults 12-14
London Silver Vaults
Chancery Lane
London WC2A 1QS
Stockists and suppliers of antique tableware and flat-ware. Also decorative commemorative ware.

Nicole Fabre
28 Bell Street
Romsey
Hampshire SO51 8GW
Non-specialist stockist of general antiques, including a range of bed linen.

Fothergill & Crowley
D11/12 Chenil Galleries
181-183 Kings Road
London SW3
A wide selection of period costumes and antique fabrics, including a range of bed linen.

Gallery of Antique Costume & Textiles
2 Church Street
Marylebone
London NW8 8ED
Specialist antique shop concentrating on fabrics and costumes from different periods.

Thomas Goode
19 South Audley Street
London W1
A selection of period china and porcelain is always available from stock.

Nicholas Harris
564 Kings Road
London SW6
A collection of aesthetic and Oriental silverware.

Hope and Glory
131A Kensington Church Street
London W8 7LP
Specialist stockists of royal commemorative ware of different styles.

E. & C.T. Koopman & Son Ltd
The London Silver Vaults
Chancery House
53-64 Chancery Lane
London WC2A 1QX
A wide-ranging collection of antique silverware from which to choose.

The Lacquer Chest
75 Kensington Church Street
London W8
Specialists in period china and porcelain. Also decorative accessories, including découpage, held in stock.

Judith Lassale
7 Pierrepont Arcade
Camden Passage
London N1 8EF
A fascinating collection of antique toys.

Joan Latford
Stand No: G005/6
Alfies Antique Market
13-25 Church Street
London NW8
A good selection of genuine Victorian glass and china from which to choose.

Ann Lingard
Rope Walk Antiques
Rye
East Sussex
A specialist collection of china and porcelain from different periods.

Lunn Antiques
86 New Kings Road
London SW6 4LU
A source of both pre-War and antique fabrics, including a range of bed linen.

Linda Morgan Antiques
26 The Mall
Camden Passage
London N1OPD
A collection of decorative antique accessories, including a range of scent bottles.

Sue Norman
L4 Antiquarius
135 Kings Road
London SW3
A range of decorative blue and white transferware.

Jacqueline Oosthuizen
23 Cale Street
London SW3
Antique china and porcelain, including Staffordshire ware.

Powell & Mathers
Antiques
571 Kings Road
London SW6
A good selection of antique toys carried in stock.

Raffles
40/42 Church Street
London NW8 6DR
Antiques and decorative arts, including boxes.

Rogers de Rin
76 Royal Hospital Road
London SW3
Antique china, including majolica. Also decorative accessories, including papier mâché and table linen.

Royal Doulton
167 Piccadilly
London W1
Main stockists of Royal Doulton china.

The Shaker Shop
25 Harcourt Street
London W1
Specialist stockists of Shaker furniture and gifts.

Manfred Schotten
The Crypt
109 High Street
Burford
Oxford
Oxfordshire
An unusual shop with a stock entirely devoted to genuine Victorian sporting equipment. Every sport (cricket, croquet, golf, fishing, etc) is catered for.

Vic Schuler
94 Syon Lane
Isleworth
Middlesex TW7 59Q
Non-specialist stockists of general antiques, as well as such decorative accessories as Toby jugs.

Jean Sewell (Antiques) Ltd
3 Camden Street
Off Kensington Church Street
London W8 7EP
A collection of antiques, including china, from a range of different periods.

Keith Skeel Antiques
Showroom: 94-98 High Street
Islington
London N1 8EG
Non-specialist stockists of general antiques and decorative accessories.

Robert Stephenson
1 Elyston Street
London SW3
A specialist stockist of genuine antique carpets, with a good range from which to choose.

S. & J. Stodel
Vault 24
London Silver Vaults
Chancery Lane
London WC2A 1QS
A specialist shop concentrating on English and Chinese silverware of different periods.

Tobias & The Angel
68 White Hart Lane
Barnes
London SW13
A good selection of antique furniture and decorative accessories, including jugs and containers, fabrics and a range of bed linen.

Mark J. West
39B High Street
Wimbledon Village
London SW19
Shop specializing in antique glass, including scent bottles.

Agnes Wilton
5 Gateway Arcade
Camden Passage
355 Upper Street
Antique decorative accessories, including scent bottles.

XS Baggage Company
Antiquarius Antique Centre
137 Kings Road
London SW1
A good range of antique travel and sporting goods.

Basia Zarzycka
Stand E3
Chenil Galleries
181-183 Kings Road
London SW3
A collection of Victorian decorative accessories.

BATHROOM FIXTURES & FITTINGS

UK
W. Adams & Sons
Unit 5-6
Credenda Road
Bromfield Road Industrial Estate
West Bromwich
West Midlands B70 7JE
Old-style faucets or taps.

Armitage Shanks Bathrooms
Armitage
Rugeley
Staffordshire WS15 4BT
Supplier of a vast and varied selection of items. Some are Victorian designs made by Edward Jones from more than a century ago. There are also many decorated suites, corner bathtubs, bidets, faucets or taps, showers and other bathroom accessories.

Bathroom Trading Company
Unit 1A
Kempshott Park
Basingstoke
Hampshire RG23 7LP
Major importer with over 250 stockists in the UK. Traditional designs, including complementary accessories, corner washstands and vanity units.

The Bespoke Basin and Bathroom Company
Unit 128
Riverside Business Centre
Haldane Place
Wandsworth
London SW18 4UQ
Stockists and suppliers of sinks or basins and bathtubs in traditional styles. Items can be painted to suit customers' own specifications

Bristol Bathroom Company
Anchor Road
Bristol BS1 5TT
Specialist suppliers of Victorian- and Edwardian-style bathrooms, fixtures and all accessories.

Czech and Speake
39c Jermyn Street
London SW1 6DN
An exclusive selection of sanitaryware, complete with faucets or taps, shower units and accessories. Many period designs are held in stock.

The Imperial Bathroom Company
Imperial Buildings
Northgate Way
Aldridge
Walsall
West Midlands WS9 8SR
Stockists and suppliers of plain and transfer-decorated traditional bathroomware.

Pipe Dreams
72 Gloucester Road
London SW7 4QT
A comprehensive selection of bathtubs and fittings from which to choose. Many of the items are based on authentic Victorian designs.

B. C. Sanitan
Unit 12
Nimrod Way
Reading RG2 0EB
Several traditional selections that can be installed either built-in or free-standing on optional ball and clawfeet.

Sitting Pretty
131 Dawes Road
London SW6 7EA
Began as a supplier of high-quality wooden toilet seats. Made now are in oak, elm, ash, sycamore and beech. Bathroom furniture can be made to order. Also stockists for B. C. Sanitan, Heritage and Czech and Speake.

The Topstock Company
Higher Farm Barn
Milbourne Wick
Sherbourne
Dorset DT9 4PW
Suppliers of traditional-style ceramic chain pulls, the designs for which have been adapted from Victorian lavatory pulls or handles. Several colourways and finishes are available.

Traditional Bathroom Warehouse
92 Carnwath Road
Fulham
London SW6 3HW
and: 270 The Colonade
Waterloo Station
Waterloo Road
London SE1 8SF
and: 103 Regents Park Road
London NW1
Specialists stockists and suppliers of Victorian and Edwardian bathrooms. Selections include roll-top, cast-iron bathtubs with high-level lavatory cisterns. There is also an exclusive range of etched or plain bath screens.

Victorian and Edwardian Bathrooms
Hill House Interiors
Rotunda Buildings
Montpellier Circus
Cheltenham
Gloucestershire
This specialist bathroom showroom stocks products made by B. C. Sanitan, Heritage and others. There are many faucets or taps, wood panels and units from which to choose.

USA
Antique Baths and Kitchens
2220 Carlton Way
Santa Barbara
California 93109
Suppliers of good-quality reproduction plumbing fixtures and accessories for Victorian-style homes. Copper sinks and pull chain toilets are kept in stock.

Besco Plumbing and Heating
729 Atlantic Avenue
Boston
Massachusetts 02111
Victorian-style tubs, sinks, shower systems and heads are always in stock.

The Broadway Collection
250 North Troost
Olathe
Kansas 66061
Suppliers of plumbing and wooden bathroom fixtures, fittings and accessories.

Mac the Antique Plumber
885 57th Street
Sacramento
California 95819
Arguably the largest supply of antique plumbing supplies in the world.

Old Fashion Things
402 SW Evangeline Thrwy
Lafayette
Louisiana 70501
This decorative-plumbing supply company has many different styles of clawfoot bathtubs, commodes, pedestal toilets, faucets or taps and accessories always in stock.

Remodelers and Renovators Supply
PO Box 45478
Boise
Idaho 83711
Suppliers and stockists of reproduction hardware tubs sinks and so on.

Roy Electric Co Inc.
1054 Coney Island Avenue
Brooklyn
New York 11230
Suppliers of clawfoot tubs, brass and chrome showers. A huge selection of hard-to-find parts and accessories is kept permanently in stock.

Vintage Plumbing Bathroom Antiques
9645 Sylvia Avenue
Northridge
California 91324
Ornamental pedestal toilets, bathtubs and showers. Parts and accessories. Everything is antique, no reproductions.

AUSTRALIA
John and Sally Gilberts Timber Bathroom Centre
111 Langridge Street
Collingwood
Victoria 3066
Master cabinet makers specializing in the design and construction of custom-made wooden bathroom furniture.

The Renovation Centre
87 Parramatta Road
Camperdown 2050
A supplier of many different types and designs of bathrooms. Brass sink or basin tops, tiles and many other accessories held in stock.

FABRICS

UK
The Antique Textile Company
100 Portland Road
London W11 4LQ
A varying stock from which can be supplied chintz quilts, printed cottons, Kashmir and paisley shawls.

G. P. & J. Baker Ltd
PO Box 30
West End Road
High Wycombe
Buckinghamshire HP11 2QD
A wide selection of period fabrics taken largely from 18th- and 19th-century original designs. Collections include The National Trust Country House Collection and English Toile Collection.

Percy Bass
188 Walton Street
London SW3
This company stocks a wide and varied selection of fabrics and wallpapers. Upholstery and restoration work is undertaken, and drapes, shades or blinds, cornices or pelmets, bed spreads and bed heads are made according to customers' specifications. An interior design service is available.

Bennison Fabrics Ltd
16 Holbein Place
London SW1 W 8NL
Documented period fabrics, also stocked in the USA.

Bloomers
41 Cheltenham Crescent
Harrogate
North Yorkshire HG1 1DN
Suppliers of genuine antique bedspreads and Honiton and Brussels lace – trimmed runners and small tablecloths. A selection of lace edgings is also available.

Brunschwig & Fils
Chelsea Harbour Drive
London SW10 OXF

Chelsea Green Designs
26 Cale Street
London SW3 3QV
Stockists and suppliers of fine authentic paisley designs.

Cocoa
7 Queens Circus
Montpellier
Cheltenham
Gloucestershire GL50 1RX
Specialists in antique drapes, bedspreads, table linen and small fabric pieces.

The Design Archives
PO Box 1464
Bournemouth BH4 9YQ
and: 79 Walton Street
London SW3 2HP
Originally established by Courtaulds. The reproduction of fine chintzes, late 18th- and 19th-century fabrics are its specialities.

Jason D'Souza
42 Queensland Road
London N7
Creator of exclusive designs which are reproduced on linens, silks and moirés. These designs are stocked nationwide.

Elizabeth Eaton
25a Basil Street
London SW3
Specialist stockists of woven fabric borders.

Anna French Fabrics & Wallpapers
343 Kings Road
London SW3
Suppliers of cotton lace panels, many of which are taken from original 19th-century Victorian designs. Lace designs are also interpreted as prints.

The Gainsborough Silk Weaving Company Ltd
Alexandra Road
Chilton
Sudbury
Suffolk
Manufacturers of high-quality fabrics, including damasks, brocades, plain and striped satins and taffetas.

The Gallery of Antique Costume and Textiles
2 Church Street
London NW8 8ED
Also at Libertys in Regent Street, London. A good selection of bedspreads, quilts and drapes is available.

Marilyn Garrow
6 The Broadway
White Hart Lane
London SW13 ONY
Suppliers and stockists of antique French and English textiles; drapes, table linen and edgings. Lace handkerchiefs and collars are also available from stock.

Hand in Hand
3 North West Circus Place
Edinburgh EH3 6ST
A good selection of embroidered and paisley shawls is usually available. Embroidered bed and table linen, velvet and brocade drapes, quilts, lace and period accessories are also stocked.

Lelievre UK Ltd
16 Berners Street
London W1P 3DD
These fabrics are available worldwide. Superb-quality fabrics; taffetas, toiles, velvets, damasks and brocades in both plain and patterned finishes.

Liberty and Co
Regent Street
London W1
As well as their own designs, which are known worldwide, this famous store sells William Morris and Arts and Crafts textiles. It is also a stockist of many other well known furnishing fabrics.

Lunn Antiques
86 New Kings Road
London SW6 4LU
Stocks of bed linen and drapes are always available.

Iris Martin
Farthing Cottage
Clickers Yard
Yardley Road
Olney
Buckinghamshire MK46 5DX
A maker of bobbin lace and also sells antique and modern lace at modest prices.

Mrs Munro
16 Motcomb Street
London SW1X 8LB
Reproductions of 19th-century prints made on high-quality glazed cottons.

Hodsoll McKenzie
52 Pimlico Road
London SW1 8LP
Production of classic patterns in both fabrics and wallpapers.

Pallu & Lake Group Ltd
Chelsea Garden Market
Chelsea Harbour
London SW10

H. A. Percheron Ltd
97-99 Cleveland Street
London W1P 5PN
*Importers of a large range of
furnishing fabrics and trimmings from around the world.
A varying selection of traditional brocades, damasks and
velours always held in stock.*

Plain Fabrics by Post
PO Box 88
Carterton
Oxfordshire OX18 3YP
*A competitively priced selec-
tion of quality plain and
striped cottons and linens.
The company also sells white
muslin and unbleached calico,
as well as piping cord, pillow
or cushion pads and other
types of haberdashery. A
thread-matching service is also
available if required*

Osborne & Little
49 Temperley Road
London SW12 8QE
*A wide selection of period-
style fabrics and wallpapers.*

Arthur Sanderson
Hundred Acres
Oxford Road
Usbridge
Middlesex UB8 1HY
*Manufacturers of a wide range
of fabrics with adapted period-
style patterns.*

Ian Sanderson
PO Box 148
Newbury
Berkshire
*Supplier of a range of ticking,
other striped fabrics and attrac-
tive fabric borders.*

Janet Shand Kydd
The Green Room
2 Church Street
Framlingham
Woodbridge
Suffolk IP13 9BE
*A good selection of 19th- and
early 20th-century textiles,
quilts, covers and drapes from
which to choose.*

Ron Simpson Textiles
Grays Antique Market
138 Portobello Road
London W11
*Antique patchwork quilts from
North America and England.
Kashmir and paisley shawls.*

Textiles (DMC) Ltd
28 Northfield Industrial
Estate
Berisford Avenue
Wembley
Middlesex HA0 1FR
*A large selection of classical
and traditional damasks from
which to choose.*

Tissunique Ltd
10 Princes Street
Hanover Square
London W1R 7RD
*Importers and wholesalers of a
range of high-quality furnishing fabrics, wallpapers, braids
and trimmings. Also specialists in historic house reproduction work.*

Warner Fabrics
Bradbourne Drive
Tilbrook
Milton Keynes
Buckinghamshire MK7
8BE
*Stockists and suppliers of
reproductions of period fabrics
and wallpapers.*

Zimmer & Rohde
103 Cleveland Street
London W1
*A good range of striking and
distinctive furnishing fabrics.*

Zoffany
63 South Audley Street
London W1
*Specialists in traditional
designs.*

USA
Bailey and Griffin
1406 East Mermaid
Lane
Philadelphia
Pennsylvania 19118

Baker Parkertex
Lee Jofa
800 Central Boulevard
Carl Ftodt
New Jersey 07072

Bennison
73 Spring Street
New York
New York 10012
Fabrics with period patterns.

Brunschwig et Fils
979 Third Avenue
New York
New York 10022-1234
*Stockists of fine fabrics and
wallpapers. Supplier to interi-
or designers of other international houses such as Baker,
Ramm Son & Crocker.*

Clarence House
211 58th Street
New York
New York 10022
*American suppliers of Cole
and Son, Design Archives
and Hodsoll McKenzie.*

Classic Revivals
6th Floor Suite 545
1 Design Centre Place
Boston
Massachusetts 02210
*Suppliers of Houles trims and
other fine fabrics and trimmings, available through
designers and showrooms.
American suppliers of Guy
Evans and Anna French.*

Cowtan and Tout
B & D Building
979 Third Avenue
New York
New York 10022
*Designs are available nation-
wide through selected stockists.
Their high-class fabrics are
based on traditional and origi-
nal designs. Also American
suppliers of fabrics from sources
such as Jane Churchill,
Colefax and Fowler, Design
Archives, Gainsborough Silk
Weaving Co.*

The Fabric Centre
485 Electric Avenue
Fitchburg
Massachusetts 01420
*Suppliers of value fabrics for
home decorating, sold and
supplied by mail, at approximately 25-50% below aver-
age national retail prices.*

Homespun Fabrics
PO Box 323
Ventura
California 93006
*Suppliers of extra wide, 10ft
(2.5m), 100% cotton fabrics
for use in making seamless
draperies, wallcoverings and
upholstery.*

Christopher Hyland
979 Third Avenue
Suite 1714
New York
New York 10022
*American supplier of fabrics
from sources such as
Alexander Beauchamp Watts
& Co and Zoffany.*

Liberty
Rockefeller Centre
5th Avenue
New York
New York 10020

Linen and Lace
4 Lafayette Street
Washington
Missouri 63090
*Importers of a good range of
Scottish lace drapes, all of
which have been recreated
from authentic historical patterns. Also stockists and suppliers of Nottingham and
Bavarian lace lengths.*

London Lace
167 Newbury Street
Boston
Massachusetts 02116
*A large and varying selection
of reproduction lace panels and
yardage, based on designs of
c1840-1920.*

**Marlene's Decorator
Fabrics**
301 Beech Street
Hackensack
New Jersey 07601
*Suppliers of first-class quality
decorator fabrics, at a fraction
of the average national retail
cost.*

Osborne & Little
979 Third Avenue
New York
NY 10022
*Patterns faithfully reproduced
from period designs, for fabrics
and wallpapers.*

Arthur Sanderson
Suite 403
979 Third Avenue
New York
NY 10022

**Schumacher
International Ltd**
939 Third Avenue
New York
New York 10022
*Fabrics and wallpapers with
documented period patterns.*

Warner
The Warner Company
108 S Desplaines
Chicago
Illinois 60606
Showroom: 6-136 The
Merchandise Mart
Chicago
*A wide range of fabrics, wall-
coverings and borders.*

Waverly
Dept. 1
PO Box 5114
Farmingdale
New York 11736-5114
*A range of toile, cotton chintz
and tartan pattern fabrics.*

York
Linden Avenue
York
Pennsylvania 17404
*Stockists of their own selection
of fabrics, wallcoverings and
decorative accessories, as well
as other designs from which to
make selections.*

Zimmer & Rhode
41 East 11th Street
New York
New York

AUSTRALIA
Boyac
259c Auburn Road
Hawthorn
Victoria
New South Wales

St James Furnishings
88 Burwood Road
Hawthorn
Victoria
New South Wales

Wardlaws
230 Auburn Road
Hawthorn
Victoria
New South Wales

NEW ZEALAND
**James Dunlop &
Company**
Available through home
furnishing specialists in
Christchurch,
Wellington and Auckland.
*Selection of fabrics, either co-
ordinating or contrasting.*

SOFT FURNISHINGS

UK
**Elizabeth Bradley
Designs Ltd**
1 West End
Beaumaris
Anglesey
North Wales LL58 8BD
*A well known designer of a
range of different needlework
kits. The Victorian collection,
for example, is based on completely original designs and
contains everything necessary
to complete the making of each
item. Rugs, pillows or cushions and panels all feature in
the catalogue.*

**Arthur Browns'
Number Three**
64 Fulham High Street
London SW6
*Ornate finials are a specialty
of this company.*

Byron and Byron Ltd
4 Hanover Yard
off Noel Road
London N1 8BE
*Poles and finials made in a
variety of different styles and
finishes. Poles are available in
mahogany, ash, matt black,
beech, and others. Finials
include those from the
Imperial Collection and the
Biedermeir Collection.*

Cope and Timmins
Angel Road Works
Angel Road
London N18 3AY
*Suppliers and stockists of brass
and wooden poles, finials and
all fittings and accessories
needed for installation.*

**Wendy A. Cushing
Designs**
14 Ingestre Place
London W1R 3LP
*A specialist supplier of passe-
menterie materials. A vast
selection of every type and
style of braid, tassel and trim-
ming held in stock. All are
made by hand using high-
quality materials to the customers' own specifications.*

Distinctive Trimmings
17 Church Street
London W8 4LF
*A specialist supplier of all
kinds of different furnishing
trimmings, as well as related
fixtures and fittings.*

J.W.B. Drennan Ltd
Unit 67
Abbey Business Centre
15-16 Ingate Place
London SW8
*Experts in the re-upholstering
and making of drapes and
general soft furnishings.
Specialists for historical projects, as well as for cutting and
customized drapery. Complete
carpentry poles and tracking
systems are also supplied.*

Guy Evans
51a Cleveland Street
London W1P 5PQ
*Trade suppliers only of high-
class trimmings, tassels,
braids, rosettes etc.*

Laura Ashley Home
7-9 Harriet Street
London SW1
and selected branches
*Suppliers and stockists of
poles, finials and fittings in a
wide variety of styles.*

Mirror Image
Studio 15
Sulivan Business Centre
Sulivan Road
London SW6
A good and varied selection of stock, from which to choose suitable poles and fixtures and fittings.

J.T. Morgan
Shop 28
Chepstow Corner
Chepstow Place
London W2
This shop is a unique supplier and stockist of unusual haberdashery goods. Much of the stock to be found there has been bought up from redundant wholesalers, and there are many items that have been in the shop since it first started trading at the turn of the century. Trimmings, ribbons, braids, buttons, cords, silk twists and so on. All of these items can be purchased in small quantities. Services provided include pleating, dyeing and button making.

McKinney Kidstone
1 Wandon Road
London SW6
A large selection of poles, rosettes, coronas, brackets and other fixtures and fittings are available from which to choose. A mail-order service is also provided and special commissions are taken.

Henry Newman
18 Newman Street
London W1P 4AB
Trade suppliers only. A wide variety of different styles of trimmings, fringes, braids and tassels is held in stock.

Resina Designs
Unit 1
Fairseat Workshops
Chewstoke
Near Bristol BS18 8XF
A brochure is available for the collection of finials, brackets and bracket decorations. Viewing is possible by appointment only.

V. V. Rouleaux
201 Kings Road
London SW6 4SR
This is the only shop in the country to specialize exclusively in ribbons. Antique, silk, organza, lace, checks and tartans are all available, and the selection is extensive.

Sadlers
3 Gerald Mews
Gerald Road
London SW1
Major international interior designers and decorators use this exclusively trade-only drapemaker. All drapes are made by hand to the customer's own specifications. High-quality valances, swags, drapes and pelmets are all made to order.

Neil Shepherd
9 The Frame
Basildon
Essex SS15 5JZ
A soft-furnishing specialist. Swags and tails, drapes, coronas and various other specific customer requirements are all catered for.

The Silk Shop
31A Rivers Street
Bath
Avon
An extensive selection of braids, cords, fringes and tassels are all stocked and supplied. Lampshades and fabrics can be matched with trimmings, or dyed to match if this is necessary.

Smith and Brighty
184 Walton Street
London SW3 2JL
Suppliers of tassled tie-backs, all made specifically to customers' orders.

Tempus Stet Ltd
Trinity Business Centre
305–309 Rotherhithe Street
London SE16 1EY
An extensive range of drape accessories is held in stock, including tie-backs and coronas and so on.

Turnell and Gigon Ltd
Room G/04
250 Kings Road
London SW3 5UE
Suppliers and stockists of an excellent and varied selection of trimmings in many colours and styles, by Passementerie of France.

Varia Textiles
43 Acre Road
Kingston upon Thames
Surrey KT2 6EK
A large selection of brass tie-backs may be ordered. A mail-order-only service is provided however.

Vigo Carpet Gallery
6a Vigo Street
London W1
Suppliers of handstitched rugs made from original designs, many of which were produced by William Morris and others in the 19th-century Arts and Crafts movement.

USA
The Antique Quilt Source
385 Springview Road
Carlisle
Pennsylvania 17013-9405
A unique source of supply of antique quilts from the state of Pennsylvania. All are offered for sale in excellent condition. Prices vary considerably but the quality is reliable and of a high standard.

Bedroom Secrets
310E Military
Fremont
Nebraska 68025
Suppliers and stockists of a wide and varying collection of comforters, window treatments, fabrics and accessories, at discount prices.

J. R. Burrows and Company
PO Box 522
Rockland
Massachusetts 02370
Historical design merchandizers holding a good selection of Nottingham lace drapes from which to choose. Aesthetic movement wallpapers and fabrics are also held in stock. Other stock items include a range of William Morris design Axminster carpets, custom-woven Victorian Wilton and Brussels carpets and runners.

Country Curtains
Red Lion Inn
Stockbridge
Massachusetts 01262

From the Heartland
PO Box 2532
Gig Harbour
Washington 98335
A range of handmade lace doilies, runners, tablecloths, pillows or cushions.

Heirloom Rugs
28 Harlem Street
Rumford
Rhode Island 02916
Printed hooked rug patterns from chair size to room size.

Linen Lady
5360 High Street
Sacramento
California 95819
Specialist stockists and suppliers of fine lace drapes and other handmade items.

Paradise Mills Inc.
PO Box 2488
Dalton
Georgia 30722
Carpets and custom rugs designs available to the general public at direct-from-the-mill prices. Free samples and quotes can be provided on request.

Rue de France
78 Thames Street
Newport
Rhode Island 02840
Specialist suppliers and stockists of lace drapes, table runners, pillows or cushions and many other items.

Victorian House
320 Townline Avenue
Beloit
Wisconsin 53511
A wide and varying selection of antique certificates and authentic Victorian drapes.

Vintage Valances
PO Box 43326V
Cincinnati
Ohio 45243
Specialist suppliers of authentic period drapery, custom made to customers' own specifications. Research work on styles and designs is also undertaken on request.

AUSTRALIA
Claire Edmonds Quilts
PO Box 446
Edgecliff
New South Wales 2027
Suppliers of an extensive range of country-style quilts, patchwork quilts and woven throws.

Country Quilts and Curtains
Alexandra Street
Berry 2535
and: 838 King Georges Road
South Hurstville 2221
Specialists in individually designed quilts, bedspreads and drapes, made to measure and to complement the customer's decor. An exclusive selection of handmade and traditional quilts to choose from.

Functional Decor
112 High Street
South Kew
Victoria 3101
Specialist stockists and suppliers of traditional furnishings. Items always carried in stock include swags, drapes, shades or blinds and bedspreads. Colour schemes and customer advisory service offered.

Heritage Lace
99 Denmark Street
Kew
Victoria 3101
Suppliers of a range of lace panels by mail.

Linen and Lace of Balmain
213 Darling Street
Balmain
New South Wales 2041
Specialist shop concentrating on the supply of antique table linen, runners, pillowcases and similar items.

Marco Fabrics
155 Auburn Road
Hawthorn
Victoria
A wide and varying selection of antique certificates and authentic Victorian drapes.

Morris Home and Garden Wares
Shop 8
376 Victoria Avenue
Chatswood
New South Wales 2067
Stocks a wide selection of tassels and braids, throws and other soft furnishings.

Patchwork House
77 Church Street
Hawthorn
Victoria 3122
Major Melbourne supplier of Liberty fabrics, stocking all the Liberty cottons, silks and voiles. Imported pure Swiss cotton lace. All items stocked for the home patchworker; classe held in patchwork, fabric stencilling and quilting.

Potpourri
4–10 Yorkshire Street
Richmond
Victoria

St James Furnishings
142 Burwood Road
Hawthorn
Victoria

Wardlaw
230–232 Auburn Road
Hawthorn
Victoria

Wilson Showcase
PO Box 6430
St Kilda Road
Central Melbourne 3004
Victoria

NEW ZEALAND
Miss Beatrice Brown & Company
454 Mt Eden Road
Mt Eden
and: 263 Ponsonby Road
Shore City
Takapuna
Major stockists of a wide and varying range of traditional tapestries, solid colours and speciality throws. A range of screen-printed floor mats is also available.

Gallery
394 Remuera Road
Pox 28-098
Remuera
Auckland
Stockists of a range of rugs and antique and decorative fabrics of different periods.

Hollyhocks
190 Queen Street
Auckland City
White table linen, tablecloths and napkins. Pillow or cushions, duvet covers, starched sheets and pillowcases, crisp white lace. Mail order only.

Takapuna
Corner of Hurstmere Road
and Anzac Street
Auckland
Rugs and antique fabrics.

WALLPAPERS & PAINTS

UK
Baer and Ingram Wallpapers
273 Wandsworth Bridge Road
London SW6
Stocking more than 4,000 reproduction historical wallpapers, this specialist shop offers a unique service for the customer searching for a very specific decor. The samples appear in books, display boards and boxes and are split into colour and style instead of manufacturer. Guidelines are provided to help the customer decide the best design for his or her interior, taking into account both the property's age and location.

Alexander Beauchamp
1 Church Street
Douglas
Isle of Man
Design and hand-print wallpapers for exacting customer requirements, including precise character reproductions of historical designs and colourings. The Archibald Knox collection consists of designs by Knox for Liberty & Co., which were produced at around the turn of the century. Many fine examples 19th-century dado papers can also be seen.

Bio-Fa Natural Paints
5 School Road
Kidlington
Oxford
Specialist stockists and suppliers of a wide selection of emulsions, oil paints, varnishes, limewashes and silicate paints (for exterior use). All of these products are guaranteed to be made from completely natural raw materials, such as essential oils, resins and plant pigment extracts.

Jane Churchill
135 Sloane Street
London SW1
Using old and traditional designs, this company specializes in producing wallpapers and fabrics of a high and distinctive standard.

Cole & Son (Wallpapers) Ltd
PO Box 4BU
18 Mortimer Street
London W1A 4BU
Using original archive materials from the 18th century as its source, this company has assembled a wide selection of different wallpapers, borders and fabrics. A range of facsimiles of late-Victorian dado papers are also held in stock. The company is also a specialist in period-style paints and powder pigments.

Colefax & Fowler
39 Brook Street
London W1
This well-established company specializes in a range of traditional English wallpapers and chintzes, using predominantly 18th- and 19th-century designs. To complement these are many types of trompe-l'oeil wallpaper borders, braids, ropes and gothic braids.

Cornelissen & Son Ltd
105 Great Russell Street
London WC1B 3RY
This company specializes in the manufacture and supply of an extensive range of period-type paints and powder pigments for use in older-style homes. They are manufacturers of a wide selection of paints, designed both for internal and external use.

Crown Paints Berger Europe Ltd
PO Box 37
Crown House
Hollins Road
Darwen
Lancashire BB3 OBG
These internationally known manufacturers produce an extensive selection of paints, designed for both internal and external use. They also supply to their many retail outlets a range of period-style embossed Anaglypta and Lincrusta papers.

Cy-Près
14 Bells Close
Brigstock
Kettering
Northants
Makers of traditional soft distemper in a range of 24 colours, manufactured using entirely natural earth pigments. "Historical Lead Paints" are also available in any colour, made specifically to customers' requirements.

Design Archives
79 Walton Street
London SW3 2HP
A fascinating range of different paint finishes.

Green and Stone
259 Kings Road
London SW3 5EL
Specialist suppliers and stockists of a wide selection of different decorating materials, including such products as crackle varnish, stencils and glazes.

Hamilton & Weston
18 St Mary's Grove
Richmond
Surrey TW9 1UY
This company specializes in reproductions of both 18th- and 19th-century wallpapers. Of particular interest is the St James Collection, which comprises wallpapers from the late-Victorian period.

Heart of the Country
Home Farm
Swinfen
Near Lichfield
Staffordshire
Specialist suppliers and stockists of a wide range of American period-style paints. As well as being manufacturers of "Williamsburg" Buttermilk paint colours, they are also suppliers of "Old Village" – a range of ready mixed paint colours, which are quality oil-based paints ideal for either interior or for exterior use.

National Trust
c/o Farrow and Ball
Vodens Trading Estate
Wimborne
Dorset
This paint selection is available in a choice of 57 different colourways and in seven paint types.

Nutshell Natural Paints
10 High Street
Totnes
Devon
Stockists and suppliers of the "Natural Colour System", which is manufactured entirely from environmentally friendly natural raw materials. Emulsions and wall and ceiling paints are available in basic white, to which can be mixed a whole range of earth and mineral pigments and water. The result is a subtle range consisting of many different shades and hues.

John Oliver Ltd
33 Pembridge Road
London W11 3HG
This company provides a specialist service, reproducing wallpaper by matching a client's own design or sample. Also held in stock is the extensive range of De Havilland papers.

Osborne & Little
304-308 Kings Road
London SW3 5UH
A selection of wallpapers and other finishes in many bold floral designs from which to choose, taken from both 18th- and 19th-century papers and fabrics. Specialist shops are stockists nationwide. A vast selection of fabrics, wallpapers borders, trimmings and other accessories provide an excellent selection.

Papers and Paints
4 Park Walk
London SW10
A large selection including 112 colours in the "Historic Range" and distempers in 28 colours. A colour-matching service is offered.

Pine Brush Products
Coton Clanford
Staffordshire
"Colourman" water-based paints in 19 colours, reproducing an 18th- and 19th-century buttermilk paint effect.

Ramm Son & Crocker Ltd
13-14 Treadway Tech Centre
Treadway Hill
Loudwater
High Wycombe
Buckinghamshire HP10 9PE
A company that specializes in the reproduction of original papers, mainly from the 19th century.

Rose of Jericho
Old Lodge
Brigstock Parks
Kettering
Northants
Traditional soft distemper, render, limewash, lead-based oil paint mixed to match specific historical decors.

Arthur Sanderson
52 Berners Street
London W1
A wide selection of hand-printed wallpapers, many designed by William Morris. Fabrics to match and co-ordinate are also available. Nationwide stockists.

Watts & Company
7 Tufton Street
Westminster
London SW1P 3QE
A company that has been a family business for more than a hundred years has a unique collection of Victorian Gothic designs. The "Hoar Cross Collection" is a book of hand-printed wallpapers selected from the original diaper patterns designed by Pugin and G. F. Bodley. Papers can be coloured to customer specification. A sumptuous selection of woven damasks, tapestries and velvets is also available, as are braids, fringes and other trimmings and accessories.

USA

Ace Hardware
Corporation
2200 Kensington Court
Oakbrook
Illinois 50521
Stockists and suppliers of a wide-ranging collection of 40 "Historic Colours" from which to choose.

American Seal
PO Box 309
Waterford
New York 12188
The Saratoga Springs Preservation Foundation has given its seal of approval to the range of 61 colours produced by this company. See "Saratoga Colours: A Guide to Historic Paint Colours, 1790-1939" for many fascinating ideas of historic colour schemes, combinations and different finishes.

Bassett & Vollum Wallpapers
915 West Summit Street
Maquoketa
Iowa 52060
A specialist manufacturer of predominantly French hand-printed borders, in styles that were in vogue during the years 1800 to 1880.

Benjamin Moore & Company
51 Chestnut Ridge Road
Montvale
New Jersey 07645
A comprehensive selection of both interior and exterior paints and stains, and a good range of clear finishes and specialty all-weather maintenance coatings.

Bradbury & Bradbury
PO Box 155
Benicia
California 94510
Specialists in hand-printed wallpapers using Victorian, Aesthetic and Edwardian styles as inspiration. A wide selection of borders, friezes and ceiling papers is also available from which to make a choice.

Cabot Stains
100 Hale Street
Newburyport
Massachusetts 01950
Producers of historic Victorian colours that have been available since 1877.

Dufour Ltd
41 Union Square
New York
New York 10003
A specialist company providing the custom reproduction of wallpaper in historical styles according to customers' own specifications.

Finnaren and Haley Paint Inc.
901 Washington Street
Conschohocken
Pennsylvania 19428
Manufacturers of the range known as "Victorian Hues" – encompassing some 54 different colours.

Homestead Paint and Finishes
PO Box 1668
Lunenburg
Massachusetts 01462
Manufacturers of the "Old Fashioned Milk-Paint" collection, which provides a limited range eight natural interior paint colours.

Old-Fashioned Milk Paint Company
PO Box 222
Groton
Massachusetts 01450
Manufacturers of "The Genuine Old Fashioned Home-Made Milk Paint" – eight interior paint colours from which to choose.

Primrose Distributing
54445 Rose Road
South Bend
Indiana 46628
This specialist manufacturer produces the versatile selection of "Old Village Paint" colours, which can be used for furniture, general woodwork and also for walls. The colours in this range are faithful to the originals and have been mixed to 18th- and 19th-century specifications.

Schumacher
79 Madison Avenue
New York
New York 10016
Specialist suppliers of the "Victorian Society Collection" – an extensive range of fabrics and wallpapers. Other Victorian reproduction styles are also available from this source. These products are sold through interior designers and direct to historic house museums.

Martin Senour Company
PO Box 6709
Cleveland
Ohio 44101
The "Williamsbury Paint Colours" collection is an extensive range of 131 exterior and interior paint colours and finishes, designed to be suitable for renovations of period-style homes and buildings.

Sherwin-Williams Company
101 Prospect Street
Cleveland
Ohio 44115
Manufacturers of "Preservation Palatte, A Tribute to American Architectural Colours, 1800-1970" – a collection of 64 authentic exterior colours. "Preservation Palatte" consists of a range of 80 19th- and 20th-century interior colours suitable for renovations of period-style homes and buildings.

Stulb Company
PO Box 597
Allentown
Pennsylvania 18105
Specialist manufacturers of "Breinig's Ready Mixed Oil Paint" – a limited collection of 12 exterior colours from the years 1867-1913. The "Williamsburg Buttermilk Paint Colours" collection consists of 14 historic interior paint colours, all suitable for renovation work.

Richard E. Thibaut Inc.
706 South 21st Street
Irvington
New Jersey 07111
Manufacturers and suppliers of an extensive range of historical wallpapers, friezes, borders and screen-printed fabrics. These products are available through interior designers and specialist shops.

Victorian Collectibles Ltd
845 East Glenbrook Road
Milwaukee
Wisconsin 3217
The "Brillion Collection" has a huge range of 1,377 different wall, border and ceiling designs all from American artists working between the years 1850 and 1910. Reproduced using modern silk-screen technology.

Victorian Interiors
575 Hayes Street
San Francisco
California 94102
Specialist suppliers and stockists of a wide range of home decorating products. Wallpapers, decorative ceiling mouldings, embossed Anaglyptas, Lincrustas, tin ceilings, carpets and rugs, windows, cornices, custom-made draperies and other products are all available.

AUSTRALIA
Hawthorne Design and Decor
99 Denmark Street
Kew
Victoria 3101
Period-house renovation specialists using authentic reproduction wallpapers, friezes and other decorative accessories, as well as a range of soft furnishings.

Heritage Colours
165 White Horse Road
Balwyn
Melbourne
Victoria
Specialist suppliers of Haynes paint to the National Trust of Australia for use as a restoration paint. A range of 100 authentic colours is available, giving rise to h 1,000 colour variations. To help make choice easier, spacious showrooms have been decorated with period displays. Many different wallcoverings, plaster ceiling medallions, roses and so on can all be seen. Free sample "test pots" are available on request.

Honeyweather & Speight
113 Barkley Street
St Kilda
Victoria
Specialist suppliers of an extensive range of paint colours and finishes.

Porters
9 Almieda Crescent
South Yarra
Victoria
Products from this company are available in all states through selected specialist stockists.

St James Furnishings
142 Burwood Road
Hawthorn
Victoria

NEW ZEALAND
Country Colours
10 Broadway
New Market
Auckland
Specialist manufacturers and suppliers of a range of different paint finishes, coatings and colours. The Country Colours selection known as "Aalto" consists of pure acrylics and enamels, all of which are suitable for New Zealand's environment. Also stockists of "Porters" original selection, which includes a range of subtle colour washes and milk-paint products.

Macleister Painted Finishes
PO Box 1669
Christchurch
This versatile company is a specialist supplier of Scrumble, Crackle, Gilding and Bronze powder. It also provides specialist tools, furniture moulding and marbling services.

Benjamin Moore Paints
PO Box 100
Waitara
An extensive selection of imported American paints, with more than 2,000 colourways stocked. These paints are available in New Zealand exclusively from Major Decorating outlets. A full colour-matching service is provided for customers on request.

ANTIQUE & REPRODUCTION FURNITURE

UK
A Barn Full of Sofas and Chairs
Furnace Mill
Lamberhurst
Kent TN3 8LH
Specialist stockists and suppliers of genuine antique, period and secondhand sofas, chairs and other soft furnishings. A complete restoration service is available for period pieces.

Arthur Brett & Sons Ltd
40-44 St Giles Street
Norwich
Stockists and suppliers specializing exclusively in English furniture, including examples from the 19th century. A good range of oak furniture and bygones.

British Antique Interiors
Queen Elizabeth Avenue
Burgess Hill
West Sussex RH15 9RX
Manufacturers of period-style reproduction furniture, all created from reclaimed genuine antique wood.

The Chelsea Trading Company Ltd
3 Astwood Mews
London SW7 4DE
Manufacturers of reproduction traditional-style towel rails, from a range of woods .

The Classic Furniture Group
28-29 Dove Street
London W!X 3PA

The Cottage Cupboard and Cabinet Company
34 Greenside Road
Erdington
Birmingham B24 0DJ
Creators and suppliers of a wide range of country reproduction ornamental furniture.

Decorative Parlour Pieces
82 Golborne Road
London W10 5PS
Makers and stockists of small decorative items ideal for displaying in the home, and also a range of kitchenalia.

Martin Dodge Interiors
Showroom: 15-16 Broad Street
Bath
Avon BA1 5LJ
Manufacturers, suppliers and stockists of reproduction English furniture, faithfully created in authentic 18th- and 19th-century styles.

The Domestic Paraphernalia Company
Unit 15
Marine Business Centre
Dock Road
Lytham
Lancashire FY8 5AJ
Carries a wide range of small domestic paraphernalia.

Doveridge House Antiques
each Hill
Long Lane
Near Shifnal
Shropshire
An extensive selection of fine furniture and other types of decorative antiques.

Dycheling Antiques
34 High Street
Ditchling
Hassocks
Sussex BN6 8TA
A large and diverse selection of Victorian-era antique chairs is always kept in stock. A chair-search service can also be provided by arrangement with individual customers.

English Antiques Portfolio
55 Grove Park Gardens
London W4 3RY
A specialist company providing cast copies of existing furniture, especially decorative and ornate Gothic pieces. Cast Gothic radiator casings can also be created.

Essential Items
Church House
Plungar
Nottinghamshire NG13 0JA
A mail-order catalogue illustrating a wide selection of footstools stocked by this company can be provided. All footstools are reproduced from authentic traditional designs.

Kitchenalia
The Old Bakery
36 Inglewhite Road
Longridge
Preston
Lancashire PR3 3JS
Everything needed for the kitchen.

Liberty and Company
Regent Street
London W1
A large and unique collection of original Arts and Crafts furniture pieces. Many other decorative items are also permanently in stock.

The Marshall Gallery
67 Masbro Road
London W14
An interesting selection of antiques. Antique mirrors and lights are a specialty, but small pieces and soft furnishings, tassels and so on may also be found.

J. W. Mundy & Son
286 Windsor Road
Bray
Maidenhead
Berkshire SL6 2DT
Victorian-style dining chairs polished to match your furniture if required.

The Old Bakery
Punnetts Town
Near Heathfield
East Sussex TN21 9DS
Specialists in traditional upholstery. Also carries a range of hand-built reproduction horsehair-stuffed sofas and chairs. An interesting range of furnishing fabrics, wallpapers and drapes is also held in stock.

Overmantels
66 Battersea Bridge Road
London SW11 3AG
Stockists and suppliers of Victorian-style archtop mirrors in a wide variety of styles, sizes and finishes.

Rope Walk Antiques
18-22 Rope Walk
Rye
East Sussex TN31 7NA
A dealer specializing in all types of pine furniture. Items invariably carried in stock include tables, chairs, dressers, chests and similar pieces, with an interesting and ever-changing wide-ranging stock of kitchenalia.

Seventh Heaven
Chirk Mill
Chirk
Clwyd
Wales
A dealer with an extensive collection of interesting antique beds – mostly dating from the 19th century.

Keith Skeel Antiques
7-9 Elliott Place
London N1
An unusual and interesting selection of fine furniture, ornaments, panelling, table lamps, chandeliers and a range of soft furnishings. Viewing of stock is by appointment only. A full furniture restoration service is also provided.

George Smith
587-589 Kings Road
Chelsea
London SW6 2EH
Stockists of reproduction period sofas and chairs.

William Tillman
Crouch Lane
Borough Green
Near Sevenoaks
Kent
Fine reproductions of 19th-century furniture, especially tables, carried in stock.

The Victorian Brass Bedstead Company
Hoe Copse
Cocking
Near Midhurst
West Sussex
Specialist stockists and suppliers of an extensive selection of fully restored genuine Victorian-period brass and iron bedsteads. All accessories catered for.

USA
Antiquaria
60 Dartmouth Street
Springfield
Massachusetts 01109
This company provides a complete mail-order service to its customers, and a catalogue is available on request. Items are shipped anywhere throughout the USA. Specialists stockists and suppliers of a wide range of genuine antique American Victorian furniture and all types of related accessories.

Bargain John & Sons Antiques
700 S. Washington
Box 705
Lexington
Nebraska 68850
Specialists in antique furnishings dating from the years between 1840 and 1900. Oak, walnut, mahogany and rosewood pieces are usually always held in stock Victorian furniture and accessories a speciality. Convenient video tapes of the stock available can be sent out to customers by arrangement.

The Bed Factory
PO Box 335
Galion
Ohio 44833
Beautiful handcrafted beds made from iron, brass and wood. Upholstered beds are also available.

Bedlam Brass
137 Route 4 Westbound
Paramus
New Jersey 07652
A good selection of brass products from which to choose.

Joan Bogart
1392 Old Northern Boulevard
Roslyn
New York 11576
Specialist in 19th-century American furniture. Viewing is by appointment only.

Classic Wicker
8532 Melrose Avenue
Los Angeles
California 90069
Stockists and suppliers of a large selection of vintage classic wicker furniture.

Clockmakers Inc.
14 John Poulter Road
Lexington
Massachusetts 02173
A large range of Victorian clocks of many different types and sizes to be found in stock.

Dovetail Antiques
RR2 Box 194
Columbus
New Jersey 08022
An extensive selection of American antique wicker furniture, from the period c1870s to 1920s.

Hardscrabble Inc.
PO Box 4341
Martinsville
Virginia 24115
A wide range of quality hand-carved reproduction furniture.

Heirloom Reproductions
1834 West 5th Street
Montgomery
Alabama 36106
Stockists and suppliers of Victorian- and French-style reproduction furniture.

Import Connection
PO Box 1922
Tucker
Georgia 30085
Children's Victorian rockers, handcrafted in white rattan.

Leonard's Antiques
600 Taunton Avenue
Route 44
Seekonk
Massachusetts 02771
A specialist dealer in antique beds and furniture. These can be purchased in their original condition or be fully restored by "in-house" craftsmen. Handcarved custom-made beds as well as a range of reproduction furniture are also carried in stock.

Magnolia Hall
725 Andover Drive
Atlanta
Georgia 30327
A good selection of Victorian-style sofas, chairs, rockers, desks, lamps and shades from which to choose.

Michaels Classic Wicker
8532 Melrose Avenue
Los Angeles
California 90069
Specialist stockists and suppliers, carrying a good range of reproduction high-Victorian wicker furniture.

A. J. Munzinger & Company
1454 S Devon
Springfield
Missouri 5809
Reproduction Victorian-style coat trees and umbrella stands, all created from original 1880's patterns.

Prince Albert's
431 Thames Street
Newport
Specialist dealer with a large selection of Victorian furniture. Articles are bought, consigned and shipped.

Randolph Herr
111-07 77th Avenue
Forest Hills
New York 11375
Specialist stockists and suppliers of grand and upright player pianos. Video tapes are available showing the stock held, and these can be sent out by arrangement.

Schwab Wood Works
PO Box 1230
Clyde
North Carolina 28721
Supplier of antique-style, quality made handcrafted footstools. A range of different finishes is available.

Southampton Antiques
172 College Highway
Route 10
Southampton
Massachusetts 01073
A dealer specializing in genuine American antique oak and Victorian-period furniture. A large and interesting selection of furniture is always held in stock

L. & J.G. Stickley Inc.
Stickley Drive
PO Box 480
Manlius
New York 13104
Taken from the original patterns by L. & J. G. Stickley, this company produces more than 60 pieces of Mission Oak furniture. These are available through selected dealerships nationwide.

Victorian Attic
Route 25
Mattituck
New York 11952
Specialist stockists and suppliers of reproduction white wicker furniture.

Victorian Showcase
1012 Logan Street
Mcechen
West Virginia 26040
Authentic reproductions of a range of 19th-century furniture, lighting, millwork and wallcoverings. Ideal source of materials for renovation work to period buildings.

Wicker Fixer
Route 1 Box 349
Ozark
Missouri 65721
As well carrying a large selection of antique wicker for sale, wicker repairs, large and small, are also undertaken on behalf of customers.

AUSTRALIA
A Colonial Craftsman
11-13 Queens Avenue
Hawthorn
Victoria

Grosvenor Antique Centre
216 Pacific Highway
Lindfield
New South Wales 2070
Early examples of Australian and European furniture can be found here. All manner of decorative items also for sale.

The Old Country Furniture Store
402 Darling Street
Balmain
New South Wales 2041
Examples of 18th- and 19th-century country and provincial furniture can be found here. The owners travel to Europe to restock. Also sells Australian colonial furniture in antique woods that have been restored using traditional methods.

Restoration Station
98 Waterworks Road
Ashgrove
Queensland
A complete furniture restoration service available.

NEW ZEALAND
John Dixon
488 Remuera Road
Auckland

W. Holliday & Sons
20 Papanui Road
Christchurch

London Antique Shop
524 Manukau Road
Auckland
A good selection of quality antiques always held in stock.

Richard Matthews
411 Remuera Road
Remuera
Auckland

Donald Melville Antiques
360 Lake Road
Takapuna
Auckland

Portobello Antiques
417 Parnell Road
Auckland

Raphael Studios Ltd
2005 Hastings Street
Napier

Philip Rhodes
105 North Street
Palmerston North

Barry Thomas Antiques
319 Remuera Road
Remuera
Auckland
An extensive and varying selection of antique furniture from which to choose.

Vaughan Antiques
83 Victoria Street
Christchurch

Elizabeth Wilkins Antiques
16 Willis Street
Wellington

AUCTION HOUSES

UK
Aldridges
130-132 Walcot Street
Bath
Avon

Allen & Harris
St Johns Place
Apsley Road
Clifton
Bristol
Avon

Amersham Auction Rooms
Station Road
Amersham
Buckinghamshire

Anderson & Garland
Marlborough House
Marlborough Crescent
Newcastle-upon-Tyne
Tyne & Wear

Biddle & Webb
Icknield Square
Ladywood
Middleway
Birmingham
West Midlands

Bigwood Auctioneers Ltd
The Old School
Tiddington
Stratford-upon-Avon
Warwickshire

Bonhams
Montpelier Galleries
Montpelier Street
Knightsbridge
London SW7
and: Lots Road
London SW10

William H. Brown
The Auction Rooms
11-14 East Hill
Colchester
Essex

Canterbury Auction Galleries
40 Station Road West
Canterbury
Kent

Christie, Manson & Woods Ltd
8 King Street
St James's
London SW1
and: 85 Old Brompton Road
London SW7

Christie's Robson Lowe
47 Duke Street
St James's
London SW1

Churchgate Auctions
The Churchgate Saleroom
66 Churchgate
Leicester

Clark Gammon
The Guildford Auction Rooms
Bedford Road
Guildford
Surrey

Cumbria Auction Rooms
12 Lowther Street
Carlisle
Cumbria

Duncan Vincent Fine Art & Chattel Auctioneers
105 London Street
Reading
Berkshire

Hamptons Fine Art
Auctioneers and Valuers
6 Arlington Street
London SW1

Andrew Hartley
Victoria Hall Salerooms
Little Lane
Ilkley
Yorkshire

Heathcote Ball & Company
Albion Auction Rooms
Old Albion Brewery
Commercial Street
Northampton
Northamptonshire

Highams Auctions
Waterloo House
Waterloo Road
Stalybridge
Cheshire
and: 207 Deansgate
Manchester
Lancashire

Hornsey Auctions Ltd
91 New Bond Street
London W1

W. H. Lane & Son
St Mary's Auction Rooms
65 Morrab Road
Penzance
Cornwall

Lewes Auction Rooms
56 High Street
Lewes
East Sussex

Lots Road Chelsea
Auction Galleries
71 Lots Road
Worlds End
London SW10

Ludlow Antique Auctions Ltd
29 Corve Street
Ludlow
Shropshire

Mallams
26 Grosvenor Street
Cheltenham
Gloucestershire
and: 24 St Michael's
Street
Oxford
Oxfordshire

Robert McTear & Co Ltd
Royal Exchange
Salerooms
6 North Court
St Vincent Place
Glasgow

Neales of Nottingham
192 Mansfield Road
Nottingham
Nottinghamshire

Onslow's
Metrostore
Townmead Road
London SW6

Phillips
Blenstock House
7 Blenheim Street
New Bond Street
London W1
and: 10 Salem Road
London W2

Riddetts of Bournemouth
26 Richmond Hill
Bournemouth Square
Bournemouth
Dorset

Rosebery's Fine Art Ltd
Old Railway Booking Hall
Crystal Palace Station
Road
London SE19

Russell, Baldwin & Bright
Ryelands Road
Leominster
Herefordshire

Sotheby's
34-35 New Bond Street
London W1

Henry Spencer & Sons
42 Silver Street
Lincoln
Lincolnshire

Nigel Ward & Morris
Stuart House
18 Gloucester Road
Ross on Wye
Herefordshire

Wilson Peacock
26 Newnham Street
Bedford
Bedfordshire

Noel Wheatcroft & Son
The Matlock Auction
Gallery
39 Dale Road
Matlock
Derbyshire

Wolley & Wallis
The Castle Auction Mart
Castle Street
Salisbury
Wiltshire

USA
A-1 Auction Service
PO Box 540672
Orlando
Florida 32854
Specializes in the sale of American antiques.

Arman Absentee Auctions
PO Box 174
Woodstock
Connecticut 06281
Specializes in American glass, Staffordshire and English soft paste.

Barrett/Bertoia Auctions & Appraisals
1217 Glenwood Drive
Wineland
New Jersey 18630
Specializes in antique toys and collectables.

Christie's, Manson & Woods International Inc.
502 Park Avenue
New York
New York 10022

Doyle Auctioneers & Appraisers
R.D. 3
Box 137
Osborne Hill Road
Fishkill
New York 12524
Thousands of collectables offered for sale.

Gallery
17 X. Main Street
Lambertville
New Jersey 08530
Specializes in American art pottery and Arts & Crafts movement.

Gunther's International Auction Gallery
PO Box 235
24 S. Virginia Avenue
Brunswick
Maryland 21716
Specializes in political, Oriental rugs, art, bronzes and the unusual.

Charles E. Kirtley
PO Box 2273
Elizabeth City
North Carolina 27096
Specializes in Civil War and other American collectables.

Manion's International Auction House Inc.
PO Box 12214
Kansas City
Kansas 66112

Nostalgia Galleries
657 Meacham Avenue
Elmont
New York 11003

Phillips
406 E. 79th Street
New York
New York 10021

Sothebys
1334 York Avenue at
72nd Street
New York
New York 10021

Weschler & Son
905 E. Street N.W.
Washington
DC 20004

Willis Henry Auctions
22 Main Street
Marshfield
Massachussets 02050

AUSTRALIA
Abbeys Auctions
428a Station Street
Box Hill
Victoria 3128

Action Auctioneers & Valuers
5691 West Swan Road
West Swan
Western Australia 6055

E. J. Ainger Pty Ltd (Aingers)
433 Bridge Road
Richmond
Victoria 3121

Armitage Auctions
113-117 Cimitiere Street
Launceston
Tasmania 7250

John A. Bell
Parkland Road
Harborne Commercial
Centre
Osborne Park
Western Australia 6107

Gregsons Auctioneers
250 Beaufort Street
Perth
Western Australia 6000

Hamilton & Miller
130 Parramatta Road
Camperdown
New South Wales 2050

Harry Harris
800 Parramatta Road
Leichardt
New South Wales 2040

Holmes Kenwick Auctions
26 Royal Street
Kenwick
Western Australia 6107

Isles Love Auction Centre
936 Nudgee Road
Northgate
Queensland 4013

James & Co. Auctioneers
8 Trafalgar Street
Wooloongabba
Queensland 4102

Lawsons
212 Cumberland Street
Sydney
New South Wales 2000

Leonard Joel
174 Inkerman Street
St Kilda
Victoria 3182

Logan City Auctions Pty Ltd
84-86 Compton Road
Underwood
Queensland 4199

Megaw & Hogg
107 Sturt Street
Adelaide
South Australia 5000

Norms City Auctions
499 Wellington Street
Perth
Western Australia 6000

Raffan & Kelaher
42 John Street
Leichardt
New South Wales 2040

Roxbury's Auction House
2nd Floor
231 George Street
Brisbane
Queensland 4000

Small & Whitfield
Unley Road
Parkside
South Australia 5063

Theodore Bruce Auctions
80 King William Street
Adelaide
South Australia 5000

Tullochs General & Antique Auctions & Estate Clearances
3-7 George Street
Launceston
Tasmania 7250

Webster Auctioneers
180 Cimitiere Street
Launceston
Tasmania 7250

Windsor Antiques
271-273 Hobart Road
Launceston
Tasmania 7250

W. J. Young (Youngs)
229 Camberwell Road
Hawthorn East
Victoria 3122

SOUTH AFRICA
Anderson Cape
Auctioneers
Church Street
Wynberg
Cape Town

Ashbey's Galleries
43 Church Street
Cape Town

Millers Antiques
62 Siemert Road
Doornfontein
Johannesburg

Raymond & Leighton-Morris Antiques
12 Keyes Avenue
Rosebank
Johannesburg

Templare Antiques
10 Lesley Avenue
Witkoppen
Johannesburg

Stephan Welz and Co.
13 Biermann Avenue
Rosebank
Johannesburg
Represent Sotheby's.

FLORISTS

UK
John Carter
The Flower Van
Michelin House
81 Fulham Road
London SW3 6RD

Paula Pryke Flowers
20 Penton Street
Islington
London N19PS

Kenneth Turner Flowers
Brook Manor
35 Brook Street
London W1Y 1AJ

Sebastian von Mybourg Floral Pageantry and Progressive Interiors
3 Bayley Street
Bloomsbury
London WC1B 3HA

USA
The Antique Rose Emporium
Route 5
Box 143
Brenham
Texas 77833

Beverley R. Dobson
215 Harriman Road
Irvington
New York 10533

Heirloom Old Garden Roses
24062 Riverside Drive
N.E.
St Paul
Oregon 97137

Historical Roses
1657 West Jackson Street
Painesville
Ohio 44077

Roses of Yesterday & Today
802 Brown's Valley Road
Watsonville
California 95076

ASSOCIATIONS

UK
Acanthus
Voysey House
London W4 4PN
Consultancy on listed buildings and conservation areas; historic building surveys and analysis; feasibility studies on uses for old buildings; garden and landscape design.

The Architectural Association
34-36 Bedford Square
London WC1

Art Workers Guild
6 Queen Square
London WC1N 3AR
This Guild is for those professional artists, architects, craftsmen and others who are engaged in the design and practice of the arts.

The Association of British Laundry Cleaning and Rental Services
7 Churchill Court
58 Station Road
North Harrow
Middlesex HA2 7SA
This association can supply the addresses and telephone numbers of specialists in the field of cleaning old and antique fabrics and textiles, for example, chintz, linen, silk, brocades and lace.

The British Ceramic Tile Council
Federation House
Station Road
Stoke-on-Trent
Staffordshire ST4 2RT
Offers advice on all aspects of tiles and tiling.

C. B. Brooking
Woodhay
White Lane
Guildford
Surrey GU4 8PU
The Brooking Collection preserves a huge selection of all sorts of architectural elements rescued from demolition. The Collection comprises up to 20,000 building components and also provides a unique record of the development of architectural details, with particular reference to features such as windows, doors, fireplaces, decorative ironwork etc. An information service is also available.

The Building Conservation Trust
Apt 39
Hampton Court Palace
East Molesey
Surrey KT8 9BS
An independent educational charity established to promote the better care of buildings of all types and ages.

Cadw - Welsh Historic Monuments
2 Fitzalan Road
Cardiff CF2 1UY
Awards grants for repairing historic buildings in Wales.

Chartered Institution of Building Services Engineers (CIBSE)
Delta House
222 Balham High Road
London SW12 9BS
Free advice on plumbing, heating and ventilation.

Chartered Society of Industrial Artists and Designers (S.I.A.D.)
29 Bedford Square
London WC1
Association of professional interior designers. Will supply details of designers specializing in period houses.

English Heritage
25 Saville Row
London W1X 2BT
Preserves and promotes some of England's historical and archaeological heritage. Offers specialist and technical advice on repair, maintenance and preservation and gives grants for repairing historic buildings throughout England.

The Guild of Master Craftsmen
166 High Street
Lewes
East Sussex
A trade association which puts clients in touch with experienced craftsmen who carry out restoration work.

Historic Homes of Britain
21 Pembroke Square
London W8

Historic Houses Association
38 Ebury Street
London SW1 0LU

Interior Decorators and Designers Association
Crest House
102-104 ChurchRoad
Teddington
Middlesex TW11 8PY
Association of interior decorators and designers.

London Stained Glass Repository
Glaziers Hall
9 Montague Close
London SE1 9DD

National Association of Decorative and Fine Arts Societies
38 Ebury Street
London SW1 0LU

The National Register of Warranted Builders
3 John Street
London WC1

The National Trust
36 Queen Anne's Gate
London SW1H 9AS

The National Trust for Scotland
5 Charlotte Square
Edinburgh EH2 4DU

Paint Research Assocation
Waldegrave Road
Teddington
Middlesex TW11 8LD
Literature available on paints, pre-treatment products and masonry coatings.

Save
68 Battersea High Street
Battersea
London SW11 3AD
Organization for saving Britain's heritage.

The Society for the Protection of Ancient Buildings
37 Spital Square
London E1 6DY
The Society supplies the names and addresses of specialist architects and also other professionals. It also issues technical publications on historic buildings repairs and advises against conjectural restoration of period details.

The Victorian Society
1 Priory Gardens
Bedford Park
London W4 1TT
A conservation amenity group dedicated to the preservation of Victorian and Edwardian buildings.

The Wallpaper History Society
Victoria and Albert Museum
London SW7 2RL
Can offer advice on documented period wallpapers and also wallcovering designs.

The William Morris Society
26 Upper Mall
Hammersmith
London W6

USA
**The Center for Historic Houses
The National Trust for Historic Preservation**
1785 Massachusetts Avenue
Washington
DC 20036
This section of the National Trust is geared particularly to the needs of home-owners.

The National Trust for Historic Preservation
1785 Massachusetts Avenue
Washington
DC 20036
The Trust publishes journals and administers many of the country's finest historic houses and gardens. Modest annual membership fee.

The New York Landmarks Conservancy
141 Fifth Avenue
New York
New York 10010
Publishes a listing of services in the New York City area, from archaeologists and architects to roofers and stone masons. The book is annually updated, and can be ordered from the Landmarks Conservancy.

Preservation Associates, Inc.
117 S. Potomac Street
Hagerstown
Maryland 21740
A nationally oriented firm providing a broad selection of specialized preservation consulting and also rehabilitation services. They are experienced with State and Federal laws and regulations as well as having technical expertise in rehabilitation projects. Will guide projects through government regulations, technical and design phases and the actual rehabilitation work.

The Victorian Society
219 S. 6th Street
Independence Mall
West Philadelphia
Pennsylvania 19106
Membership includes lectures, annual meetings in cities with a Victorian heritage and publications including "The Nineteenth Century".

AUSTRALIA
Antiques Dealers Association
PO Box 24
Mealvern
Victoria

Design Institute of Australia
50 Burwood Road
Hawthorn
Victoria
Branches of this Institute are in all states of Australia.

Society of Interior Designers of Australia
H.I.A. House
Jolimont Parade
East Melbourne
Victoria
Branches of this Society are to be found in all states of Australia.

PLACES TO VISIT

UK
Alnwick Castle
Alnwick
Northumberland

The American Museum
Claverton Manor
Bath
Avon
A selection of interesting mid 19th-century rooms are on display.

Brodick Castle
Isle of Arran

Calke Abbey
Ticknall
Near Melbourne
Derbyshire
This fascinating house, built in the year 1701, contains a treasure trove of Victoriana, in terms of furniture and range of decorative styles.

Cardiff Castle
Cardiff
South Glamorgan
Wales
A Gothic showpiece for the visitor.

Castell Coch
Whitchurch
South Glamorgan
Wales

Chettle House
Chettle
Blandford
Dorset
A lovely Queen Anne house with an interior that was remodelled during the 19th century.

Church Farm House Museum
Greyhound Hill
London NW4
This museum concentrates mostly on the extensive range of 19th-century domestic items. There are two period finished rooms – the kitchen, c1820, and the dining room, c1850.

Clifton Hotel
Viewfield Street
Highlands
Nairn IV12 4HW
This creeper-clad Victorian house is positively crammed full of fascinating antiques, artefacts and books.

Cragside House
Rothbury
Morpeth
Northumbria NE65 7PX
House designed by Norman Shaw. Aesthetic interiors. First house in the world to be lit by water-powered electricity.

Ettington Park Hotel
Alderminster
Stratford upon Avon
CV37 8BS
A Victorian Gothic mansion. Some parts date back much earlier. Gilded ceilings, fine antiques and original paintings to be seen.

Felbrigg Hall
Roughton
Norwich NR11 8R

18 Folgate Street
Spitalfields
London
This 1724 house has decorated and furnished rooms from 1724 to early 20th century.

Inverlochy Castle
Torlundy
Fort William PH33 6SN
A magnificent castle much admired by Queen Victoria.

Knebworth House
Knebworth
Hertfordshire

Leighton House
12 Holland Park Road
London W14
Built 1860s-70s. Features the famous "Arab Hall".

Linley Sambourne House
18 Stafford Terrace
London W8
Aesthetic interior.

Osborne House
York Avenue
East Cowes
Isle of Wight
Built 1845-6.

Russell Cotes Art Gallery and Museum
East Cliff
Bournemouth BH1 3AA

Thoresby Hall
Ollerton
Nottinghamshire

Waddesdon Manor
Waddesdon
Near Aylesbury
Buckinghamshire
HP18 0JH
Built in 1874. Fine late-Victorian formal gardens.

Wightwick Manor
Wightwick Bank
Wolverhampton
West Midlands WV6 8EE
This manor house, which was built in 1887, was heavily influenced by William Morris. It contains numerous fine examples of William Morris's and William de Morgan's work. The gardens are Victorian and also Edwardian in style.

USA
Asa Paker House
Jim Thorpe
Pennsylvania

Bartow Pell Mansion
895 Shore Road
NorthPelham Bay Park
Bronx
New York
New York 10464

The Breakers
Newport
Rhode Island

Chateau-sur-Mer (Wetmore Mansion)
Newport
Rhode Island

Cooper Hewitt Museum
2 East 91st Street
New York
New York

Gallier House
New Orleans
Louisiana

Heritage Square Museum
Exit 43 off 111 Pasadena
Freeway
Los Angeles
California

Lansdowne
Natchez
Mississippi

Lockwood-Mathews Mansion
Norwalk
Connecticut

Lyndhurst
Tarrytown
New York

Morris Jumel Mansion
1765 Jumel Terrace
New York
New York 10032
A Palladian mansion with period rooms decorated in English Colonial, American and French Empire and Federal styles.

Morse-Libby House (Victorian Mansion)
Portland
Maine

Old Merchants House
29 East 4th Street
New York City
New York
Open to the public.

Roosevelt House
New York City
New York

Ulysses S. Grant Home
500 Bouthillier Street
Galena
Illinois 61036
See Other Useful Addresses.

OTHER USEFUL ADDRESSES

The publishers are grateful to the following museums, home-owners, interior designers, hotels and guest houses for allowing special photography for this book:

UK
Christophe Gollut
116 Fulham Road
London SW3 6HU
Interior designer who specializes in using furniture of the 18th and 19th centuries in eclectic Continental-influenced interiors. Christophe Gollut favours a rich, mellow mood.

The Convent
Hall Place
3 Lyndhurst Terrace
Hampstead
London NW3 4QA
A high-Victorian Gothic "domestic palace" which is a listed Grade II building. It was constructed in the mid Victorian years by Sir Gilbert Scott's Associates. For further information contact David Warbeck.

Kit Kemp
18 Thurloe Place
London SW7
Interior designer.

Tessa Kennedy
Studio 5
91-97 Freston Road
London W11 4BD
Interior designer.

The Marshall Gallery
67 Masbro Road
Brook Green
London W14
Jason and Deidre Marshall run this "old curiostiy" antique shop which stocks a rich variety of Victoriana.

The Pelham Hotel
15 Cromwell Place
London SW7
Hotel owned by interior designer Kit Kemp.

Keith Skeel Antiques
94-98 High Street
Islington
London N1 8EG
Antique shop featuring all sorts of eccentricities.

USA
Belle of the Bends
508 Klein Street
Vicksburg
Mississippi 39180
An Italianate mansion built in 1876. Open as a guest house.

Belle Vue
Route 1
Box 38
Shepherds Grade Road
Shepherdstown
West Virginia 25443
A guest house run by Gay Shepherd-Henderson.

The Belvedere Mansion
1008 Park Avenue
Galena
Illinois 61036
Built in 1857 for J. Russel Jones this mansion is furnished with formal Victorian pieces and run by Joe Fessler and Richard Burlingame. The house is open to the public.

Cedar Grove
2300 Washington Street
Vicksburg
Mississippi 39180
A Greek Revival mansion built with sun-dried bricks in 1840 and completed in 1858. Open as a guest house.

Dezoya House
1203 Third Street
Galena
Illinois 61036
Built c.1830 in a regional adaptation of Federal style from native limestone by builders from Virginia. All the original posts, beams and laths are hand-split and made from local oak. The house is furnished with a variety of antiques and art from 1790-1820 and is open as a guest house. It is currently owned by Carol and Bill Preston who also run a historical restoration service.

The Durfee House
1007 West 24th Street
Los Angeles
California 90007
A "Pink Lady" in St James Park Historic District of Los Angeles. Historic Cultural Monument No. 273, the house was built c.1880 in Eastlake style. Owned by Edward and Anne Dorrs.

The Garth Woodside Mansion
RR 1
Hannibal
Missouri 63401
Built as a summer home in 1871 this is an example of Second Empire architecture, the mansard roof is made of slate. The mansion is run by Irv and Dianne Feinberg as a bed and breakfast inn.

Keith Knost Associates
123 East German Street
Sheperdstown
West Virginia 25443
Interior designer.

Old Merchants House
29 East 4th Street
New York
New York
Open to the public.

Rockliffe Mansion
1000 Bird Street
Hannibal
Missouri 62304
A mansion of Neo-classical design which has visible touches of classical Greek Revival. There is also some influence of Art Nouveau decoration in the interior. The construction of the house was begun in 1898 and was completed in 1900. It is open as a guest house and managed by Wayne Scott.

The Steamboat House
605 So. Prospect
Galena
Illinois 61036
A two-storey Gothic Revival house built in 1858 for Captain Daniel Smith Harris. The decor is mid-Victorian. Open as a guest house and owned by Elisabeth Sacco McClellan.

Ulysses S. Grant Home
500 Bouthillier Street
Galena
Illinois 61036
Open to the public, this brick house was designed by William Dennison in 1860. It was presented fully furnished to Grant upon his return from the Civil War in 1865. The house is typical of the Italianate bracketed style with its rectilinear shapes, projecting eaves, low-pitched roof and balustraded balconies over covered porches. It has been restored to its original 1870s appearance and is furnished with period pieces and many of the original items belonging to the Grant family. Tours are available. The home is owned and operated by the Illinois Historic Preservation Agency. Pete Campbell is the site attendant.

Lyn von Kirsting
Indigo Seas
123 N. Robertson Blvd
Los Angeles
California 90048
A shop selling fabrics, linens, all kinds of soft furnishings, pillows or cushions as well as a vairety of shell-decorated items, in particular boxes. The shop belongs to interior designer Lyn von Kirsting. She also runs a restaurant called "The Ivy", at the same address.

EUROPE
Alberto Pinto
61 Quai d'Orsay
75007 Paris
Interior designer.

T. & E. Design AG
Frohburg Street 58
8832 Wollerau
Switzerland
Interior design company run by Edda and Tim Abegg.

Directory compiled by Frances Page.

GLOSSARY

Acanthus: A carved ornament of conventionalized, serrated leaves, used on columns and mouldings.

Aesthetic movement: A decorative arts movement with a strong Japanese influence, which flourished in Britain from c.1870 to the late 1880s. A precursor to Art Nouveau, it also overlapped with the Arts and Crafts movement.

Alloy: A metal such as bronze, brass or pewter made by melting together two or more elements such as copper, zinc and tin.

Ambrotype: Early type of photograph in the United States - see Daguerreotype.

Anaglypta: Type of wallpaper with heavily embossed pattern. Primarily used on dados and ceilings and painted and varnished for protection and ease of cleaning.

Andiron: An iron bar used to support the end of a log in a hearth.

Aniline: A product of coal tar used in dyeing and other industrial arts.

Animaliers: French (but also German) sculptors of small, lifelike models of wild and domestic birds and animals, usually in bronze.

Antimacassars: Also known as '"tidies" - crocheted or knitted doilies placed on the backs and arms of upholstered furniture to protect it from dirt and grease.

Anthemions: Honeysuckle or palm-like ornamentation.

Arabesques: Interwoven, symmetrical patterns of branches, tendrils and scrolls, commonly found in Islamic designs.

Arcading: A row of open or closed arches supported on columns or pilasters, usually forming a covered passageway.

Architrave: A collective name for the mouldings (jambs, lintels etc) surrounding doors, windows and archways.

Armoire: The French name for a large cabinet or cupboard or linen press.

Art glass: A general term for late 19th-century and early 20th-century decorative glassware.

Art Nouveau: A style of decoration characterized by curves and flowing lines, asymmetry and flower and leaf motifs, prevalent from the 1880s to 1914.

Arts and Crafts movement: Late 19th- and early 20th-century group of artists and craftsmen who rejected machine-made goods in favour of those made by traditional methods. One of the founders of the movement was William Morris.

Automata: Mechanized toys, dolls, music boxes etc, with concealed clockwork movements, made for the amusement of both children and adults.

Ball-and-claw: A carving depicting an animal's claw holding a ball, primarily used as feet on items of furniture such as chairs and tables.

Balloon back: Popular Victorian dining- or drawing-room chair with rounded back.

Balloon framing: A simple method of timber-framed construction, common in the United States.

Baluster: A small pillar supporting a stair rail, usually circular in section and curvaceous in outline.

Balustrade: A row of balusters connected by a rail.

Barge-board: A wide, flat board used to seal the space below the roof, in-between the tiles and the wall on a gable end. They usually feature decorative carving or pierced decoration. (Also known as a vergeboard.)

Baroque style: An extravagant and heavily ornate style of architecture, furniture, ceramics, glassware and decoration that had its origins in 17th-century Italian architecture. Characterized by the abundant use of cupids, cornucopias and other such decoration set in symmetrical, curvaceous designs. A precursor of the lighter, more frivolous and colourful Rococo style.

Baseboard: A moulded wooden skirting board attached to the base of a wall and usually running around the perimeter of a room.

Batiste: A fine fabric of linen, cotton or wool.

Bentwood: Artificially curved wood used in the manufacture of furniture, especially chairs.

Bergère: A type of chair or sofa featuring cane panels at the sides and back.

Bevelled glass: A type of glass or mirror with edges cut to slope off at an angle.

Biedermeier: An essentially middle-class style of furniture, interior decoration and Bohemian glass and porcelain that originated in Austria and Germany after the Napoleonic wars. The furniture was mostly hand-crafted in walnut and softwoods such as cherry and pear and displayed geometric forms and, often, sophisticated motifs.

Bisques: Dolls made from an unglazed white porcelain. Also, pottery that has undergone the first firing before being glazed.

Blue and white: A widely used decorative ceramic colour scheme in which cobalt blue is used as an underglaze.

Bone china: Chinaware made primarily from calcium phosphate (bone-ash).

Boullework: First perfected by Charles André Boulle (1642-1732), a cabinetmaker in the service of Louis XIV. A complicated form of inlay work, using gold, silver, or brass and pewter, ivory and mother-of-pearl, set in tortoiseshell or wooden panels used to decorate furniture.

Bric-a-brac: Knick-knacks, curiosities and other treasured odds and ends.

Brocatelle: A stiff, heavy-figured silk and linen fabric.

Brussels carpet: A flat-weave carpet with a looped, uncut pile.

Butler's tray: A portable tray, usually rectangular, with handholds at each end and mounted either on legs or on a folding stand. Used for serving drinks and removing glasses.

Button-backed: Padded upholstery with a buttoned, quilted effect; achieved by pulling a strong thread through the covering material and stuffing to the framework or webbing, and concealing it on the outside with buttons.

Cabriole legs: Outwardly curving legs usually deployed on drawing- and dining-room chairs, notably from 1830-80 and often combined with a balloon back.

Canterbury: A wooden stand incorporating divisions for holding sheet music and books.

Capitals: The head or top part of a column.

Capstan table: A variant of a large, circular drum table with draws set into a deep frieze and supported on a central pedestal or tripod.

Carolean: Styles of architecture, decoration and furniture originating during the reigns of Charles I and II of England.

Cartouche: A scroll-like ornament with rolled ends.

Caryatid: A female figure deployed in place of a column to support an entablature.

Chair rail: see Dado rail.

Chaise volante: Literally, a "flying chair" - lightweight, made of *papier mâché* or wood and designed to be moved easily around a room.

Chenille: A thick, velvety cord made of silk or wool and often used for table covers.

Chesterfield: A well-padded, over-stuffed sofa, usually button-backed, with the back and arms of the same height.

Cheval mirror: A large mirror supported on a frame and designed to swivel to various angles of inclination within it.

Chevron: A V-shaped heraldic symbol representing two rafters of a house butting up to each other at an angle.

Chimney breast: The stone, brick or cement structure that projects into a room and contains the fireplace flue.

Chinoiserie: Furniture, ornaments and decoration made in Europe in the Chinese style.

Chintz: A cotton fabric usually printed in several colours on a white or pale ground.

Chippendale style: Furniture, usually made of mahogany, made to the designs of Thomas Chippendale (1718-89). His work included a variety of influences, including Chinese, Rococo and Gothic styles.

Clapboard: Overlapping, wedge-shaped boards that form the external covering of a timber-framed structure.

Cloak-pin tie-backs: Circular drape or curtain tie-backs, usually made of ornamental gilt metal and attached to the wall by a stem. Drapes or curtains were either draped behind or wound round them.

Coal-tar dye: A type of dye primarily used to colour fabrics and wallpapers and derived from the thick, opaque liquid formed by distilling coal.

Colonial style: All-embracing term used to describe North American architecture, furniture and decoration dating from the early 17th century pioneer settlements to the establishment of federal government in 1789.

Colourwash: A technique for decorating walls and ceilings in which a thin veil of colour (or colours) is brushed out over a contrasting or complementary basecoat.

Commode: Either a small sideboard, an ornamental chest of drawers or a chair containing a chamber pot.

Console: A decorative scroll-shaped bracket.

Corbel: A projecting stone or timber block, often carved supporting a horizontal member such as a beam.

Cornice: Either a projecting moulding positioned along the top of a building or a window, or a plaster moulding covering the join between a ceiling and a wall, often at the top of the frieze. (Also known as a moulding.)

Cretonne: A boldly printed fabric suitable for drapes or curtains and upholstered furniture.

Crumb cloth: A cloth temporarily laid over a floor or carpet, usually under a dining table, and designed to catch spills and crumbs.

Dado: A skirting or rail, usually made of wood, running around the walls of a room at approximately the height of a chair back. Also, the space below that rail and above the baseboard or skirting board.

Daguerreotype: An early form of photograph taken using a process invented by Louis Daguerre (1789-1851), and involving the mercury vapour development of silver iodide exposed on a copper plate.

Damask: A silk or linen fabric incorporating a woven pattern.

Davenport: A small ornamental writing desk, first made by the English furniture maker Gillows for a Captain Davenport. Also a large sofa.

Deal: A softwood, usually fir or pine.

Decalcomania: A type of glassware decorated at home by gluing scraps - images either cut from magazines or sold in sets by craft shops - to the inside of clear glass vessels, and then coating them with enamel or whitewash.

Découpage: The craft of applying decorative paper cutouts to wooden, fabric or cardboard panels, screens, boxes etc. (Originated in the 18th century.)

Diaper: A diamond-shaped motif.

Distemper: A water-based paint.

Divan: A couch or bed without sides or a back.

Dog grate: see Andiron.

Drab: A light grayish-brown or greenish-brown colour.

Dumb-waiter: A movable platform or trolley for transporting food either to or around a dining room.

Eastlake style: Architecture and furniture, prevalent in North America, built according to the designs of the English architect and designer Charles Eastlake (1836-1906).

Eaves: That part of a roof which overhangs the wall.

Ebonized: Wood stained and polished black to simulate ebony.

Eglomisé mirror: A mirror in which gold or silver foil has been applied to the reverse of the glass. The foil was then engraved and painted black.

Electroplating: A technique for covering or plating metal wares with silver or other precious metals.

Elevation: One of the external faces of a building.

Empire style: A style of furniture and furnishings popular in France c.1804-30, and the United States c.1810-30. Solid and stately in style, the furniture was characterized by the use of sombre-looking woods such as mahogany, ebony and rosewood, and was mostly uncarved but generously ornamented with brass inlay and ormolu mounts in the form of, for example, burning torches, urns, lions' masks, eagles and swans. Later, papyrus leaves, crocodiles, sphinxes and other Egyptian motifs were also used on all sorts of furnishings and fittings. In the United States the style was adapted to include local motifs such as fruit, flowers and the American eagle.

Enamelling: A technique for applying (and firing) a vitrified, glossy coating to metal, wooden or ceramic surfaces.

Encasement: The practice of enclosing fixtures and fittings such as bathtubs and sinks or basins in wooden surrounds.

Encaustic tile: A decorative and glazed fired tile, incorporating patterns made of different coloured clays.

Epergne: An ornamental centrepiece for the table, such as a glass flower stand.

Escutcheon: A metal plate around a keyhole.

Etagère: *see* Whatnot.

Etruscan style: A late 18th-century offshoot of Neo-classicism introduced by the architect and designer Robert Adam c.1774, and based on the architecture, ornamental wares and a style of decoration originating in Etruria (now Tuscany and Umbria), an ancient Italian state situated north of the River Tiber.

Fanlight: A window above a door, usually semi-circular, with glazing bars radiating out like a fan. (Also known as a transom window in the United States.)

Faux bamboo and faux marbre: "Fake" bamboo and marble, created by embellishing plain wooden or plaster surfaces with translucent paints and glazes to simulate the appearance of the natural materials.

Federal style: Architecture and furniture from the early years of American independence (1789-1830); the latter is generally adorned with patriotic or military symbols such as the eagle.

Fender: A screen or guard placed in front of a fireplace to prevent hot coals from damaging the surrounding floor or carpet.

Festoon: A drape or curtain ruched to hang in folds.

Field: The area of a wall above a dado and below a frieze.

Fillet: A moulding, usually of gilded wood but sometimes metal fretwork, used as a trim for wall coverings or panels of stretched fabric.

Finials: Ornamental foliage on top of a spire, gable etc.

Fire-dogs: *see* Andiron.

Fish-tails: The folded hanging drapery of a valence or pelmet, falling in overlapping loops. The lining of the drapes revealed by the folds is often in a contrasting colour.

Flats: Toy soldiers, commonly made of lead.

Flatware: Objects of flattened form, such as plates, saucers, shallow dishes and salvers, as opposed to cups, bowls and tureens. In silverware the term also refers to articles of tableware made from flat sheet without a cutting edge, such as spoons, forks, sifters and slicers.

Fleur-de-lys: A heraldic floral motif, French in origin.

Flock wallpaper: A textured wallpaper made of fine particles of wool (or other fibres) applied over a cloth, but more usually a paper base to form a raised pattern.

Fluted: Ornamented with channels or grooves (flutes).

French-polish: A varnish, consisting of shellac dissolved in white spirit, applied to furniture.

Fresco: An ancient form of decoration in which paint is applied to walls covered with damp plaster.

Fretwork: Ornamental plasterwork or woodwork embellished with a repeat cut or perforated pattern.

Frieze: Either the section of a wall situated between the architrave and the moulding or cornice or, simply, a decorated band running along the top of a wall.

Gable: That part of a wall situated just below the end of a pitched roof and cut into a triangular shape by the sloping sides of the roof.

Gasolier: A gas-burning chandelier.

Georgian style: 18th-century style characterized by the proportions and ornaments of Classical architecture, applied universally to buildings, furniture and decorative art forms.

Gesso: A plaster of Paris used, usually on wood, to provide a smooth surface for gilding or painting.

Geyser: An early type of water heater.

Gilding: A wafer-thin layer of gold or gold substitute applied over a plaster, ceramic or wooden surface.

Glazing bars: The bars, usually made of wood, that hold panes of window glass in place. (Also known as astragals.)

Gothic Revival: A revival of the original Gothic style of architecture which flourished from the 11th to the 15th centuries and was characterized by soaring, slender lines, pointed or ogee arches and tracery. The 19th century Gothic Revival included elaborate Gothic motifs applied to European furniture and metalwork. Leading exponents of the Gothic Revival included Augustus Pugin, William Burges, William Morris, Bruce Talbert and Charles Eastlake.

Gothick: 18th and early 19th-century spelling of Gothic, and today denoting the delicate applied ornament which was fashionable before the full-scale Gothic Revival of 1840 onward.

Greek key pattern: A geometrical decoration made of continuous right-angled lines.

Grisaille: A monochrome form of *trompe l'oeil*.

Grotesque: Ornamental figures, animals or birds depicted in fantastic or ornamental form.

Half-timbered: A method of construction in which vertical and horizontal timbers are used to make up the frame of a wall, which is then filled in with lath and plaster (nogging), sticks and mud or clay (wattle and daub), stone, or brick.

Hassock: A firmly stuffed cushion.

Hearth: The floor of a fireplace.

Hepplewhite style: Style of furniture based on the designs of George Hepplewhite (d.1786), and characterized by elegant chairs with straight, tapering legs and oval, heart-shaped or shield-shaped backs.

Hipped roof: A roof with four sloping sides.

Hob: A ledge on the back side of a fireplace or grate for warming a pot or kettle.

Inglenook: A recessed space beside a fireplace, usually housing a bench.

Insertions: Semi-transparent drapes or net curtains hung in-between a window and the main drapes or curtains.

Isznik pottery: Coarse-bodied Turkish earthenware, either coated with a white slip or tin-glazed and decorated with bright colours under a glassy quartz glaze.

Jacobean: Architecture, furniture and decoration characteristic of the period of James I of England (1603-25).

Japanned: Painted and varnished in imitation of Oriental lacquerwork.

Joinery: Doors, windows, stairs and other wooden fixtures and fittings.

Kelim: Flat carpet with geometric patterns, produced chiefly in Turkey and featuring distinctive colourways such as pink, acid green and black.

Lambrequins: A strip of drapery hung over a window, doorway or mantel shelf.

Limewash: A milky like mixture of slaked lime, water and pigment used to coat porous plaster and stone walls.

Lincrusta: A type of wallpaper with a thick embossed pattern, commonly applied to dados and ceilings and designed to be painted and varnished.

Linen: Cloth made of lint or flax.

Linen press: Large cabinet or cupboard with drawers, doors and sliding shelves for storing linen and clothes.

Linoleum: Durable floor covering made from compressed cork, ground wood and linseed oil, backed by burlap or strong canvas.

Lit-en-bateau: Literally a "boat-bed", featuring a scrolled head and footboards of equal height, and sometimes ornamented with ormolu mounts.

Louis Quatorze style: The style inspired by the Court of the Sun King, Louis XIV (reigned 1643-1715) and his palace at Versailles. Broadly consisted of a more opulent Baroque modified by Classical lines and marked by flamboyant craftsmanship. Cabinet-making was notable for its fine veneers and intricate marquetry, exotic woods, tortoiseshell, lacquerwork and precious metals.

Louis Quinze style: (1720-50) - *see* Rococo style.

Louis Seize style: A Classical (Greek) reaction to the fussiness of Rococo that began some 20 years before Louis XVI style, in 1754.

Lustres: A candlestick or vase ornamented with pendants of cut-glass.

Lustreware: Pottery decorated with a metallic glaze.

Majolica: A form of earthenware painted to look like colourful glazes of 16th-century Italian majolica.

Mansard roof: A roof with two slopes, the lower one almost vertical to allow extra space for rooms in the loft or attic.

Marbling: Marble simulated with paints and glazes.

Marquetry: A decorative veneer on furniture made up of shaped pieces of wood or other materials such as ivory, metals and mother-of-pearl, arranged in a pattern of contrasting colours.

Massing: The positioning of pieces, such as ceramics, in a display so that no one item dominates the group at the expense of another.

Mechanicals: Greeting cards with moving parts, for example, "pop-up" cards.

Medallion: A circular ornament, such as a ceiling rose sometimes incorporating a bas relief.

Moiré: A cloth made of mohair, silk or other fabrics and incorporating a regular wavy pattern with a water-like appearance.

Moquette: A canvas-backed furnishing fabric with a thick-cut velvet pile.

Mosaic: A design or pattern made up of different coloured pieces of material, usually marble but also glass, fabric etc.

Moulding: An ornamental section of wood or plaster, such as a cornice or a picture rail.

Neo-classical style: A style of architecture and decoration based on the forms of Ancient Greece and Rome. Characteristic elements included chains of Classical motifs such as garlands of flowers and husks, palmettes (palm leaves), anthemions, round and oval paterae (plaques), urns and cameos.

Newel post: An upright post at the end or corner of a staircase, usually attached to both the handrail and the string. Also, on a circular staircase, the central post around which the stairs curve.

Oil cloth: A canvas impregnated with linseed oil and used as a floor covering.

Ogee: An S-shaped section of moulding or architrave.

Ogive: A pointed arch or window.

Opaline glass: Glassware predominantly of a milky white hue, but also featuring subtle gradations of colour across its surface.

Ormolu: Pale yellow gilt or bronzed metallic ware, normally covered with a protective coat of clear lacquer.

Ottoman: A low, stuffed, backless seat, sometimes in the form a chest.

Overmantel: A decorative treatment above a fireplace, often incorporating a mirror or painting.

Paisley pattern: A design incorporating a cone-like, ornamental motif used on Paisley shawls.

Palmette: A decorative motif based on the fan-shaped leaf of a palm tree.

Pantry: A small room used to store food and tablewares.

Papier mâché: A lightweight material made of paper pulp and glue, usually decorated to resemble wood or plaster.

Parapet: A low wall running along the edge of a roof.

Parian ware: A type of porcelain that looks like fine marble.

Parisiennes: Fashion dolls depicting adults or adolescents wearing copies of contemporary fashions.

Parquet: Flooring made up of wooden blocks fitted together to form a pattern.

Pastille burner: A device for burning incense.

Pediment: Originally a triangular structure crowning the front of a Greek building, but also a triangular or rounded structure situated over the top of a portico, door, window or niche.

Pelmet: A fabric or fabric-covered device fixed above a window and designed to conceal a drape rod and the top of the drapes or curtains. (Also known as a valance.)

Pendant: An ornament hanging down from a ceiling.

Pharonic: Ancient Egyptian patterns and motifs.

Piano nobile: The principal floor of a house, containing the reception rooms.

Piazza: A broad veranda.

Picture rail: A wooden or plaster moulding running along the top of a wall and designed to hang pictures from.

Pier glass: A tall mirror, originally hung on the wall in-between two windows.

Pier table: A table designed to be placed in-between two windows.

Pilaster: A square column built into, and partly projecting from a wall, or used to frame a doorway or fireplace etc.

Plush: A luxurious fabric, similar to velvet but with a longer and more open pile.

Polychromy: The art of decorating in many colours.

Porcelain: A thin, white earthenware, either transparent or semi-transparent and first made in China.

Porphyry: A hard, variegated rock, most commonly purple and white in colour.

Porte cochère: A porch wide enough to allow access for a carriage.

Portico: A number of columns situated along the side of a building, or a colonnade forming a porch at the entrance to a building.

Portière: A drape or curtain hung over a door or doorway.

Press-moulded glass: Glassware given its shape and pattern by the application of pressure in a mould.

Primary colours: Those colours or pigments - red, yellow and blue - from which all other colours can be mixed from.

Purdonium: A coal-scuttle or bucket.

Push plate: A small panel, usually made of brass, fixed above or below the pull or handle of a door and designed to protect the painted or varnished surface from dirt or grease.

Putti: Cherubs or very young boys, usually winged, and most commonly found in Renaissance and Baroque art and sculpture.

Quarry tile: An unglazed floor tile.

Quatrefoil: A four-lobed circle or arch formed by cusping.

Ragging: A form of decoration, usually applied to walls, in which one, two or more semi-transparent paints or glazes are applied over a contrasting or complementary coloured basecoat.

Rattan: Wicker or cane work made from the long thin stems of climbing palms.

Register grate: A fire grate with a moveable iron plate housed in the flue designed to regulate the updraft.

Repp: Corded cloth, usually woollen.

Riser: The vertical surface of a step.

Rococo: A style of architecture, decoration and furniture first popularized in France in the 1720s during the reign of Louis XV. Derived from *rocaille* or shell decoration, it is in fact a nonsense word which embraces shell, foliage, swept and delicately curved ornamentation unrelated to the underlying structure. In essence, a freer development of Baroque.

Roll-top: A writing desk featuring a sliding, curved cover made from thin slats of wood.

Romanesque: A style of architecture marking the transition from Roman to Gothic, and characterized by round arches and vaults.

Rose: *see* Medallion.

Scagliola: A decorative finish made from hardened and polished chips or plaster and marble.

Sconce: A wall bracket for holding candles and other forms of lighting.

Scroll: A spiral or curved ornamentation.

Serge: A strong twilled fabric made of silk or worsted.

Shades: displays of imitation flowers, stuffed birds, shells and miniature figures under glass domes, particularly fashionable during the high-Victorian period.

Shingles: Wooden tiles or panels used to clad the exterior walls, especially on American Shingle-style houses.

Skirting board: A flat moulding running round the base of a wall. (Also called a baseboard.)

Slip: Liquid clay used as a finish or as a decorating medium on pottery, or as a medium for casting hollow-ware and figures.

Spandrel: The approximately triangular space between the curve of an arch and the rectangular frame above it. Also, the space between two arches and the horizontal moulding or cornice that runs above them.

Spattering: The technique of applying a fine spray or spatter of different coloured paints and glazes over a surface to simulate porphyry and other variegated stones.

Spill holder: Cylindrical or wall-hanging vase, designed to hold spills or matches for lighting candles and pipes. They were usually made from porcelain, pottery or brass.

Spindle: A thin, turned column of wood, mostly used in staircases.

Sponging: The technique of applying semi-translucent paints and glazes to a surface to produce subtle gradations of colour when simulating, for example, marble.

Strapwork: An ornamentation of crossed and interlaced fillets, either applied or carved in wood, stone or plaster, and often used in screens and on ceilings and mouldings or cornices.

Stretcher: A brick positioned so its long face is visible.

String: One of the two sloping members that hold the end of the treads and risers in a staircase.

Stucco: A fine cement or plaster used on the surface of walls, mouldings and other architectural ornaments. Primarily used for exterior rendering.

Swag: A piece of fabric draped between two supports; a carved or painted decoration resembling such a fabric; or a garland of ribbons, flowers, fruit or foliage. (Also known as a festoon.)

Terraced house: A house that forms one of a whole straight or curving line of at least three such houses attached to each other. (Known as a row house in the United States).

Terra-cotta: Unglazed fired clay used for making tiles, architectural ornament, garden pots etc.

Terrazzo: A polished finish for floors and walls made of marble or stone chips set into mortar.

Toile: A thin cotton or linen.

Tracery: Surface ornamentation of intersecting ribwork, usually in the upper part of a Gothic window, forming a pierced pattern.

Transom: The horizontal member across the top of a door, or across the top or middle of a window.

Transom light: In the United States, a window or pane above a door, whether rectangular or arched. (Known as a fanlight in Britain.) Also, a window that is hinged along its top edge.

Trefoil: A three-lobed circle or arch formed by cusping.

Trivet: A bracket with three projections for fixing on the top bar of a grate, and used to support a pot or kettle.

Trompe l'oeil: Literally "a trick of the eye"; a decorative effect, such as a painting of architectural detail or a vista, that gives the illusion of reality.

Valance: A hanging border of drapery attached to the top of a window (as a pelmet) or around the sides of a bed.

Vaseline glass: Yellowy green glass, made with uranium oxide and popular for low-cost vases and other decorative ornaments.

Veneer: A thin slice of wood applied as a decorative surface to a more common and less attractively grained and figured wood.

Veranda: A roof-covered but otherwise open gallery, porch or balcony supported by posts.

Verdigris: A green coating of basic cupric carbonate that forms in the atmosphere on copper, brass or bronze.

Vergeboard: *see* Bargeboard.

Vernacular: A term describing humble, often rural architecture, with little or no stylistic pretension, or in a purely regional style, or in a manner based on a naive misunderstanding of high-style architecture.

Vestibule: An entrance hall, or the enclosed section at the head of a hall and just inside the front door.

Voile: Thin, semi-transparent material.

Wainscot: A simple, early form of wooden panelling, either full height or on the lower half of a wall. (Also called wainscotting.)

Weatherboard: *see* Clapboard.

Witches balls: A type of decalcomania incorporating mirrored glass and often hung in cottage windows to ward off witches, who were scared of their own reflections.

Whatnot: A lightweight, compact stand with three or more shelves on which to put knick-knacks, books or ornaments. The French equivalent is an *étagère*.

Woodgraining: The art of simulating the appearance of natural wood using paints and glazes.

Wilton carpet: A carpet that has a looped pile cut to give it a soft finish.

BIBLIOGRAPHY

Banham, Joanna, Sally Macdonald and Julia Porter, *Victorian Interior Design*, Cassell (1991)

Barrett, Helena and John Phillips, *Suburban Style*, Macdonald Orbis (1987)

Beeton, Mrs, *Book of Household Management*, London (1906)

Blom, Benjamin, *A Monograph of the Works of McKim Mead and White 1879-1915*, New York (1973)

Boorstin, Daniel J., *The Americans: The National Experience*, Vintage Books, New York (1965)

Bridgeman, Harriet and Elizabeth Drury (eds.), *The Encyclopedia of Victoriana*, Country Life (1975)

Briggs, Asa, *Victorian Things*, Penguin (1990)

Calder, Jenni, *The Victorian Home*, Batsford (1977)

Calloway, Stephen, *The Elements of Style*, Mitchell Beazley (1991)

Calloway, Stephen and Stephen Jones, *Traditional Style*, Pyramid Books (1990)

Cochran, Chris, *Restoring a New Zealand House*, New Zealand Historic Places Trust (1980)

Clark, Robert Judson, *The Arts and Crafts Movement in America 1876-1916*, Princeton University Press (1973)

Clarke, Allen, *The Effects of The Factory System*, London (1899)

Condit, Carl Wilbur, *American Building: materials and techniques from the first colonial settlements to the present*, University of Chicago Press (1982)

Cooper, Jeremy, *Victorian and Edwardian Furniture and Interiors*, Thames and Hudson (1987)

Cooper, Nicholas, *The Opulent Eye: Late Victorian and Edwardian taste in interior design*, The Architectural Press

Dixon, Roger & Stefan Muthesius, *Victorian Architecture*, New York and Toronto, Oxford University Press (1978)

Dubrow, Eileen and Richard, *American Furniture of the 19th Century*, Schiffer (1983)

Dubrow, Eileen and Richard, *Made in America 1875-1905*, Schiffer

Eastlake, Charles, *Hints on Household Taste*, London (1878)

Edis, Robert, *The Decoration and Furniture of Town Houses*, London (1890)

Edwards, R. (ed.), *The Connoisseur Period Guides: Regency 18120-1830, Victorian 1830-1860*, London (1976-8)

Escott, T.H.S., *Social Transformations of the Victorian Age*, Seeley and Co. (1897)

Evans, Ian, Clive Lucas and Ian Stapleton, *Colour Schemes for Old Australian Houses*, The Flannel Flower Press, Sydney

Gere, Charlotte, *Nineteenth-century Decoration - The Art of the Interior*, Weidenfeld & Nicolson (1989)

Greene, Harlan, Charleston, *City of Memory*, Legacy Publications, Carolina (1987)

Griffith, Helen C. (ed.), *Southern Interiors*, Oxmoor House (1988)

Guild, Robin, *The Victorian House Book*, Sidgwick & Jackson (1989)

Hamilton, Jean, *Wallpaper*, Victorian & Albert Museum (H.M.S.O. 1983)

Hamlin, Talbot, *Greek Revival Architecture in America*, Oxford University Press (1944)

Handlin, David P., *American Architecture*, Thames and Hudson (1985)

Hartley, Dorothy, *Food in England*, Futura (1985)

Jenner, Michael, *London Heritage*, Michael Joseph (1988)

Johnson, Alan, *How to Restore and Improve your Victorian House*, David & Charles (1984)

Jones, Owen, Plans, *Elevations, Sections and Details of the Alhambra*, London (1842)

Kennedy, Roger G., *Greek Revival America*, National Trust for Historic Preservation/Stewart Tabori &Chang, New York (1989)

Kerr, Robert, *The Gentleman's House*, London (1864)

Kyle Leopold, Allison, *Victorian Splendour*, Stewart, Tabori & Chang (1986)

Lancaster, Osbert, *A Cartoon History of English Architecture*, John Murray

Lane, Terence and Jessie Serle, *Australians at Home*, Oxford University Press (1990)

Lasdun, Susan, *Victorians at Home*, Weidenfeld & Nicolson

Lipman, Jean, and Alice Winchester, *The Flowering of American Folk Art (1776-1876)*, Viking, New York (1974)

Lockett, Terence, A., *Collecting Victorian Tiles*, Antique Collectors Club (1979)

Loudon, John Claudius, *An Encyclopedia of Cottage, Farm, and Villa Architecture and Furniture*, London (1833)

Marshall, John and Ian Willox, *The Victorian House*, Sidgwick and Jackson (1986)

Miller, Judith and Martin, *Miller's Understanding Antiques*, Mitchell Beazley (1989)

Miller, Judith and Martin Miller, *Period Details*, Mitchell Beazley (1987)

Miller, Judith and Martin, *Period Finishes and Effects*, Mitchell Beazley (1992)

Miller, Judith and Martin, *Period Style*, Mitchell Beazley (1989)

Moss, R. and G. Winkler, *Victorian Exterior Decoration*, Henry Holt & Company, New York (1987)

Moss, R. and G. Winkler, *Victorian Interior Decoration: American Interiors 1830-1900*, Henry Holt & Co. (1987)

Muthesius, Hermann, *Das Englische Haus*, Berlin (1904)

McCorquodale, *The History of Interior Decoration*, Phaidon

Naylor, Gillian, *William Morris by himself*, Macdonald Orbis (1988)

Ohrbach, Barbara Milo, *Antiques at Home*, Clarkson N. Potter, Inc (1984)

Orrinsmith, Lucy, *The Drawing Room, Its Decoration and Furniture*, U.S. (1877)

Pomada, Elizabeth and Michael Larsen, *The Painted Ladies Revisited*, E.P. Dutton, New York (1989)

Robertson, E. Graeme, *Decorative Cast Iron in Australia*, Viking O'Neil (1984)

Salmond, Jeremy, *Old New Zealand Houses 1800-1940*, Reed Books (1986)

Savage, George, *Dictionary of 19th-century Antiques*, Barrie and Jenkins (1978)

Schmidt, Carl T., *The Victorian Era in the United States*, New York (1971)

Scully, Vincent J., *The Shingle Style and The Stick Style*, Yale University Press/Oxford University Press, London (1971)

Shaw, Peter, *New Zealand Architecture*, Hodder & Stoughton

Slesin, Suzanne and Stafford Cliff, *English Style*, Thames & Hudson

Spofford, Harriet, *Art of Decoration Applied to Furniture*, (1878)

Stewart, Di, *The New Zealand Villa - Past and Present*, Viking Pacific (1992)

Swedberg, Robert and Harriett, *Victorian Furniture Books I, II, III*, Wallace Homestead Book Company

Thomson, D., *England in the 19th Century*, Pelican (1950)

Thornton, Peter, *Authentic Decor*, Weidenfeld & Nicolson

Turner, Mark and Lesley Hoskins, *The Silver Studio of Design*, Webb & Bower (1988)

Viney, Graham, *Colonial Houses in South Africa*, Struik Winchester (1987)

Vogt, A.M., *The Nineteenth Century*, The Herbert Press (1989)

Wainwright, Clive, *The Romantic Interior*, Yale University Press (1989)

Waldhorn, Judith and Sally Woodbridge, *Victoria's Legacy*, 101 Productions, San Francisco (1978)

Wissinger, Joanna, *Victorian Details*, Running Heads Inc.

INDEX

ACKNOWLEDGMENTS

The authors and publishers would like to thank the following house-owners and museums:
Edda and Tim Abegg, Rosie and Michael Addison, The American Museum in Bath, Lee Anderson, The Inn at Antietam,
Jane Baigent, Wendy Barber and John Hinchcliffe, Bartow Pell Mansion, The Belle of the Bends, Raf Borello,
Bowne House, Peter Campbell at the Ulysses S. Grant House, Cedar Grove, Mike Chalon, Chilston Park Hotel,
Jane Churchill, The Classic Furniture Group, Coline Covington, The Cooper Hewitt Museum, Cragside,
Jane Cumberbatch, Randy Danforth, Anne Dore, June Ducas, The Durfee House, Clifford Ellison,
Irv and Dianne Feinberg at Garth Woodside Mansion, Joe Fessler and Richard Burlingame at Belvedere Mansion,
Suzie Forge, The Gamble House, George Williams House, Christophe Gollut, Roderick Gradidge, Jacques Grange,
The Grange, Griswold House, Tom Heaton, Suzanne Henderson, Heritage Square Museum, Tom Hickman,
Lynn and Nigel Howard, Jonathon Hudson, Husted House, Indigo Seas, Richard Irving, The Ivy Restaurant,
Trisha Jamieson, Richard Jenrette, Kearfoot-Bane House, Tim and Kit Kemp, Tessa Kennedy, Keith Knost, Baldassare Larizza,
Leighton House, Robert Levins, Linley Sambourne House, Jason and Deidre Marshall at the Marshall Gallery,
Lord and Lady McAlpine, Elizabeth McClellan at the Steamboat House, Old Merchant's House, Judith and Martin Miller,
The Morris Jumel Mansion, National Trust for Scotland, Tom Parr, The Pelham Hotel, Alberto Pinto, Plas Teg, Sarah Polden,
William and Carol Preston at Dezoya House, Buddy Rau, Elsbeth Riley-Smith, The Russell Cotes Art Gallery, James Ryan,
Salve Regina College, The Second House Museum, Wayne Scott of the Rockcliffe Guest House,
Gay Shepherd-Henderson at Belle Vue, Keith Skeel, Annie and Lachie Stewart, St Mary's College in Twickenham,
Colin Tennant, Gabi Tubbs, Lyn von Kirsting, Merikay Waldvogel, David Warbeck at Hall Place,
Mary Wondrausch, Woodland Terrace in Pennsylvania, Melissa Wyndham.

The following kindly gave permission to reproduce photographs and illustrations in this publication:
KEY: *b* BOTTOM; *m* MIDDLE; *l* LEFT; *r* RIGHT; *t* TOP
9 br, 12 r The Bridgeman Art Library; 9 tr, 9 bl, 15 t The Stapleton Collection; 10 l, 10 r by kind permission of the
Board of Trustees of the Victoria and Albert Museum; 15 tr 26 tl, 26 tr Mark Fiennes (Arcaid); 21 bl Geraldine Barry;
27 l Richard Bryant (Arcaid); 27 r NTPL/Rupert Truman; 34 bl, 35 tm, 36 tl, 36 tm, 37 tl, 37 lm Dennis and Sheila Curran;
36 m Seldon & Son catalogue; 37 bl Steven Box & Co catalogue and The Sanitary Engineering and Ventilation Co;
37 bm Agnews; 37 br, 39 lm Pryke & Palmer catalogue; 39 lm H. & C. Davis Co pattern book; 40 tl James Hagger;
41 tl George Jackson & Sons; 41 tml, 41 bl Clark & Fenn; 42 tm Taylor and Maw Bros, A.J. Bicknell & Co and
Woodward's National Architect catalogues; 42 tr Macfarlane's Castings catalogue; 45 tr Hampton & Sons;
82-3, 87, 88, 91, 92, 95, 96 Christie's Auctioneers and Sothebys Auctioneers; 82 l William Hockley Antiques;
82 m T. G. Wilkinson Antiques; 83 r Lesley Bragge Antiques; 91 (no 3) George Smith; 91 (no 4) Andrew Hartley.

The following suppliers kindly allowed special photography for this publication.
Their addresses are listed in the Directory, see page 224.
The Antique Traders, Arenski, Kate Bannister, Basia Zarzycka, Bennison Fabrics Ltd, Nicholas Boston, Britannia,
Coles & Son Wallpapers Ltd, Cork Brick Antiques, Crown Berger, Richard Dennis, Design Archives,
The Dining Room Shop, Bryan Douglas, Nicholas Fabre, Fothergill & Crowley, Gainsborough Silk Weaving Co Ltd,
The Gallery of Antique Costume & Textile, Hamilton Weston (Bradbury & Bradbury), Ian Harris at N. Bloom & Son,
Nicholas Harris, Claire Hobson at Thomas Goode, Hope & Glory, E. & C.T. Koopman & Son Ltd, The Lacquer Chest,
Judith Lasalle, Joan Latford, Lelievre, Ann Lingard at Rope Walk Antiques, Lunn Antiques, Linda Morgan Antiques,
Sue Norman, Old Pine, Jacqueline Oosthuizen, Osborne & Little, Powell & Mathers Antiques, Raffles, Rogers de Rin,
Royal Doulton, Sanderson, Manfred Schotten, Vic Schuler, Schumacher, Jean Sewell Antiques, The Shaker Shop,
Keith Skeel, Robert Stephenson, S. & J. Stodel, Tobias & the Angel, Watts & Co Furnishings Ltd,
Mark J. West, Agnes Wilton, Steven Woodham, XS Baggage Company.

Thanks also to Roderick Gradidge for contributing to the section on American Victorian Architecture and to
Robin Wyatt for contributing to the section on British Victorian Architecture and the chapter on Interior Details.